BEST-EVER
Comfort Food

BEST-EVER
Comfort Food

Over 200 recipes for childhood favourites,
family traditions, school dinners, and
mother's home-cooked classics

CONTRIBUTING EDITOR: Bridget Jones

HERMES
HOUSE

This edition is published by Hermes House,
an imprint of Anness Publishing Ltd,
Blaby Road, Wigston, Leicestershire LE18 4SE
Email: info@anness.com
Web: www.hermeshouse.com; www.annesspublishing.com

If you like the images in this book and would like to investigate using
them for publishing, promotions or advertising, please visit our
website www.practicalpictures.com for more information.

Publisher: Joanna Lorenz
Editorial director: Helen Sudell
Project editor: Simona Hill
Designer: Design Principals
Production Controller: Wendy Lawson
Editorial reader: Debbie Millett

ETHICAL TRADING POLICY
Because of our ongoing ecological investment programme, you, as
our customer, can have the pleasure and reassurance of knowing
that a tree is being cultivated on your behalf to naturally replace the
materials used to make the book you are holding. For further
information about this scheme, go to
www.annesspublishing.com/trees

A CIP catalogue record for this book is available from the
British Library.

NOTES
Bracketed terms are intended for American readers.
For all recipes, quantities are given in both metric and imperial
measures and, where appropriate, in standard cups and spoons.
Follow one set of measures, but not a mixture, because they
are not interchangeable.

Standard spoon and cup measures are level.
1 tsp = 5ml, 1 tbsp = 15ml, 1 cup = 250ml/8fl oz.
Australian standard tablespoons are 20ml. Australian readers should
use 3 tsp in place of 1 tbsp for measuring small quantities.
American pints are 16fl oz/2 cups. American readers should use
20fl oz/2.5 cups in place of 1 pint when measuring liquids.

Electric oven temperatures in this book are for conventional ovens.
When using a fan oven, the temperature will probably need to be
reduced by about 10–20°C/20–40°F. Since ovens vary, you should
check with your manufacturer's instruction book for guidance.

The nutritional analysis given for each recipe is calculated per portion
(i.e. serving or item), unless otherwise stated. If the recipe gives a
range, such as Serves 4–6, then the nutritional analysis will be for the
smaller portion size, i.e. 6 servings. The analysis does not include
optional ingredients, such as salt added to taste.

Medium (US large) eggs are used unless otherwise stated.

PUBLISHER'S NOTE
Although the advice and information in this book are believed to be
accurate and true at the time of going to press, neither the authors
nor the publisher can accept any legal responsibility or liability for any
errors or omissions that may have been made nor for any
inaccuracies nor for any loss, harm or injury that comes about from
following instructions or advice in this book.

CONTENTS

ENTERING the COMFORT ZONE

COMFORT FOOD: HAPPY MEMORIES, FAVOURITE AND FAMILIAR DISHES, EASY ENTERTAINING, PRIVATE INDULGENCES, CALM AND CONTENTMENT.

We all have our favourite comfort foods; they might be creamy, sweet, spicy, or salty, and they appeal directly to our body's feel good responses. Foods that we enjoy eating often have pleasant associations and are hard to resist. Our favourite dishes might be based on childhood memories of times when we felt safe and secure, enjoyable holidays abroad, or special celebration treats. Eating pleasurable food is deeply satisfying; it relieves us of our hunger and makes us feel content. When our hunger is satisfied after a meal that we have enjoyed, all is well with our world. We have restored our blood-sugar levels to an even balance, and our mood is restored to good humour.

Everybody likes to eat, and while not all of us like to cook, it's true that most of us are capable of rustling up the kinds of things that we do like to eat. Many favourite comfort foods are simple offerings that can be made quickly and easily: hot toast dripping with salty butter and

Above: Cheese is one of the most popular and versatile comfort foods. Enjoy it on its own, or with fruit and crackers.

Above: Everybody has a favourite tipple, and social drinking is a comfortable and pleasant way to relax and entertain.

flavourful, fruity jam; a thick slab of moist cake with a mug of strong coffee; a soft cheese and crunchy salad sandwich, topped with tangy pickle; or home-baked cookies dunked in a cup of tea. With ease of cooking in mind, all of the recipes in this book are no-fuss, everyday recipes, made with ingredients that are readily available. None of them

involve complicated cooking methods, though some do take time to cook. What they have in common is an appeal to a basic instinct in all of us. Food nurtures the body and

Below: Foods that contain carbohydrate (the pasta), protein (the meat), and fat (the melted cheese) in a single dish are nourishing and satisfying.

Below: Fatty foods, particularly of the carbohydrate variety, make us feel full quickly. Carbohydrates release energy slowly, and when covered in salt, taste delicious too.

Above: Sweet and sugary foods give instant comfort. They taste good and provide an instant lift to flagging energy levels. Indisputably, home-baked cakes and cookies taste better and will keep you feeling fuller for longer than store-bought confectionery.

Above: Creamy and spicy foods can be very satisfying. The heat is uplifting, and the spiciness provides a sensory taste explosion on the palate.

nourishes the soul. Eating is essential, and we all enjoy good, flavourful food, preferably in the company of good friends or family. To that end, here is a delicious collection of 200 appealing, tried-and-tested recipes from all over the world. They taste divine, will satisfy our appetites, feed our families and make us feel good.

Comfort food does not necessarily mean unhealthy eating, although a few of these recipes might best be kept for special treats. It's really about unhurried menu planning, choosing familiar ingredients, pleasurable shopping trips and effortless food preparation. Food at its best is always home-made, and knowing it's been made using the freshest ingredients, just before it's about to be consumed, adds to our nurturing instincts. A home-cooked dish of piping hot food as we arrive

home on a cold day is a welcome pleasure; the warmth of the kitchen and the aroma of cooking both add to our emotional response to food. Likewise a warm, milky drink in the evening, before we go to bed, will make us content and sleepy. Some foods are calming and warming, while others are energy-giving, and make us feel alert and ready to face the day. For many of us, the types of food that we like to eat may be a subconscious reaction to their effect once consumed.

Enjoying food and its different aromas, tastes and textures, and learning to cook the foods that we take pleasure in eating should be habit-forming. With so many delicious recipes at your disposal, and suitable suggestions for every meal and every possible occasion, you should never be stuck for a mealtime suggestion ever again.

Right: Sharing good food and conversation with family and friends fulfils a basic and nurturing need in us all.

THE COMFORT ZONE

Turning to food when times are tough is quite natural as our bodies recognize eating as a positive activity. Occasional indulgences are an enjoyable part of life — feel good about them and celebrate the benefits of a wide variety of comfort foods.

BEAT THE BLUES

EATING CERTAIN FOODS DEFINITELY HELPS TO LIFT THE SPIRITS. SWEET FOODS HAVE PLEASANT ASSOCIATIONS AND MEMORIES OF TREATS AND REWARDS GIVEN WHEN WE WERE LITTLE. HOMELY CARBOHYDRATE-RICH FOODS, SUCH AS TOASTED CRUMPETS OR MUFFINS, ARE AN INSTANT REMEDY.

There are plenty of reasons why we might feel at a low ebb, and at times like these, food is a good source of solace. If your mood is down temporarily, then preparing yourself a quick snack might be the answer. Low blood sugar levels produce a poor mood, so if you're feeling low because you haven't eaten recently, or haven't eaten enough of the right kinds of food, your body is sending out a clear signal.

Food is nurturing, and while a little of what we fancy does do us good, we need to make sure that what we are eating is feeding our bodies with nutrition, as well as feeding our souls.

Carbohydrates keep blood sugar levels up, and the complex starchy and wholegrain type, found in bread, rice, pasta, potatoes, fruit, pulses and legumes, help to keep blood-sugar levels steady. These foods maintain a good mood, stabilize energy levels, good concentration and they keep productivity levels up at work or school. On the other

Below: Complex carbohydrates should make up a large percentage of each meal, particularly if you are a person that feels below par on a regular basis. Choose from bread, pasta, rice, pulses, legumes, fruit and nuts, and keep stocked up with these ingredients, so that you can reach for them the moment you feel hungry.

hand, carbohydrates such as chocolate and sweet, sugary, snack foods are quickly absorbed into the body giving us a short-term boost, and producing a good mood quickly. These types of treats are cheap, very appealing when we're hungry, and take no effort to prepare. The downside is that the "good mood feeling" won't last for long. For that, you need to eat a filling and healthy carbohydrate meal first and finish with a little sweet treat.

The B group vitamins are important for converting food into energy and supplying the brain with the oxygen that is important for a bright and positive outlook. They are also important for a healthy nervous system. Eating a mixed diet ensures an adequate supply of B group vitamins: meat and offal, fish, eggs, nuts and seeds, wholegrains and vegetables supply the range of vitamins that make up this group.

Vitamin C and minerals, such as magnesium, manganese and zinc, are also vital for overcoming stress and helping us to feel good and healthy. Small and frequent meals and snacks help to keep blood-sugar levels up, so

Above: Sugary foods appeal to all our senses. They look appealing, smell delicious and the taste is guaranteed to meet our expectations.

between meals reach for a piece of fruit, or a slice of toast, and keep home-made biscuits for really special treats.

Below: Canned fish is a good ingredient to keep to hand in the store cupboard. The protein that it contains helps us to stay alert.

Quick fixes

When you're feeling low, try a fast fix to help lift your spirits. Toast is a good one to start with, since cutting a thick slice of bread takes no effort and the aroma as it toasts is instantly appealing. Likewise, making a hot chocolate drink with real chocolate is extremely satisfying. If you like to bake, fill the kitchen with wafts of sweet aromas; buttery shortbread has minimal ingredients so is quickly mixed and fast to bake. Its melt-in-the-mouth taste is pure heaven.

TOPPING MUFFINS OR CRUMPETS

Freshly toasted crumpets or English muffins are reassuringly good with all sorts of toppings.

Savoury

• Spread with lots of garlic butter.
• Fill split toasted muffins with hot crisp chips (French fries), then add ketchup or mayonnaise.
• Spread with mustard, top with cheese and grill (broil) until golden.
• Top with tomatoes and bacon, then grill until aromatic and cooked.
• Top with cooked ham and a poached egg.

Sweet

• Spread with soft cheese and jam (jelly).
• Spread with peanut butter and chocolate spread.
• Pile on soft cheese and honey or maple syrup.
• Spread with unsalted (sweet) butter, chopped banana and drizzled honey.

Above: Chocolate heaven for a chocoholic.

REAL HOT CHOCOLATE

All hot milky drinks are soothing and sleep-inducing. A steaming mug of good chocolate is guaranteed to take your mind off worries and woes. Sipping the smooth, dark liquid and dunking your favourite biscuits is a tonic and a treat. You need good-quality, dark chocolate for this.

Break up 115g/4oz plain (semi-sweet) chocolate and melt it in a heatproof bowl over a pan of barely simmering water. Bring 400ml/14fl oz/1⅔ cups milk to the boil in a separate pan. When the chocolate has melted stir in a little of the milk, then whisk in the remainder until frothy. Pour into a mug and sweeten to taste.

Little Mexican fritters, known as churros, are the traditional accompaniment for hot frothy chocolate, but doughnuts or rich butter cookies are also delicious dunked in chocolate.

SHORTBREAD ROUNDS

These are rich, buttery and melt-in-the-mouth. They're very indulgent, but unquestionably good for the spirits. They are also easy to make, and doing a bit of baking is a good way of taking time out.

Cream 450g/1lb/2 cups butter with 225g/8oz/1 heaped cup caster (superfine) sugar until very soft and pale (a food processor is ideal for this). Sift 450g/1lb/4 cups plain (all-purpose) flour, 225g/8oz/scant 1½ cups ground rice or rice flour and 5ml/1 tsp salt together, and stir this into the creamed mixture. Pulse in a food processor to combine the ingredients. When the mixture resembles fine breadcrumbs, knead it lightly into a ball – do not overwork this dough or it will become greasy. Shape it into a long roll, measuring about 7.5cm/3in in diameter, wrap in clear film (plastic wrap) and chill until firm.

Preheat the oven to 190°C/375°F/Gas 5. Cover two baking sheets with non-stick baking parchment. Sprinkle some demerara sugar on a piece of greaseproof (waxed) paper or baking parchment and roll the dough in this. Cut the roll into slices, about 1cm/½in thick, and place well apart on the baking sheets. Bake for 20–25 minutes, until very pale gold. Sprinkle with golden caster sugar and leave to cool for 10 minutes, until firm enough to handle. Transfer the shortbread rounds to a wire rack to cool. Makes 24.

Above: Crumpets and English muffins.

Above: Churros dunked in real hot chocolate.

Above: Shortbread and tea.

TIRED OUT

WHEN ENERGY LEVELS ARE FLAGGING, GIVE BOUGHT CONVENIENCE FOODS A MISS. OPT, INSTEAD, FOR OLD FAVOURITES, SUCH AS BEANS ON TOAST, THAT ARE DELICIOUSLY FAMILIAR AND FULL OF FOOD VALUE TO GIVE YOUR BODY A BOOST.

When we're feeling exhausted and in need of instant comfort, fast fixes are the way to go. Often our response to feeling tired is to reach for high-energy foods or a drink of caffeinated coffee in the hope that they will give us energy. Try chunky sandwiches filled with fruity jam (jelly), or mashed banana sandwiches. Both will help energy levels to rise. There are plenty of healthy and simple ideas to try that are full of nutritious ingredients yet taste delicious too.

Some foods just make you feel wide awake and full of energy. Refreshing flavours, zesty seasonings and a bit of colour work wonders. Opt for uplifting drinks to go with simple snacks or a bowl of breakfast cereal – try fresh fruit and vegetable juices, smoothies that are packed full of nutrients, and fresh fruit shakes. Use herbs and seasonings that are enlivening – sunny basil and head-clearing mint are good with savoury snacks. Fresh root ginger or pickled ginger is good in sandwiches.

When the body needs energy, go for fruit, legumes, wholemeal (whole-wheat) bread and pasta which will slowly release energy into the bloodstream, ensuring long-term recovery. This is particularly important after any form of exercise that leaves the muscles depleted of their energy supplies.

Bread and pasta, particularly wholemeal types, are good sources of complex carbohydrates. Savoury snacks on toast, such as tinned spaghetti hoops, cheese, and scrambled eggs are great

Left: Porridge and stewed fruits will give your body a good and healthy start to the day, keeping energy levels steady.

for filling you up, replacing spent energy, providing fibre and protein as well as B vitamins and minerals.

Snacks full of goodness

Being too tired to cook a proper meal should not mean missing out on balanced eating. This is the time to snack on raw food, such as fruit and vegetables that taste good just as they are. A thin slice of cheese on wholegrain crackers is a good source of protein, calcium and B vitamins. Dried fruit and nuts are tasty and good for you; keep unsalted brazils, pecans, walnuts and hazelnuts in stock. Fruit and vegetable drinks and snacks are natural tonics that help fight tiredness and restore energy. Ideally you should satisfy hunger levels with a snack and once energy levels are back on track, cook a simple supper.

Iron is vital for the production of haemoglobin used for transporting oxygen in red blood cells. Good sources of iron include offal (variety meats), red meat, egg yolks, and dark green leafy vegetables. Vitamin C is important for iron absorption, especially to improve the availability of iron from vegetable sources.

BEANS ON TOAST

Easy and great for replenishing lost energy, especially with wholemeal (whole-wheat) breads, good old beans on toast are great on their own but can also be transformed with the addition of other ingredients.
• Toast one side of the bread, brush the other with garlic oil and grill (broil) until golden. Sprinkle with shredded basil before adding the beans.
• Mix crushed garlic, lemon zest and chopped parsley into the butter.
• Use garlic or herb bread instead of toast.

Right: This childhood favourite is great for any time of day. Thick-sliced white bread, loaded with butter and topped with hot baked beans, will fill you up and restore your energy levels.

BANANA AND PECAN SMOOTHIE

Smoothies are easy to make and drink, are full of restorative nutrients and taste sublime. Nuts contribute vitamin E and essential fatty acids, while bananas and maple syrup provide energy. When you're too tired to cook, why not whizz up a fruit and nut smoothie?

Below: Nourishing banana and pecan smoothie.

Process 50g/2oz/½ cup pecan nuts in a food processor or blender until finely chopped. Add 2 large bananas and process to a thick paste, scraping down the nuts occasionally. Add 150ml/¼ pint/⅔ cup milk and a dollop of maple syrup and process until smooth. Pour over crushed ice and serve at once. Serves 2.

Below: Bananas are also a useful source of carbohydrate while they are still firm, before they soften and become sweet and sugary.

Above: Pecan nuts are a healthy snack, perfect to nibble throughout the day.

Below: A peanut butter and jelly sandwich is a nutritious childhood favourite.

PEANUT BUTTER AND JELLY SANDWICH

This traditional American snack provides sustenance, flavour and texture, and when extra fruit is added, it has extra vitamin value.

For variety, thickly slice a baguette or cut individual brioche in half to make open sandwiches. Top each half with peanut butter, jam and fresh fruit. For closed sandwiches, try light rye bread. Spread with peanut butter. Mix in some fresh fruit, such as blueberries, blackcurrants or redcurrants; diced apple, mango or papaya; sliced strawberries; or quartered kiwi-fruit slices. Spread the fruit and jam mixture over the peanut butter. Top with more bread or serve as an open sandwich. Serve with your favourite drink. Serves 1.

UNDER THE WEATHER

SPOT THE SYMPTOMS BEFORE YOUR BODY HAS TIME TO DIP INTO ILLNESS AND USE COMFORT EATING TO FIGHT COLDS AND SIMILAR EVERYDAY ILLNESSES. THE BEST SORT OF FOOD TO GIVE THE BODY A LIFT WHEN ILLNESS THREATENS IS LIGHT AS WELL AS NURTURING AND NUTRITIOUS.

Combining comfort eating with traditional home cures enhances the feeling of well-being, and boosts the system to fight off mild, everyday infections. Vitamin C, found in oranges, kiwi fruit and lemons, is said to help fight off colds if taken at the first signs of symptoms.

Many herbs provide gentle remedies that are protective and help to stimulate the body's immune system. Combining natural remedies with healthy foods is a positive way to counteract feeling ill.

Small, simple and familiar

When you're feeling under the weather eating small meals regularly is the solution. When you have a poor appetite, small quantities of food can be reassuring and are more appealing that a huge meal. Simple flavours are easier on the taste buds than complex seasonings. Since our senses of taste and smell are often reduced, the appearance and texture of foods are more important. Familiar foods and basic dishes made with just a few flavourful ingredients are

Left: Manuka honey has strong antiseptic qualities, and a taste you'll appreciate if you're feeling off-colour.

more likely to arouse our interest than unusual or experimental recipes. Treats and/or childhood favourites such as mushroom omelette or boiled eggs with toast soldiers are always popular since they appeal to our early memories and are very easy to eat.

Nurturing liquids

Caring for an ill person starts with providing the right hot drink. Hot toddies, with a touch of alcohol, are intended to soothe and induce sleep. Honey is a natural antiseptic and very soothing for sore throats. Lemon is often used for its vitamin C content, to help fight off infection. Ginger is an interesting ingredient – it has a warming, yet refreshing, flavour; it is also a well-known aide for overcoming nausea and sickness. Ginger tea is easily made by infusing slices of fresh root ginger in boiling water, then sweetening it with

HOMEMADE LEMONADE

This uncooked lemonade is made in minutes. It is a cooling and comforting source of vitamin C – just the drink to help fight off an irritating cold.

Mix the finely grated rind and juice of 2 lemons with 600 ml/1 pint/ 2½ cups chilled still or sparkling mineral water. Stir in 50g/2oz/¼ cup sugar until it has completely dissolved. Alternatively, add 30ml/2tbsp honey or to taste. Serve at once. Serves 3.

Above: Fresh lemons contain vitamin C.

Above: Make fresh lemonade to feed a cold, and try it served warm in winter.

honey to taste. Milky drinks are soothing and sleep-inducing at night. Cold drinks are often welcome, particularly lemonade, which provides vitamin C.

Warming and satisfying soups are easy to eat and digest. Chicken soup is the classic choice as it is nutritious and simple in flavour. Simple vegetable soups, such as leek and potato, are usually better than any that are spicy.

Light and good

Thin bread lightly spread with butter, made into delicate sandwiches, for example with cucumber, tomato, ham or chicken, are just what's needed at times of illness and will provide comfort. Simple vegetables, such as baked or mashed potatoes, are also appealing.

Lightly grilled fish or egg dishes are nutritious, as are boiled or poached eggs, or omelettes with simple fillings. Proper custard made with eggs is nutritious. Baked egg custards are not too sweet, and they can be served with fresh fruit (such as berries or diced kiwi fruit) for added vitamin C.

Fruit makes a good snack – bananas that are not too ripe are an excellent food for a queasy stomach as they rarely cause an upset. Fruit salad made with soft fruits is a nice treat for recovery.

CHICKEN SOUP

A nutritious, flavourful chicken soup that is light on salt is best made with good stock and vegetables.

Melt a little butter in a large pan and add 2 chopped onions, 2 chopped potatoes, 1 diced carrot and 1 diced celery stick. Cook gently for 5 minutes, until the vegetables are softened slightly but not browned. Stir in 750ml/1½ pints/3 cups good chicken stock and bring to the boil. Reduce the heat, cover and simmer for 30 minutes.

Mix 25g/1oz/¼ cup plain (all-purpose) flour with 150ml/¼ pint/⅔ cup milk and stir this into the soup. Bring to the boil, stirring. Add 175g/6oz diced, cooked chicken and heat gently for 5 minutes. Finally, add 300ml/½ pint/1¼ cups single (light) cream and stir in seasoning to taste. Serve sprinkled with chopped parsley. Serves 4.

Right: Chicken soup is a traditional remedy for illness of many kinds.

HOT TODDY

A hot toddy has to be all things: soothing, calming and warming. Combine ginger to settle a swirling tummy, honey to soothe a sore throat and a tipple to lift the spirits.

Pare the rind off 2 lemons and place in a pan with 4 slices of fresh root ginger, 5ml/1tsp honey and 175ml/6fl oz/¾ cup water. Bring the ingredients to the boil, then remove from the heat and leave to infuse for 5 minutes. Stir in 175ml/6 fl oz/¾ cup Scotch whisky, Irish whiskey or American bourbon and warm through. Strain into warmed glasses. Serves 2.

Above: A hot toddy is good for colds.

MUSHROOM OMELETTE

Simple to make and easy to eat, omelettes are a good choice when your appetite has all but disappeared.

To make the filling melt 15g/ 1 tbsp butter and add 75g/3oz/generous 1 cup sliced mushrooms. Cook for 5 minutes. Stir in 15g/1 tbsp plain (all-purpose) flour and 85ml/3 fl oz/⅓ cup milk. Boil, stirring, and season to taste. Whisk two eggs with 15ml/1 tbsp water and seasoning. Melt a little butter in a frying pan and pour in the egg. Allow to cook, then turn and cook on the other side until browned. Turn out on to a plate and add the filling. Serves 1.

Above: Mushroom omelettes taste delicious.

THE MORNING AFTER

HAVING A HANGOVER, THE REWARD FOR OVER-INDULGENCE, IS PROBABLY THE LEAST OF YOUR CONSIDERATIONS WHEN YOU'RE LOOKING FORWARD TO AN EVENING OUT. THE MORNING AFTER IS A DIFFERENT STORY THOUGH. FEELING TOO ILL TO FACE THE DAY? HELP IS AT HAND.

A few drinks in the company of good friends lift the spirits and provide a heady feeling that most of us enjoy. A few drinks too many, though, can have us feeling regretful the following day. This isn't a state to be endured. Food is a great healer, and there are plenty of comforting recipes that will lift the day, give you back your zing and get you back on track.

Alcohol has a severe dehydrating effect, so even though you may have drunk a lot of liquid, it will leave you feeling thirsty. Drinking water is the best cure, and lots of it. After over-indulging, the body needs a pick-me-up by way of extra B vitamins, vitamin A, C and E, plus minerals and fatty acids. So good balanced eating is essential for counteracting the effects of alcohol.

Protein foods, such as fish, meat and poultry, eggs, some dairy products, fresh fruit and vegetables, and a balance of carbohydrates are important. Most people do not feel like eating a large meal in the morning, so the breakfast – or brunch – should be welcome food that will calm the stomach, as well as the head.

Eating substantial complex carbohydrate foods, such as bread, pasta or rice, while consuming plenty of alcohol-free liquid, helps to minimize a hangover and keep the body hydrated.

Eating to feel better

Having a hangover is the classic comfort-food zone. For the worst cases, plain toast, porridge and cereals with milk are a good choice. Breakfast cereals that are fortified with B-group vitamins are good for replenishing supplies when absorption has been inhibited by alcohol. Fruit in yogurt is refreshing and nutritious – bananas are easy to digest, and low-fat yogurt with honey works wonders. Pears are light in flavour, easy to digest and not too disruptive. Papaya, mango, kiwi and orange all provide useful antioxidant vitamins.

Intense hunger often accompanies a modest hangover. A hearty cooked brunch works wonders, if eaten a few hours after waking up. Grilled tomatoes and bacon, poached or scrambled eggs, mushrooms and plenty of warm crusty bread might all appeal. If cooking is too much trouble, cooked ham or finely sliced cheese in wholemeal rolls is plain, comforting and satisfying.

Semi-sweet breads, such as currant buns or brioche, or American muffins with fresh and dried fruit and bran are a perfect choice. Blueberry muffins are refreshing, and they go well with bananas in yogurt.

Below: Home-baked muffins are a delicious start to a hangover day.

BACON SANDWICH

A brilliant morning-after cure, bacon sandwiches provide vitamins, minerals and comforting familiarity. Use your favourite ingredients – back bacon or thin and crispy rashers (slices). Use soft or crisp rolls, or thick slices of fresh bread. The cut sides of the rolls or the bread can be toasted, if liked. Butter the rolls or bread and spread with sauce, if required, such as ketchup or brown sauce. Grill (broil) or fry the bacon to taste, allowing 4 rashers for each sandwich. Place the bacon in the rolls or between two slices of bread and serve at once.

Add red bell pepper, avocado and spring onions (scallions) for antioxidant vitamins to counteract the alcohol.

Left: Grilled bacon smells divine.

Above: Hangovers are not the best start to the day, but seeking comfort in food will definitely help you start to feel better. Many foods have healing qualities, and there are plenty of simple recipes that are energy-giving.

PRAIRIE OYSTER

This is an alcohol-free version of the original morning-after drink, traditionally served with a large measure of spirits. Use a perfectly fresh, free-range egg. Mix 5ml/1tsp Worcestershire sauce with 5ml/1tsp white wine vinegar and 5ml/1tsp tomato ketchup in a tall glass. Slide 1 raw egg yolk into the glass, taking care not to break it, and season with cayenne pepper. Do not stir. Down the mixture in one gulp.

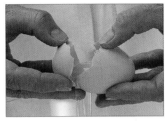

Above and right: If swallowing a raw yolk does not appeal, mix the ingredients instead with freshly squeezed orange juice.

BLOODY MARY

The last resort in terms of health, hair of the dog is a dose of alcohol to stimulate the system and dull it at the same time. This is not the best sort of morning-after cure as far as your health goes, but as a rare fix, and for anyone with a cast-iron stomach, fruit juice laced with vodka is an option, as in a bloody Mary. Buck's fizz, sparkling white wine or champagne with freshly squeezed orange juice (half and half) is more civilized and hugely refreshing. Everyone has his or her favourite recipes for this old-fashioned hangover cure. Some put tomato ketchup in it, others add a splash of sherry.

Put a slice of lemon and 2–3 ice cubes in a tall glass. Add 5ml/1 tsp Worcestershire sauce, 5ml/1 tsp lemon juice, a pinch of celery salt, about six drops of Tabasco and six twists of pepper from a mill. Stir and fill the glass to about 4cm/1½in from the top with tomato juice, then pour in a measure of vodka. Stir well. Serves 1.

Right: For a severe hangover, starting the day with more alcohol might be the only answer.

FRIDAY NIGHT FEELING

IN ON YOUR OWN? FEELING LONELY? WANT A STRESS-FREE EVENING TO WIND DOWN FROM THE WEEK AT WORK? TIME SPENT NURTURING YOURSELF WHEN YOU'RE IN ON YOUR OWN IS TIME WELL SPENT. CHOOSE INFORMAL, EASY TO PREPARE FAST-FOOD TREATS FOR INSTANT COMFORT.

Preparing for the weekend usually means re-fuelling for a different type of activity; even if it just means catching up with the housework. Weekend menu

planning should cater for more relaxed cooking, and Friday evening is the night to start. Comfort cooking is about enjoying kitchen time – there's no particular rush, the recipes are familiar, favourite music brightens or calms, and the ambience is one of caring and sharing. The ingredients can be basic and may be shopped for in advance, or a brief shopping session may be part of the positive activity.

Relaxing cooking sessions should be simple. Make use of all the ready-washed and prepared ingredients:
• vegetables and salads that do not require washing, trimming and peeling
• cuts of poultry and meat that cook quickly, such as diced and stir-fry cuts or thin escalopes and steaks
• cooked meats and poultry
• fish and seafood that are cooked in

Left: Preparing the evening meal is a pleasant ritual that has a more relaxed approach at the weekend.

minutes or ready-cooked
• couscous and fresh pasta that are ready in minutes
• deli produce and good-quality canned or bottled ingredients
• breads and bakes, including long-life, part-baked breads.

Favourite and familiar

Instead of following complicated or unfamiliar recipes, preparing old favourites is fun and hassle-free. Enjoying time spent in the kitchen preparing a recipe that is tried and trusted, as well as enjoyed by all who will share it, can be a nurturing experience. Knowing you'll enjoy the finished results before the meal is even cooked makes the dinner a treat to look forward to. Best of all, the pressure is off because the results are guaranteed and while the meal cooks there is time to turn attention and thoughts to other things.

Below: Cheese risotto.

CHEESE RISOTTO

Risottos are the easiest food to prepare. They take little effort, minimal ingredients and taste absolutely delicious. Serve with wine.

Bring 1 litre/1¾ pints/4 cups beef, chicken or vegetable stock to the boil, reduce the heat so that it is simmering. Cook 1 chopped onion in 25g/1oz/ 2tbsp butter in a pan over gentle heat until soft and lightly browned.

Add 275g/10oz/1½ cups risotto rice and cook for 2 minutes, stirring to coat all the grains in butter. Pour in 120ml/ 4fl oz/½ cup dry white wine,increase the heat slightly. When the wine has evaporated, gradually add the stock, a ladleful at a time, allowing the rice to absorb each addition before adding more. After 20–30 minutes, the rice should be tender but firm and creamy.

Remove from the heat. Add a knob of butter. Stir in 75g/3oz/1 cup grated cheese and season to taste. Cover and leave to rest for 3–4 minutes. Serves 4.

HOMEMADE BURGERS AND RELISH

Easy to make and terrific to eat, these are real Friday chill-out fare. Mix 450g/1lb lean minced (ground) beef with 1 chopped shallot, 30ml/2 tbsp chopped parsley, 30ml/2 tbsp tomato ketchup and seasoning. Divide the mixture into four. Knead each portion into a ball, then flatten it into a burger.

Make a spicy relish by cooking 1 chopped shallot, 1 crushed garlic clove and 1 finely chopped and seeded green chilli in 15ml/1 tbsp olive oil for a few minutes, until softened. Add a 400g/14oz can of ratatouille and simmer for 5 minutes.

Preheat the grill (broiler) and cook the burgers for about 5 minutes on each side, until browned and cooked through. Meanwhile, split the burger buns. Arrange lettuce leaves on the bun bases, add the burgers and top with warm relish. Add the bun tops. Serve with chunky chips (French fries).

Right: Who can resist home-made burgers and relish?

TEX-MEX CHILLI POTATOES

Chilli provides heat and flavour for plain jacket potatoes. This is classic comfort food to lift the spirits.

Brush 2 large potatoes with a little oil, prick, and bake at 220°C/425°F/ Gas 7 for about 30 minutes before beginning to cook the chilli.

Cook 1 chopped onion with 1 crushed garlic clove and ½ diced red (bell) pepper in a little oil for about 10 minutes, until soft but not browned. Add ½ seeded and diced small red chilli, 5ml/1 tsp ground cumin and a pinch of cayenne pepper. Stir in a 200g/7oz can tomatoes, 2.5ml/½ tsp tomato paste, 60ml/4 tbsp water and 2.5ml/½ tsp each of oregano and marjoram. Boil, reduce the heat and cover. Simmer for 25 minutes.

Add a drained 200g/7oz can kidney beans and cook, uncovered, for 5 minutes. Stir in some chopped fresh coriander (cilantro) and seasoning. Halve the potatoes, top with chilli and add a dollop of soured cream to each.

Left: Baked potatoes are great when you are weary. They don't need to be watched while they cook, and they always taste divine.

MIDNIGHT SNACKS

MUNCHING IN THE MIDDLE OF THE NIGHT BRINGS BACK MEMORIES OF CHILDHOOD ESCAPADES. LATE-NIGHT SNACKS HAVE TO BE REASSURING BECAUSE THERE ARE TIMES WHEN YOU JUST CAN'T HELP YOURSELF, BUT ALSO LIGHT SO THEY DON'T CAUSE DISCOMFORT WHEN YOU REALLY DO WANT TO SLEEP.

Midnight snacking often happens in phases, and can last for days or weeks on end. This type of snacking often goes hand-in-hand with sleeplessness, or may be a usual reaction to arriving home after a late night. When you're feeling hungry

Above: Midnight cookie binges can be pleasantly habit-forming.

SPREAD ON TOAST

When there is no time to mess about, your favourite spread on hot buttered toast is the hot option. You have to be ready for high-comfort-factor occasions – if your shopping list is non-existent, at least make sure the stock of things to spread on toast is always topped up. There should always be bread and butter in the freezer so that it can be thawed in seconds in the microwave if necessary. Slice a good loaf thickly before freezing so that individual slices can be toasted from frozen.

Spread-wise, yeast extract (such as Marmite or Vegimite) has to be top on the list. Honey, jam (jelly) or chocolate spreads work for some people, marmalade for others.

Speed is essential for things spread on toast. The butter has to be soft to spread easily; the toast thick, fresh and hot; the plate has to be warmed so that condensation does not form under the toast, giving it a soggy bottom; a hot drink must be prepared; and the whole lot has to be consumed promptly.

in the middle of the night and in need of comfort, there are some excellent recipes to test.

Raiding the food stores

All-milk drinks are calming and sleep-inducing, especially in winter. Look out for malt extract. It is similar to runny honey in texture, dark in colour and sweet with a strong malt flavour. It provides magnesium, important for the nervous system, and phosphorus. Stir a spoonful or two into a mug of hot milk.

Home-baked cookies, scones and American muffins are all deeply satisfying. Freeze some for times of need, and they can be thawed in seconds in a microwave oven. Plain muffins or those with fruit additions taste best. Chocolate is a mood-enhancing ingredient, and just a few chips in an otherwise plain recipe will do the trick, making the cake more of a treat.

Sandwich fillings and toasties

Preparing a sandwich can be a good way of diverting the mind from sleeplessness, as it requires more thought than stirring up a hot drink.

Cheese is rich and quite heavy, but it is a calming food. Chutneys and pickles that are sharp-sweet, spicy and soothing complement cheese. Dried apricots taste good with strong cheese and lettuce leaves or watercress. Toasted sandwiches are good for making a comparatively small amount of cheese go a long way.

Bananas, chocolate spread, jam and honey are all comforting foods to sandwich between substantial slices of crusty bread. Fruit buns and teabreads are good plain, but better with butter.

For grand-scale indulgence plain vanilla ice cream sandwiched between your favourite chocolate cookies makes a feast for the midnight hour.

Left: Marmite on toast. You either love it or hate it.

Below left: A scone topped with a dollop of home-made fruity jam (jelly) and a trickle of cream is the best midnight treat.

Below: Ice cream eaten straight from the tub always feels decadent, but if you can leave the ice cream to soften slightly, you'll get all the benefit of the creamy flavour, it'll taste even better.

CHEESE AND PICKLE SANDWICH

Old-fashioned cheese and pickle sandwiches always satisfy hunger pangs. This is the door-step sandwich zone: bread must be fresh and hunky; crusts are de rigueur.

Bring basic pickle to life by adding a little chopped fresh fruit – pear, apple, banana, mango or peach – with a good squeeze of lemon or lime juice. Ready-to-eat dried fruits are good; try apricots, pineapple, mango or peach. Diced red or green (bell) peppers and chopped spring onion (scallion) also pep up a standard pickle.

Cheddar and similar hard cheeses are traditional, but you could try others: Jarlsberg or Gruyere with tangy, spicy pickle; Danish blue or Stilton for a punchy flavour; or ripe brie for a rich and creamy taste.

Left: The ultimate cheese and pickle sandwich.

LATE-NIGHT COOKIE STACK

These are dangerous cookies. Take a pile of them to bed and all that will be left next morning will be crumbs in the sheets. They are a must with a tall glass of ice-cold milk or stacked with an obscene amount of ice cream.

Preheat the oven to 180°C/350°F/ Gas 4 and grease two baking sheets. Cream 75g/3oz/6 tbsp butter with 75g/3oz/6 tbsp golden caster (superfine) sugar and 75g/3oz/6 tbsp soft light brown sugar until pale and fluffy. Beat in 1 large (US extra large) egg and 2.5ml/ ½ tsp vanilla essence. Sift 150g/5oz/1¼ cups self-raising flour, 25g/1oz/¼ cup cocoa powder (unsweetened) and 1.5ml/¼ tsp salt over the mixture. Add 100g/4oz/ 4 squares chopped chocolate (or chocolate chips) and fold the dry ingredients into the creamed mixture.

Place four heaped tablespoons of the mixture well apart on each baking sheet. Spread the mixture with the back of a wetted spoon and bake for 12 minutes, until risen and set. Leave on the sheets for a minute to firm up, then cool on a wire rack. Repeat with the remaining mixture. Makes 12 large or 20 small cookies.

Right: Not for the faint-hearted, this sweet concoction will satisfy all hunger pangs.

BACK FROM SCHOOL

FOND MEMORIES OF TEA-TIME TREATS THAT WERE READY TO GREET US WHEN WE ARRIVED HOME FROM SCHOOL PROVIDE A STORE OF COMFORT FOOD FOR LIFE. DELICIOUS SMALL-SCALE SNACKS THAT ARE VISUALLY APPEALING AS WELL AS FILLING ARE GUARANTEED TO BE DEMOLISHED IN AN INSTANT.

Sandwiches are nutritious, but it's really the filling that makes them appealing. Bread, preferably wholemeal (whole-wheat) or at least containing some whole grains, provides complex carbohydrates for long-term energy. Pitta breads, French breads, crusty country loaves, soda bread, rolls, bagels and fruit breads are all made for filling.

Salad vegetables are ideal for savoury sandwiches – cucumber, tomato, spring onion and grated carrot are delicious with medium- or low-fat soft white (farmer's) cheese. Canned fish, such as sardines, salmon or tuna, are good with salad vegetables or on their own. Egg sandwiches are a real favourite and so simple – hard boiled, chopped and mixed eggs go well with sliced tomatoes or salad cress. Adding mayonnaise masks the filling's flavour – spreading generously with butter is better.

Sweet fillings comfort as well as taste moreish. Bananas go well with jam (jelly), honey or chocolate spread. Diced fresh fruit or small whole berries can be stirred into jam for added nutritional value. Nut butters provide protein and good fat; read the labels to avoid products that have a high salt content and contain hydrogenated oils or palm oil, which is high in saturated fat.

Make 'n' bake

Home-baking is an all-round comforter, making the cook feel as good as those who share the results. Make baking a family activity and all the cooks can share the results. Children love cooking, and making cakes or rolling dough is fun.

While some bought cakes and biscuits (cookies) are made with large quantities of sugar, hydrogenated oils, colouring and flavouring, home-made goodies can be full of ingredients that make a valuable contribution to the diet. Using butter makes the biscuits and cakes taste divine and adds that melt-in-the-mouth flavour. Nuts, dried and fresh fruit, and even vegetables can be used in cake recipes.

Above: Sweet treats are better when they're home-made.

Home-baked products freeze well and small portions can be removed as required, so a whole batch of cakes or biscuits does not have to be consumed in one sitting. Small cakes or slices of larger cakes thaw quite quickly at room temperature or in seconds in a microwave oven. Slice large cakes before freezing them and interleave the slices with pieces of freezer film or non-stick baking parchment.

Sweet treats

There are so many dessert treats that are fun to make and have a high nutritional value as well as satisfying every sweet tooth.

Fruit jellies can be made very simply by dissolving gelatine in fruit juice. Pour this over small fresh berries or diced fruit in individual bowls, cover and set in the refrigerator. The result is a treat that also provides a portion of fruit.

Milk-based desserts are fun to make and nutritious, and many are just right for afternoon tea. Pancakes are brilliant for sharing – both cooking and eating – and for teaching children how to prepare food and use the stove. Custards are not too sweet, and they can be served with fruit to follow sandwiches for a well-balanced light meal.

Above: Promoting an interest in food from an early age creates tomorrow's cooks.

JAM SANDWICHES

Make these nutritious as well as irresistible – it's a great opportunity for introducing a grainy bread, either wholemeal or a malted loaf with whole grains. Cut the bread thick or use rolls. Spread with soft cheese (try medium or low fat) and top with jam. Add sliced banana for food value and flavour before topping with the second slice.

Below: Jam (jelly) sandwiches are simple to make. They taste better with fresh fruit added. Try chopped banana.

JAMMY SWEETHEARTS

Process 225g/8oz/2 cups plain (all-purpose) flour and 175g/6oz/¾ cup butter in a food processor until the mixture resembles fine breadcrumbs. Add 130g/4½oz/⅔ cup caster (superfine) sugar and 1 egg yolk and pulse to combine the ingredients. Turn the mixture out on to a floured surface and knead until smooth. Shape into a ball and wrap in cling film (plastic wrap), then chill for 30 minutes.

Preheat the oven to 180°C/350°F/Gas 4. Roll out the dough thinly and cut out 6cm/2½in rounds. Place half the rounds on greased baking sheets. Use a small heart-shaped cutter, about 2cm/¾in in diameter, to cut out the centres of the remaining rounds and place on baking sheets. Bake for about 12 minutes, until pale golden, then cool on a wire rack.

Beat 50g/2oz/¼ cup unsalted (sweet) butter and 90g/3½oz/scant 1 cup icing (confectioners') sugar together until creamy. Add a few drops of vanilla essence if you like. Sandwich the plain and cut-out biscuits together with the buttercream and fill the cut outs with a little jam. Makes 20.

Right: Jammy sweethearts.

HOT BUTTERED PANCAKES

Sift 300g/11oz/2¾ cups plain (all-purpose) flour with 5ml/1tsp each of bicarbonate of soda (baking soda) and cream of tartar. Stir in 75g/3oz/6 tbsp caster (superfine) sugar and make a well in the middle. Add 2 beaten eggs and 5ml/1 tsp lemon juice, then gradually beat in 400ml/14fl oz/1⅔ cups milk. Beat the dry ingredients with the eggs, adding the milk little by little to make a smooth, thick batter. Do not add all the milk until the batter is smooth, then add enough milk to make a batter the consistency of double (heavy) cream. Leave to stand for 30 minutes.

Heat a griddle pan and grease it lightly with butter. Drop spoonfuls of the batter on the griddle, leaving space between them, and cook until they are just set, bubbling on the surface and golden underneath. Turn and cook the second side. Transfer to a plate covered with a dishtowel and keep warm until all the batter is cooked. Adjust the heat under the pan so that it does not become too hot and brown the outside of the pancakes before the batter is set and bubbly. Serve the pancakes hot with butter – a little jam, honey or maple syrup can be added. Serves 4.

Left: Frying pancakes have a delicious aroma.
Right: Pancakes dripping with butter.

A FRIEND IN NEED

RECIPES THAT HELP MAKE YOU FEEL CONTENT AND FULL, ARE EASY TO EAT AS WELL AS FAMILIAR ARE GOOD CHOICES WHEN IT COMES TO SPENDING TIME WITH FRIENDS IN NEED. EVERYONE APPRECIATES DELICIOUS-TASTING SIMPLE FOODS.

Simple savoury foods that are full of flavour are good to share. Everyone loves fast food, it's tasty and full of energy, but the great thing about home-made versions is that they are usually more filling meals.

Pouring out problems is the ideal excuse for sharing a plate of fries, with ketchup and mayo or any other favourite dip. Hot dogs and pizza are in the same category. Fillings and toppings must be punchy – spicy salami or chorizo, big meaty frankfurters, lots of garlic, plenty of herbs. Some breakfast favourites also work well on shared platters. Try good sausages grilled (broiled) until golden and served with a tomato chutney or salsa to dip, or grilled bacon with a stack of American-style thick pancakes and maple syrup to drizzle over them. Mini meatballs are good with garlic-laden cucumber and yogurt dip (with a hint of mint).

If inspiration is lacking and time short, bread and cheese is calming and good for sharing. Long crusty French baguettes, heated and aromatic, with big wedges of blue cheese and creamy ripe brie can be accompanied by little cornichons, wedges of sharp-sweet apple and crunchy pickled onions.

Friendly encounters

Meeting for afternoon tea can be a treat, and an opportunity for a good chat. Cucumber sandwiches on wholemeal (whole-wheat) bread, or finger rolls filled with smoked ham, go well with afternoon tea; toasted tea cakes or English muffins are ideal. Afternoon tea will sustain you until an evening meal and because the food is light you can justify having a sweet treat. Danish pastries or a jam (jelly) and cream sponge will round off the afternoon. Jam tarts are a treat, that are extremely good topped with cream.

Above: A plate of fries, with salt and vinegar shaken over it, is an instant pick-me-up that's hard to resist. Eat them when they're piping hot and freshly cooked for the best taste.

CREAM TEA

Fresh scones with thick cream and fruity jam are the perfect accompaniment to a refreshing drink of tea.

Preheat the oven to 230°C/450°F/ Gas 8. Rub 50g/2oz/¼ cup diced butter into 450 g/1lb/4 cups self-raising flour with a pinch of salt added. Stir 15ml/ 1 tbsp lemon juice into 400ml/ 14fl oz/1⅔ cups milk and leave to stand for a minute, then stir this into the dry mixture to make a soft, but manageable, dough. Knead the dough lightly into a ball on a well-floured surface, then roll it out to at least 2.5cm/1in thick. Use a 5cm/2in cutter to stamp out rounds and place them on a greased baking sheet. Brush with a little milk and bake for about 20 minutes, until risen and golden brown. Cool on a wire rack.

Serve the scones with butter, jam and clotted cream or whipped double (heavy) cream. Makes about 12.

Left: A cream tea with jam (jelly) and cream is a quintessentially English tradition.

HOT DOGS

Fry ½ of a sliced onion for each hot dog in a little oil or butter until soft and lightly browned. Poach or grill (broil) frankfurters, 1 per bread roll, for 3–5 minutes, until they are thoroughly reheated (they are ready-cooked). Split and toast hot dog buns and spread with mustard and/or ketchup or relish. Add the frankfurters and onions and serve at once.

Update the basic hot dog by adding grilled spring onions (scallions) or thinly sliced raw onion (red for a mild flavour) instead of fried onions, with some shredded sage, mint, oregano or marjoram. Sliced tomato and peppery watercress are good. Sliced avocado is deliciously creamy with smoky frankfurters. Instead of toasted hot dog rolls, use a warm crusty baguette, flat breads, such as pitta, naan or chapati, or wraps.

Left: Hot dogs are classic American street food.

Below: The Italian love of pizza is shared the world over.

BRESAOLA AND ROCKET PIZZA

With a punchy topping, home-made pizza tastes much better than the bought alternatives, and it does not have to involve hours of hard labour.

Preheat the oven to 200°C/400°F/ Gas 6. Make up a 150g/5oz packet pizza base mix according to the instructions – usually adding about 120ml/4 fl oz/½ cup lukewarm water and kneading for 5–10 minutes, until the dough is smooth and elastic. Divide the dough in half and roll each piece out into a 23cm/9in round. Place on baking sheets.

Cook 225g/8oz/3¼ cups sliced mixed wild mushrooms in a little butter with 2 chopped garlic cloves for about 5 minutes over high heat, until the mushrooms are softened but not over-cooked. Spread the pizza bases with pesto – about 30ml/2 tbsp on each – and top each with 4 slices bresaola and 2 sliced tomatoes, placed around their edges. Spoon the mushrooms into the middle. Divide 75g/3oz/⅓ cup cream cheese between the pizzas, dotting it over the topping. Bake for 15–18 minutes. Sprinkle with rocket (arugula) and serve. Serves 4.

SPOIL YOURSELF

COMFORT EATING SHOULD BE PART OF EVERY WEEK. LUXURIOUS TREATS ARE IDEAL FOR DAYS OFF,
WHEN YOU HAVE ONLY YOURSELF TO PLEASE. AFTER ALL, THE CHANCE TO NURTURE YOURSELF IS AN
INVESTMENT IN YOUR WELL-BEING.

Cooking for yourself is all about pandering to your own palate, particularly so if your usual routine is to cook for a busy family. Choosing foods that you adore and tailoring a menu just for yourself can feel quite liberating, so make the most of time spent alone and catering for yourself.

This is the time to make your favourite dish, whether it's something really simple to create, such as a smoked salmon and cream cheese bagel with a glass of chilled wine, a simple snack such as corn chips with guacamole, or something that requires more complicated cooking skills and ingredients. Since eating your favourite foods is about nurturing yourself, make time to enjoy a leisurely meal without distractions. Listening to relaxing music, or eating outside in the garden on a warm day may contribute to the unhurried pace and ambience.

Quality not quantity

Choose the finest-quality ingredients that you can afford, rather than opting for quantity. The following are a few suggestions for simple treats that can be assembled from quality ingredients.
• Smoked halibut with crème fraiche on warm blini
• Gravadlax with light rye bread
• Smoked duck or venison with grated raw celeriac tossed with olive oil and snipped chives, served with warm crusty bread
• Salad of cooked asparagus drizzled with a little olive oil and lemon juice and served with the best mayonnaise, and thin bread with butter
• Smoked ham or pork with diced beetroot (beets) drizzled with honey, cider vinegar and walnut oil, served with good whole-meal walnut bread.
Choose an appropriate wine to serve with your treat and enjoy.

Above: What could be more of a treat than a glass of red wine?

CORN CHIPS WITH SALSA AND GUACAMOLE

Dice 4 seeded tomatoes and mix with 30ml/2 tbsp chopped fresh basil, the juice of ½ lime, 20ml/2 tsp good-quality sweet chilli sauce, 1 finely chopped small red onion, salt and freshly ground black pepper. Cover and leave to marinate for 1–2 hours.

For guacamole, mash the flesh from 4 ripe avocados with the juice of ½ lime and 1 seeded and diced mild green chilli. Add salt and pepper to taste. If you like, add some chopped spring onions (scallions) or diced tomato.

Brush 8 yellow corn tortillas (about 300g/11oz) with a mixture of chilli and sunflower oil on both sides, stacking them up as you do so. Cut the stack into 6 wedges. Place on a grill (broiler) pan and toast under a hot grill for about 30 seconds on each side, until browned.

Place the corn chips in bowls and leave to cool. Serve with the salsa and guacamole. Serves 4.

Right: Dips and salsas are summer treats.

CHUNKY CHOCOLATE ICE CREAM

Whisk 4 egg yolks with 75g/3oz/6 tbsp caster (superfine) sugar and 5ml/1 tsp cornflour (cornstarch) until thick and foamy. Heat 300ml/½ pint/1¼ cups milk until just about to boil, then pour it into the egg mixture, stirring all the time. Pour this custard back into the pan and cook over a gentle heat, stirring, until thickened. Remove from the heat.

Break 150g/5oz/5 squares chocolate into pieces and stir them into the custard. When melted, cover, leave to cool, then chill. Whip 300ml/½ pint/1¼ cups whipping cream until thick, then fold it into the chocolate custard. Freeze the mixture in an ice-cream churn or in an appropriate container. If choosing a container, whisk the mixture twice during freezing. Fold in 50g/2oz/2 squares each of chopped dark, white and milk chocolate after whisking for the last time and freeze until firm. Serve decorated with chocolate. Serves 4.

Left: Delicious chunky chocolate ice cream.

Simple is best

Ripe fruit is simple, colourful and succulent. Serve it with rich Greek (US strained plain) yogurt or other full fat (whole) milk yogurt, clotted or whipped cream or crème fraiche. Select the best dessert cookies, or indulgent chocolate cookies as accompaniments. Pour small glasses of chilled dessert wine to sip with sweet dishes.
- Serve papaya and mango with wedges of lime
- Sprinkle strawberries with a little caster (superfine) sugar and kirsch
- Serve perfect strawberries or ripe figs with freshly ground black pepper
- Soak ready-to-eat dried fruit, such as apricots, figs and peaches, in brandy overnight, then drain them before serving with mascarpone. Reserve the brandy as a liqueur
- Whip double (heavy) cream with chocolate liqueur and serve as a dip for strawberries; use orange liqueur and serve the fruit with fresh apricot halves
- Serve vanilla ice cream with grated lime zest and freshly grated nutmeg.

Round off with a few good-quality chocolates and make your favourite blend of coffee.

Right: Lox and cream cheese bagels.

SMOKED SALMON AND CREAM CHEESE

Preheat the oven to 200°C/400°F/ Gas 6 and warm 2 bagels for 4–5 minutes. Slice them in half horizontally and spread generously with cream cheese. Top with smoked salmon – about 150g/5oz for both – and season with black pepper. Serve with lemon wedges. Serves 2.

BREAKFAST TO BRUNCH

There are times when a slice of toast, a banana or cereal is all you have time for first thing in the morning. Weekends and holidays are the time to indulge in extravagant and lazy breakfasts. This is a chapter full of wonderful ideas for memorable breakfast events, from flaky morning pastries to fabulous fry-ups.

DANISH PASTRIES

*EVEN THOUGH THESE WORLD-FAMOUS PASTRIES ARE TIME-CONSUMING TO MAKE, THE PROCESS IS
ENJOYABLE AND THE RESULTS ARE INCOMPARABLY WONDERFUL, ESPECIALLY WITH THE COFFEE FILLING.*

MAKES SIXTEEN

INGREDIENTS
45ml/3 tbsp near-boiling water
30ml/2 tbsp ground coffee
40g/1½oz/3 tbsp butter
115g/4oz/½ cup caster
  (superfine) sugar
1 egg yolk
115g/4oz/1 cup ground almonds
1 egg, beaten
275g/10oz/1 cup apricot jam (jelly)
30ml/2 tbsp water
175g/6oz/1½ cups icing
  (confectioners') sugar
50g/2oz/½ cup flaked (sliced)
  almonds, toasted
50g/2oz/¼ cup glacé
  (candied) cherries

For the pastry
275g/10oz/2½ cups plain
  (all-purpose) flour
1.5ml/¼ tsp salt
15g/½oz/1 tbsp caster
  (superfine) sugar
225g/8oz/1 cup butter, softened
10ml/2 tsp easy-blend (rapid-rise)
  dried yeast
1 egg, beaten
100ml/3½fl oz/scant ½ cup chilled
  water

1 To make the pastry, sift the flour, salt and sugar into a bowl. Rub in 25g/1oz/2 tbsp butter. Stir in the yeast. In a separate bowl, mix the egg and water together, add to the flour mixture and mix to a soft dough. Lightly knead for 4–5 minutes. Place in a plastic bag, seal and chill for 15 minutes.

2 Put the remaining butter for the pastry between two sheets of baking parchment and beat with a rolling pin to make an 18cm/7in square. Chill.

3 Roll out the dough on a floured surface to a 25cm/10in square. Put the butter in the middle of the dough square, angled like a diamond, then bring up each corner of the dough to enclose it fully.

4 Roll out the pastry thinly to measure about 35cm/14in in length. Turn up the bottom third of the pastry, then gently fold down the top third. Seal the edges together with a rolling pin. Wrap the pastry in clear film (plastic wrap) and chill for 15 minutes.

5 Repeat the rolling and folding three more times, turning the pastry after folding each time so that the short ends are at the top and bottom. Allow the pastry a 15-minute rest between each turn.

6 To make the filling, pour the hot water over the coffee and infuse for 4 minutes. Strain through a fine sieve. Cream the butter and sugar together. Beat in the egg yolk, ground almonds and 15ml/1 tbsp of the coffee.

7 Divide the dough and filling equally into three. Roll one dough portion to an 18 × 35cm/7 × 14in rectangle. Spread with filling and roll up from a short end. Cut into six equal slices. Roll another portion into a 25cm/10in round, and cut into six equal segments.

8 Put a spoonful of filling at the widest end of each segment. Roll the pastry towards its point to form a crescent.

9 Roll out the remaining dough into a 20cm/8in square; cut into four. Place some filling in the centre of each piece, and shape by making cuts from each corner almost to the centre, then fold four alternate points to the centre.

10 Preheat the oven to 220°C/425°F/Gas 7. Space the pastries well apart on greased baking sheets. Cover loosely with oiled clear film and leave to rise for about 20 minutes, until almost doubled in size. Brush with the egg and bake for 15–20 minutes until lightly browned and crisp. Cool on wire racks.

11 Put the jam in a pan with the water; bring to the boil, then sieve. Brush the jam over the warm pastries. Mix the icing sugar with the remaining coffee to make a thick icing. Drizzle the icing over some of the pastries and decorate some with almonds or chopped glacé cherries. Leave to set before serving.

Energy 387Kcal/1623kJ; Protein 5.1g; Carbohydrate 48.1g, of which sugars 34.6g; Fat 20.8g, of which saturates 9.4g; Cholesterol 76mg; Calcium 65mg; Fibre 1.3g; Sodium 161mg.

CROISSANTS

PERFECT CROISSANTS CONSIST OF PUFFED AND FLAKY LAYERS OF YEAST DOUGH. THEIR PREPARATION, WHICH IS A SOOTHING, CREATIVE PROCESS, IS NOT TO BE RUSHED; EATING THEM IS BREAKFAST BLISS.

MAKES FOURTEEN

INGREDIENTS

- 350g/12oz/3 cups unbleached white bread flour
- 115g/4oz/1 cup fine plain (all-purpose) flour, preferably French
- 5ml/1 tsp salt
- 25g/1oz/2 tbsp caster (superfine) sugar
- 15g/½ oz fresh yeast
- 225ml/scant 8fl oz/scant 1 cup lukewarm milk
- 1 egg, lightly beaten
- 225g/8oz/1 cup butter

For the glaze
- 1 egg yolk
- 15ml/1 tbsp milk

COOK'S TIP

Make sure that the block of butter and the dough are about the same temperature when combining, to ensure the best results.

VARIATION

To make chocolate-filled croissants, place a small square of milk or plain (semisweet) chocolate or 15ml/1 tbsp coarsely chopped chocolate at the wide end of each triangle before rolling up as in step 8.

1 Sift the flours and salt together into a large bowl. Stir in the sugar. Make a well in the centre. Cream the yeast with 45ml/3 tbsp of the milk, then stir in the remainder. Add the yeast mixture to the centre of the flour, then add the egg and gradually beat in the flour until it forms a dough.

2 Turn out on to a lightly floured surface and knead for 3–4 minutes. Place in a large lightly oiled bowl, cover with lightly oiled clear film (plastic wrap) and leave in a warm place, for about 45–60 minutes, or until doubled in bulk.

3 Knock back (punch down), re-cover and chill for 1 hour. Meanwhile, flatten the butter into a block about 2cm/¾in thick. Knock back the dough and turn out on to a lightly floured surface. Roll out into a rough 25cm/10in square, rolling the edges thinner than the centre.

4 Place the block of butter diagonally in the centre and fold the corners of the dough over the butter like an envelope, tucking in the edges to completely enclose the butter.

5 Roll the dough into a rectangle about 2cm/¾in thick and approximately twice as long as it is wide. Fold the bottom third up and the top third down and seal the edges with a rolling pin. Wrap the dough in clear film and chill for about 20 minutes.

6 Repeat the rolling, folding and chilling twice more, turning the dough by 90 degrees each time. Roll out on a floured surface into a 63 x 33cm/25 x 13in rectangle; trim the edges to leave a 60 x 30cm/24 x 12in rectangle. Cut in half lengthways. Cut crossways into 14 equal triangles with 15cm/6in bases.

7 Place the dough triangles on two baking sheets, cover with clear film and chill for 10 minutes.

8 To shape the croissants, place each one with the wide end at the top, hold each side and pull gently to stretch the top of the triangle a little, then roll towards the point, finishing with the pointed end tucked underneath. Curve the ends towards the pointed end to make a crescent. Place on two baking sheets, spaced well apart.

9 Mix together the egg yolk and milk for the glaze. Lightly brush a little glaze over the croissants, avoiding the cut edges of the dough. Cover the croissants loosely with lightly oiled clear film and leave to rise, in a warm place, for about 30 minutes, or until they are nearly doubled in size.

10 Meanwhile, preheat the oven to 220°C/425°F/Gas 7. Brush the croissants with the remaining glaze and bake for 15–20 minutes, or until crisp and golden. Transfer to a wire rack and leave to cool. The croissants are best warm, with butter, if liked, and good quality fruit conserve.

Energy 253Kcal/1059kJ; Protein 4.3g; Carbohydrate 28.5g, of which sugars 3.2g; Fat 14.4g, of which saturates 8.7g; Cholesterol 50mg; Calcium 72mg; Fibre 1g; Sodium 251mg.

AMERICAN PANCAKES WITH GRILLED BACON

THESE SMALL, THICK, BUTTERY PANCAKES WILL BE EATEN IN SECONDS, SO MAKE PLENTY. THE BATTER CAN BE MADE THE NIGHT BEFORE, READY FOR BREAKFAST ... OR A LATE-NIGHT SNACK ATTACK.

MAKES ABOUT TWENTY

INGREDIENTS
175g/6oz/1½ cups plain (all-purpose) flour, sifted
pinch of salt
15ml/1 tbsp caster (superfine) sugar
2 large eggs
150ml/¼ pint/⅔ cup milk
5ml/1 tsp bicarbonate of soda (baking soda)
10ml/2 tsp cream of tartar
oil, for cooking
butter
maple syrup
crisply grilled (broiled) bacon, to serve

1 To make the batter, mix together the flour, salt and sugar. In a separate bowl, beat the eggs and milk together, then gradually stir into the flour, beating to a smooth, thick consistency. Add the bicarbonate of soda and cream of tartar, mix well, then cover and chill until ready to cook.

2 When you are ready to cook the pancakes, beat the batter again. Heat a little oil in a heavy frying pan or griddle. Drop dessertspoonfuls of the mixture into the pan, spaced well apart, and cook over a fairly high heat until bubbles appear on the surface of the pancakes and the undersides become golden brown.

3 Carefully turn the pancakes over with a palette knife or fish slice (metal spatula) and cook briefly until golden underneath, then transfer them to a heated serving dish. Top each pancake with a little butter and drizzle with maple syrup. Serve with grilled bacon.

Energy 46Kcal/196kJ; Protein 1.8g; Carbohydrate 7.9g, of which sugars 1.3g; Fat 1.1g, of which saturates 0.3g; Cholesterol 23mg; Calcium 25mg; Fibre 0.3g; Sodium 12mg.

IRISH GRIDDLE SCONES

ALSO CALLED POTATO CAKES OR GRIDDLE CAKES, THESE DELICIOUS MORSELS ARE GREAT WITH BUTTER AND JAM, OR WITH BACON FOR A HEARTY MORNING-AFTER BREAKFAST OR BRUNCH.

MAKES SIX

INGREDIENTS
    225g/8oz floury potatoes, cut into
      uniform chunks
    115g/4oz/1 cup plain (all-purpose)
      flour
    2.5ml/½ tsp salt
    2.5ml/½ tsp baking powder
    50g/2oz/4 tbsp butter, diced
    25ml/1½ tbsp milk
    bacon rashers (strips), to serve
    butter, for greasing

1 Cook the potatoes in a pan of boiling water until tender.

4 Add the mashed potatoes and mix thoroughly with a fork. Make a well in the centre and pour in the milk. Mix to form a smooth dough.

5 Turn out on to a lightly floured surface and knead gently for about 5 minutes until soft and pliable. Roll out to a round 5mm/¼ in thick. Cut in half, then cut each half into three wedges.

6 Before you cook the scones, fry a batch of bacon rashers to serve with them. Keep warm in a low oven, until the scones are ready.

7 Grease a griddle or frying pan with a little butter and heat until very hot. Add the cakes and fry for 3–4 minutes until golden brown on both sides turning once. Serve hot with the bacon rashers.

2 Drain the potatoes and return them to the pan over a high heat. Using a wooden spoon, stir the potatoes for 1 minute until moisture has evaporated. Transfer to a bowl and mash well, making sure there are no lumps.

3 Sift together the flour, salt and baking powder into a bowl. Rub in the butter with your fingertips until it has the consistency of fine breadcrumbs.

Energy 156Kcal/653kJ; Protein 2.6g; Carbohydrate 21.2g, of which sugars 1g; Fat 7.3g, of which saturates 4.5g; Cholesterol 18mg; Calcium 36mg; Fibre 1g; Sodium 221mg.

SCRAMBLED EGGS WITH ANCHOVIES

SCRAMBLED EGGS ARE WEANING FOOD AND THEY RATE HIGH IN THE COMFORT ZONE. JUST PLAIN ON LOTS OF BUTTERY TOAST, THEY WORK WONDERS FOR LIFTING THE SPIRITS. IN A GROWN-UP VARIATION, AS HERE, THEY ARE STYLISH FOR BRUNCH OR AN IMPROMPTU SUPPER FOR TWO.

SERVES TWO

INGREDIENTS
    2 slices bread
    40g/1½oz/3 tbsp butter, plus
      extra for spreading
    anchovy paste, such as
      Gentleman's Relish, for spreading
    2 eggs and 2 egg yolks, beaten
    60–90ml/4–6 tbsp single (light)
      cream or milk
    salt and ground black pepper
    anchovy fillets, cut into strips,
      and paprika, to garnish

COOK'S TIP
These creamy scrambled eggs are delicious in baked potatoes instead of on toast. Serve with a salad and a glass of crisp white wine for a tasty meal.

1 Toast the bread, spread with butter and anchovy paste, then remove the crusts and cut into triangles. Keep warm.

2 Melt the rest of the butter in a medium non-stick pan, then stir in the beaten eggs, cream or milk, and a little salt and pepper. Heat very gently, stirring constantly, until the mixture begins to thicken.

3 Remove the pan from the heat and continue to stir until the mixture becomes very creamy, but do not allow it to harden.

4 Divide the scrambled eggs among the triangles of toast and garnish each one with strips of anchovy fillet and a generous sprinkling of paprika. Serve immediately, while still hot.

Energy 410Kcal/1701kJ; Protein 13.8g; Carbohydrate 11.3g, of which sugars 1.3g; Fat 35g, of which saturates 17.5g; Cholesterol 489mg; Calcium 104mg; Fibre 1.5g; Sodium 358mg

OMELETTE ARNOLD BENNETT

CREATED FOR THE WRITER ARNOLD BENNETT, WHO DINED AT THE SAVOY HOTEL IN LONDON, THIS CREAMY, SMOKED HADDOCK SOUFFLÉ OMELETTE IS A FAVOURITE BREAKFAST TREAT.

SERVES TWO

INGREDIENTS
175g/6oz smoked haddock fillet,
  poached and drained
50g/2oz/4 tbsp butter, diced
175ml/6fl oz/¾ cup whipping or
  double (heavy) cream
4 eggs, separated
40g/1½oz/⅓ cup mature Cheddar
  cheese, grated
ground black pepper
watercress, to garnish

COOK'S TIP
In a comfort food emergency, when smoked haddock may not be available, use drained and flaked canned tuna or salmon instead.

1 Remove the skin and any bones from the haddock fillet and discard. Carefully flake the flesh using a fork.

2 Melt half the butter with 60ml/4 tbsp of the cream in a fairly small non-stick pan, then add the flaked fish and stir together gently. Cover the pan with a lid, remove from the heat and set aside to cool slightly.

3 Mix the egg yolks with 15ml/1 tbsp of the cream. Season with pepper, then stir into the fish. In a separate bowl, mix the cheese and the remaining cream. Stiffly whisk the egg whites, then fold into the fish mixture. Heat the remaining butter in an omelette pan, add the fish mixture and cook until browned underneath. Pour the cheese mixture over and grill (broil) until bubbling. Garnish and serve.

Energy 850Kcal/3518kJ; Protein 38.6g; Carbohydrate 2.6g, of which sugars 2.6g; Fat 76.2g, of which saturates 43.3g; Cholesterol 653mg; Calcium 291mg; Fibre 0g; Sodium 1151mg.

MUFFINS <u>WITH</u> BACON, EGGS <u>AND</u> QUICK HOLLANDAISE SAUCE

THIS TASTY BREAKFAST IS IDEAL FOR BIRTHDAYS, ANNIVERSARIES OR OTHER DAYS WHEN YOU WANT TO TREAT SOMEONE SPECIAL. THE SAUCE IS MADE IN A BLENDER OR FOOD PROCESSOR, WHICH TURNS IT FROM A SLIGHTLY DIFFICULT RECIPE INTO AN EASY OPTION.

2 Fill a large frying pan with water and bring to the boil. Add the vinegar and regulate the heat so that the water simmers. Crack the eggs into the water and poach them for 3–4 minutes, or slightly longer for firm eggs.

3 Split and toast the muffins while the eggs are cooking. Spread with butter and place on warmed plates.

4 To make the hollandaise sauce, process the egg yolks and white wine vinegar in a blender or food processor. Melt the butter. With the motor still running, very gradually add the hot melted butter through the feeder tube. The hot butter will cook the yolks to make a thick, glossy sauce. Switch off the machine as soon as all the butter has been added and the sauce has thickened. Season to taste.

5 Arrange the bacon on the muffins and add a poached egg to each. Top with a spoonful of sauce and grind over some black pepper. Serve immediately.

COOK'S TIPS
• Eggs that are a week or more old will not keep their shape when poached so, for the best results, use very fresh free-range organic eggs.
• To make sure that you don't break the yolk, crack the eggs into a cup before carefully adding them to the gently simmering water.

SERVES FOUR

INGREDIENTS
   350g/12oz rindless back (lean) bacon rashers (strips)
   dash of white wine vinegar
   4 eggs
   4 English muffins
   butter, for spreading
   salt and ground black pepper
For the hollandaise sauce
   2 egg yolks
   5ml/1 tsp white wine vinegar
   75g/3oz/6 tbsp butter

1 Preheat the grill (broiler) and cook the bacon for 5–8 minutes, turning once, or until crisp on both sides.

Energy 612Kcal/2549kJ; Protein 32.6g; Carbohydrate 30.2g, of which sugars 2.4g; Fat 41.1g, of which saturates 18.3g; Cholesterol 429mg; Calcium 143mg; Fibre 1.3g; Sodium 1880mg.

EGGS RANCHEROS

THERE ARE MANY VARIATIONS ON THIS POPULAR DISH, WHICH IS GREAT FOR BREAKFAST OR BRUNCH.
THE COMBINATION OF CREAMY EGGS WITH ONION, CHILLI AND TOMATOES WORKS WONDERFULLY WELL.

SERVES FOUR

INGREDIENTS
oil, for frying
2 corn tortillas, several days old, cut
  into strips
2 fresh green jalapeño chillies
1 garlic clove
4 spring onions (scallions)
1 large tomato
8 eggs, beaten
150ml/¼ pint/⅔ cup single (light)
  cream
chopped fresh coriander (cilantro)
salt and ground black pepper

1 Heat 1cm/½in oil in a frying pan until very hot, watching it closely. Fry the tortilla strips until golden, turning occasionally; drain on kitchen paper.

2 Spear the chillies on a long-handled metal skewer and roast them over the flame of a gas burner until the skins blister and darken. Do not let the flesh burn. Alternatively, dry fry them in a griddle pan until the skins are scorched. Place them in a strong plastic bag and tie the top to keep the steam in. Set aside for 20 minutes.

3 Meanwhile, crush the garlic and chop the spring onions finely. Cut a cross in the base of the tomato. Place it in a heatproof bowl and pour over boiling water to cover. After 3 minutes lift the tomato out using a slotted spoon and plunge it into a bowl of cold water. Leave for a few minutes to cool.

4 Drain the tomato, remove the skin and cut it into four pieces. Using a teaspoon scoop out the seeds and the core, then dice the flesh finely.

5 Remove the chillies from the bag and peel off the skins. Cut off the stalks, then slit the chillies and scrape out the seeds. Chop the flesh finely. Put the eggs in a bowl, season with salt and pepper and beat lightly.

6 Heat 15ml/1 tbsp oil in a large frying pan. Add the garlic and spring onions and fry gently for 2–3 minutes until soft. Stir in the diced tomato and cook for 3–4 minutes more, then stir in the chillies and cook for 1 minute.

7 Pour the eggs into the pan and stir until they start to set. When only a small amount of uncooked egg remains visible, stir in the cream so that the cooking process is slowed down and the mixture cooks to a creamy mixture rather than a solid mass.

8 Stir the chopped coriander into the scrambled egg. Arrange the tortilla strips on four serving plates and spoon the eggs over. Serve at once.

Energy 324Kcal/1355kJ; Protein 18.4g; Carbohydrate 17.8g, of which sugars 3.1g; Fat 20.9g, of which saturates 8.3g; Cholesterol 477mg; Calcium 146mg; Fibre 1.2g; Sodium 254mg.

KITCHIRI ᵂᴵᵀᴴ RED LENTILS

THIS LENTIL AND RICE DISH IS A DELICIOUS INTERPRETATION OF ORIGINAL INDIAN KITCHIRI, WHICH WAS ADAPTED BY THE BRITISH TO USE SMOKED FISH INSTEAD OF DHAL AND RENAMED KEDGEREE. SLIGHTLY SPICY AND FULL OF CALMING CARBOHYDRATE, THIS IS PERFECT FOR A LAZY BREAKFAST.

SERVES FOUR

INGREDIENTS
  50g/2oz/¼ cup red lentils, rinsed
  1 bay leaf
  225g/8oz/1 cup basmati rice
  4 cloves
  50g/2oz/4 tbsp butter
  5ml/1 tsp curry powder
  2.5ml/½ tsp mild chilli powder
  30ml/2 tbsp chopped flat leaf parsley
  salt and freshly ground black pepper
  4 hard-boiled eggs, quartered, to
    serve (optional)

1 Put the lentils in a pan, add the bay leaf and cover with cold water. Bring to the boil, skim off any foam, then reduce the heat. Cover and simmer for 25–30 minutes, until tender. Drain, then discard the bay leaf.

2 Meanwhile, place the rice in a pan and pour in enough cold water to cover it. Swirl the rice and water, then drain it in a sieve. Repeat once more, then return the drained rice to the pan. Cover with 475ml/16fl oz/2 cups boiling water. Add the cloves and a generous pinch of salt. Cook, covered, for 10–15 minutes, until all the water is absorbed and the rice is tender. Discard the cloves.

3 Melt the butter in a frying pan over a gentle heat, then add the curry and chilli powders and cook for 1 minute.

4 Stir in the lentils and rice and mix well until they are coated in the spiced butter. Season the mixture to taste and cook for 1–2 minutes until heated through. Stir in the parsley and serve with the hard-boiled eggs, if using.

Energy 335Kcal/1397kJ; Protein 7.2g; Carbohydrate 52g, of which sugars 0.4g; Fat 10.7g, of which saturates 6.5g; Cholesterol 0mg; Calcium 19mg; Fibre 0.6g; Sodium 80mg.

GRIDDLED TOMATOES ᴼᴺ SODA BREAD

NOTHING COULD BE SIMPLER THAN THIS BASIC DISH, TRANSFORMED INTO SOMETHING SPECIAL BY ADDING A DRIZZLE OF OLIVE OIL, BALSAMIC VINEGAR AND SHAVINGS OF PARMESAN CHEESE.

SERVES FOUR

INGREDIENTS
  olive oil, for brushing and drizzling
  6 tomatoes, thickly sliced
  4 thick slices soda bread
  balsamic vinegar, for drizzling
  salt and freshly ground black pepper
  shavings of Parmesan cheese, to
    serve

COOK'S TIP
Using a griddle pan reduces the amount of oil required for cooking the tomatoes and gives them a barbecued flavour.

1 Brush a griddle pan with olive oil and heat. Add the tomato slices and cook for 4–6 minutes, turning once, until softened and slightly blackened. Alternatively, heat a grill (broiler) to high and line the rack with foil. Grill (broil) the tomato slices for 4–6 minutes, turning once, until softened.

2 Meanwhile, lightly toast the soda bread. Place the tomatoes on top of the toast and drizzle each portion with a little olive oil and vinegar. Season to taste and serve immediately with thin shavings of Parmesan.

Energy 142Kcal/602kJ; Protein 4.7g; Carbohydrate 28.8g, of which sugars 8.1g; Fat 1.7g, of which saturates 0.2g; Cholesterol 0mg; Calcium 72mg; Fibre 3.1g; Sodium 188mg.

FRIED POTATOES <u>WITH</u> CHORIZO <u>AND</u> EGG

THIS SUMPTUOUS SPANISH BREAKFAST WILL SET YOU UP FOR A DAY OF HARD PHYSICAL WORK IN THE GARDEN.

SERVES FOUR

INGREDIENTS
6 fresh jalapeño chillies
60ml/4 tbsp vegetable oil
1 onion, finely chopped
450g/1lb waxy potatoes, scrubbed
   and cut in 1cm/½in cubes
few sprigs of fresh oregano, chopped,
   plus extra, to garnish
75g/3oz/1 cup freshly grated
   Parmesan cheese (optional)
225g/8oz chorizo sausage, sliced
4 eggs

1 Dry roast the jalapeños in a griddle pan, turning them frequently so that the skins blacken but do not burn. Place them in a strong plastic bag and tie the top to keep the steam in. Set aside for 20 minutes.

2 Remove the jalapeños from the bag, peel off the skins and remove any stems. Cut them in half, scrape out the seeds, then chop the flesh finely.

3 Meanwhile, heat half the oil in a large heavy frying pan which has a lid. Add the onion and fry, stirring occasionally, for 3–4 minutes, until translucent, then add the potato cubes.

4 Stir to coat the potato cubes in oil, then cover the pan and cook over a moderate heat for 20–25 minutes, until the potatoes are tender. Shake the pan occasionally to stop them from sticking to the bottom.

5 When the potatoes are tender, push them to the side of the frying pan, then add the remaining oil.

6 When the oil is hot, spread out the potatoes and add the jalapeños. Cook over a high heat for 5–10 minutes, stirring carefully so that the potatoes turn golden but do not break up.

7 Add the oregano and Parmesan, if using. Mix gently, spoon on to a heated serving dish or plates and keep hot.

8 Fry the chorizo in any oil remaining in the pan until cooked and browned. Add to the potatoes. Fry the eggs to taste using the chorizo fat or fresh oil, as preferred. Add to the potatoes and serve at once, sprinkled with oregano.

Energy 186Kcal/776kJ; Protein 2.2g; Carbohydrate 19.9g, of which sugars 2.7g; Fat 11.4g, of which saturates 1.4g; Cholesterol 0mg; Calcium 13mg; Fibre 1.5g; Sodium 13mg.

BLACK PUDDING SNACKETTES

THIS IS A TRENDY TAKE ON THAT BREAKFAST FAVOURITE, FRIED BLACK PUDDING. MAKE IT WITH BLACK PUDDING OR MORCILLA – THE SPANISH BLACK PUDDING SEASONED WITH GARLIC AND OREGANO. THESE SNACKETTES ARE POPPED AWAY ONE AFTER THE OTHER, SO BE SURE TO MAKE PLENTY.

SERVES FOUR

INGREDIENTS

15ml/1 tbsp olive oil
1 onion, thinly sliced
2 garlic cloves, thinly sliced
5ml/1 tsp dried oregano
5ml/1 tsp paprika
225g/8oz black pudding (blood sausage), cut into 12 thick slices
1 thin French stick, sliced into 12
30ml/2 tbsp fino sherry
sugar, to taste
salt and ground black pepper
chopped fresh oregano, to garnish

COOK'S TIP

If you can find real *morcilla*, serve it neat: simply fry the slices in olive oil and use to top little rounds of bread. If you cannot find black pudding, you can use red chorizo instead.

1 Heat the olive oil in a large frying pan and fry the sliced onion, garlic, oregano and paprika for 7–8 minutes until the onion is softened and has turned golden brown.

2 Add the slices of black pudding, then increase the heat and cook them for 3 minutes, without stirring. Turn them over carefully with a spatula and cook for a further 3 minutes until crisp.

3 Arrange the rounds of bread on a large serving plate and top each with a slice of black pudding. Stir the sherry into the onions and add a little sugar to taste. Heat, swirling the mixture around the pan until bubbling, then season with salt and black pepper.

4 Spoon a little of the onion mixture on top of each slice of black pudding. Scatter the oregano over and serve.

Energy 513Kcal/2164kJ; Protein 16.2g; Carbohydrate 77.4g, of which sugars 4.8g; Fat 16.7g, of which saturates 5.1g; Cholesterol 24mg; Calcium 213mg; Fibre 3.2g; Sodium 1208mg.

CHEER-ME-UPS

The very thought of preparing some dishes is enlivening. This chapter is full of foods that are just right for times when other things are going wrong. Tempting sarnies and toddler suppers are included along with grown-up recipes that bring back memories of happy times. From boiled eggs with toast fingers to sticky buns, there's a recipe to cheer up every mood.

JAMMY TOAST

THE SIMPLEST SNACKS WITH MINIMAL INGREDIENTS ARE OFTEN THE TREATS THAT TASTE THE BEST.
FLAVOURING THE BUTTER IS NOT ESSENTIAL BUT MAKES A NICE TOUCH.

SERVES TWO

INGREDIENTS
75g/3oz/6 tbsp butter
a little natural vanilla essence
 (extract)
grated rind of 1 lemon (optional)
4 slices bread
20ml/4 tsp jam (jelly)

1 Cream the butter with vanilla to taste
until thoroughly combined. Mix in the
lemon rind, if using.

2 Toast the bread on both sides. Serve
piping hot or leave to cool on a rack
until crisp if preferred. Spread thickly
with flavoured butter and jam, and eat
at once.

Energy 445Kcal/1854kJ; Protein 4.4g; Carbohydrate 38.1g, of which sugars 13.1g; Fat 31.7g, of which saturates 19.8g; Cholesterol 80mg; Calcium 90mg; Fibre 1.7g; Sodium 475mg.

SMOKED MACKEREL PÂTÉ

SOME OF THE MOST DELICIOUS DISHES ARE ALSO THE EASIEST TO MAKE. SERVE THIS POPULAR PÂTÉ
WITH THIN MELBA OR HOT WHOLEMEAL (WHOLE-WHEAT) TOAST FOR A DEEPLY SATISFYING SNACK.

SERVES SIX

INGREDIENTS
4 smoked mackerel fillets, skinned
225g/8oz/1 cup cream cheese
1–2 garlic cloves, finely chopped
juice of 1 lemon
30ml/2 tbsp chopped fresh chervil,
 parsley or chives
15ml/1 tbsp Worcestershire sauce
salt and cayenne pepper
chopped fresh chives, to garnish

1 Break up the mackerel, discarding
the skin and bones, and place in a food
processor. Add the cream cheese,
garlic, lemon juice and chervil, parsley
or chives.

2 Process the ingredients until
combined but with a slightly coarse
texture, not completely smooth.

3 Add the Worcestershire sauce, salt
and cayenne pepper to taste. Process to
mix, then spoon the pâté into a dish,
cover with clear film (plastic wrap) and
chill for at least 30 minutes.

4 Sprinkle with chopped chives to
garnish and serve.

Energy 402Kcal/1661kJ; Protein 13.8g; Carbohydrate 0.4g, of which sugars 0.4g; Fat 38.4g, of which saturates 15.3g; Cholesterol 106mg; Calcium 55mg; Fibre 0g; Sodium 643mg.

GARLIC MUSHROOMS ON TOAST

PUNCHY FLAVOUR AND RICH BUTTERY JUICES TASTE DIVINE IN THIS SIMPLE SUPPER TREAT.

SERVES FOUR

INGREDIENTS
4 large slices bread
75g/3oz/6 tbsp butter, plus extra
   melted butter for brushing bread
3 shallots, finely chopped
2 garlic cloves, finely chopped
675g/1½lb field (portabello) or
   chestnut mushrooms, thickly sliced
75ml/5 tbsp dry white wine
45ml/3 tbsp chopped fresh parsley
salt and ground black pepper

1 Toast the bread on both sides under a hot grill (broiler). Alternatively, heat a ridged griddle until very hot and toast the bread on both sides until quite dark. Brush the toasted bread with melted butter and keep warm.

2 Melt the butter in a frying pan, add the shallots and garlic, and cook for 5 minutes until golden. Add the mushrooms and toss well. Fry over a high heat for 1 minute.

3 Pour in the wine and season well. Boil over high heat until the wine evaporates and the mushrooms are moist and buttery. Lightly stir in the parsley. Pile the mushrooms on the toast and serve immediately.

Energy 297Kcal/1240kJ; Protein 8.1g; Carbohydrate 25.9g, of which sugars 2.9g; Fat 17.3g, of which saturates 10.2g; Cholesterol 40mg; Calcium 107mg; Fibre 3.3g; Sodium 420mg.

CINNAMON TOAST

THIS IS AN OLD-FASHIONED SNACK THAT IS WARMING AND SOOTHING ON A COLD DAY. CINNAMON TOAST IS PERFECT WITH A HOT CHOCOLATE DRINK OR WITH FRESH FRUIT.

SERVES TWO

INGREDIENTS
75g/3oz/6 tbsp butter
2 teaspoons ground cinnamon
30ml/2 tbsp caster (superfine) sugar
4 slices bread
prepared fresh fruit (optional)

1 Cream the butter with the cinnamon and half the sugar.

2 Toast the bread on both sides. Spread with the butter and sprinkle with a little extra sugar. Serve at once, with pieces of fresh fruit, if you like.

Energy 451Kcal/1877kJ; Protein 4.4g; Carbohydrate 39.6g, of which sugars 14.6g; Fat 31.7g, of which saturates 19.8g; Cholesterol 80mg; Calcium 94mg; Fibre 1.7g; Sodium 471mg

CROQUE MONSIEUR

A POPULAR FRENCH SNACK THAT LITERALLY TRANSLATED MEANS "CRUNCH (OR MUNCH) GENTLEMAN".
TRADITIONALLY FRIED, BUT OFTEN TOASTED, THIS IS IDEAL WHEN INSTANT COMFORT IS REQUIRED.

SERVES TWO

INGREDIENTS
a little butter, for spreading
4 thin slices of country-style bread
75g/3oz Gruyère or Cheddar
cheese, sliced
2 lean honey roast ham slices
ground black pepper
flat leaf parsley, to garnish

1 Preheat a sandwich toaster or the grill (broiler). Lightly butter the bread and place the cheese and ham on 2 slices. Top with the other slices of bread and press firmly together.

2 Cook in the sandwich toaster or under the grill until browned on both sides. Serve hot, garnished with parsley.

Energy 480Kcal/2010kJ; Protein 20.9g; Carbohydrate 48.6g, of which sugars 3.1g; Fat 22.9g, of which saturates 14g; Cholesterol 65mg; Calcium 452mg; Fibre 2.1g; Sodium 1072mg.

WELSH RAREBIT

THIS HAS BEEN A FAVOURITE SNACK FOR GENERATIONS. TRADITIONALLY, THE CHEESE IS MELTED WITH
BUTTER, A LITTLE BEER, MUSTARD AND SEASONING, THEN SPREAD ON TOAST, BUT THIS IS A QUICK AND
QUIRKY VERSION. USE GOOD MELTING CHEESE, SUCH AS CHEDDAR, MONTEREY JACK OR CAERPHILLY.

SERVES TWO

INGREDIENTS
2 thick slices bread
butter, for spreading
10ml/2 tsp spicy or mild mustard
100g/3¾ oz Cheddar cheese, sliced
pinch of paprika or cayenne pepper
ground black pepper

1 Preheat the grill (broiler) and lightly toast the bread on both sides. Spread with butter and mustard, then top with the cheese. Heat under the grill until the cheese melts and starts to brown.

2 Sprinkle a little paprika or cayenne on the cheese. Season with pepper.

Energy 363Kcal/1516kJ; Protein 17.3g; Carbohydrate 24.3g, of which sugars 1.6g; Fat 21.5g, of which saturates 13.7g; Cholesterol 59mg; Calcium 457mg; Fibre 1.1g; Sodium 687mg.

BOILED EGG WITH TOAST SOLDIERS

IT IS A GOOD IDEA TO GET BACK TO BASICS OCCASIONALLY AND THIS IS ONE OF THE FIRST EATING EXPERIENCES MOST PEOPLE HAVE. EGGS AND TOAST ARE NUTRITIOUS, WARMING AND COMFORTING. TOAST SOLDIERS HAVE A SMILE-A-DIP QUALITY THAT IS JUST UNBEATABLE.

SERVES ONE

INGREDIENTS
  1 egg
  4 thin slices bread
  a little butter, for spreading
  salt

1 Place the egg in a small pan and pour in hot, not boiling, water to cover. Bring to the boil and cook for 3 minutes for a very soft egg, 4 minutes for a soft yolk and firm white, or 8 minutes for a hard egg.

2 Toast the bread while the egg is boiling and cut it into fingers. Serve the freshly boiled egg with toast fingers, butter and salt to sprinkle.

Energy 409Kcal/1710kJ; Protein 12.5g; Carbohydrate 40.3g, of which sugars 2.8g; Fat 23.1g, of which saturates 12.3g; Cholesterol 235mg; Calcium 154mg; Fibre 2.5g; Sodium 556mg

POACHED EGG ON TOAST

BUY THE FRESHEST EGGS AS THEIR WHITES ARE NOT TOO RUNNY, SO THEY STAY IN SHAPE DURING COOKING. ADD A LITTLE VINEGAR TO THE SIMMERING WATER TO HELP THE WHITE SET QUICKLY AND SWIRL THE WATER BEFORE DROPPING IN THE EGG. A COMFORTING SUPPER IN JUST A FEW MINUTES.

SERVES ONE

INGREDIENTS
  1 red or green (bell) pepper or a
    mixture of both
  1 spring onion (scallion), chopped
  75g/3oz/6 tbsp butter
  chilli flakes (optional)
  2 eggs
  2 thin slices toast
  salt and ground black pepper

1 Cook the pepper and spring onions in the butter until soft. Add chilli if liked.

2 Poach the eggs in a frying pan of simmering water for 2–3 minutes, until set. Arrange the peppers and eggs on toast and serve at once.

Energy 891Kcal/3692kJ; Protein 19.4g; Carbohydrate 39.4g, of which sugars 13.2g; Fat 74.3g, of which saturates 42.5g; Cholesterol 540mg; Calcium 146mg; Fibre 3.8g; Sodium 914mg

CLASSIC EGG MAYO SANDWICH

WHEN THE EGG IS PERFECTLY HARD-BOILED, THE MAYONNAISE FRESHLY MADE AND THE BREAD SOFT AND CRUSTY, THIS IS ONE OF THE MOST SATISFYING SANDWICHES TO EAT.

SERVES TWO

INGREDIENTS
    4 eggs
    4 spring onions (scallions), chopped
    1 dill-pickled cucumber, chopped
    softened butter
    4 thick slices bread
    mustard and cress, watercress, or
        rocket (arugula)
    salt and ground black pepper
For the mayonnaise
    2 egg yolks
    2.5ml/½ tsp Dijon or English (hot)
        mustard
    300ml/½ pint/1¼ cups mild olive oil
    15ml/1 tbsp white wine vinegar or a
        squeeze of lemon juice
    salt and ground black pepper

1 Make the mayonnaise. Beat 2 egg yolks with the mustard and salt in a bowl. Add half the oil a tablespoon at a time and whisk in each addition until the mixture begins to thicken. Add the vinegar or lemon juice and beat again. Add the remaining oil in a thin, steady stream, beating all the time. Season. Chill.

2 Place the eggs in a pan and cover with cold water. Simmer for 7 minutes. Drain and immerse in cold water.

3 Peel and roughly chop the eggs. Add the spring onions, cucumber and enough mayonnaise to make a thick, spreadable mixture.

4 Butter the bread. Scatter with cress, watercress or rocket and pile the filling on top. Top with bread.

Energy 680Kcal/2819kJ; Protein 15g; Carbohydrate 30.2g, of which sugars 3.5g; Fat 56.5g, of which saturates 13.6g; Cholesterol 35mg; Calcium 201mg; Fibre 2.3g; Sodium 479mg.

CHICKEN TIKKA SANDWICH

USING COOKED CHICKEN TIKKA TO FILL A SANDWICH IS A GREAT WAY OF ENJOYING THE SPICINESS OF INDIAN FOOD WITHOUT HAVING TO PREPARE OR BUY A WHOLE MEAL.

SERVES ONE

INGREDIENTS
    1 chicken tikka breast
    butter for spreading
    2 thick slices wholemeal (whole-
        wheat) bread
    mango chutney
    watercress sprigs

1 Slice the chicken tikka thinly. Butter the bread and spread one slice with a little mango chutney.

2 Arrange the chicken on the bread and top with watercress sprigs. Cover with the second slice of bread and press down gently.

Energy 360Kcal/1525kJ; Protein 35.9g; Carbohydrate 43.3g, of which sugars 16.5g; Fat 6g, of which saturates 0.7g; Cholesterol 88mg; Calcium 139mg; Fibre 2.3g; Sodium 729mg.

CHEESE SALAD BAGUETTE

ONE OF THE MOST POPULAR OF ALL SANDWICHES. CHEESE IS A STAPLE PART OF MANY PEOPLE'S DIETS AND ITS FAMILIARITY MAKES IT TRULY COMFORTING. ADD YOUR CHOICE OF SALAD AND PICKLE.

SERVES ONE

INGREDIENTS
  1 small baguette
  butter for spreading
  3 slices hard cheese, such as
    Cheddar, red Leicester, Spanish
    Manchego or Monterey Jack
  2 tomatoes, sliced
  ½ small red or white onion
  watercress sprigs
  mixed salad leaves
  salt and pepper

1 Slit the baguette open lengthways and spread with butter. Insert the cheese, cutting large slices in half so that they fit.

2 Add the tomatoes and the onion, separating the slices into rings. Season lightly with salt and pepper.

3 Insert some watercress and salad leaves and press the baguette closed.

Energy 700Kcal/2931kJ; Protein 25.8g; Carbohydrate 64.1g, of which sugars 9.4g; Fat 38.4g, of which saturates 23.9g; Cholesterol 101mg; Calcium 590mg; Fibre 4.2g; Sodium 1182mg.

CLASSIC BLT

THIS DELICIOUS AMERICAN SANDWICH IS MADE WITH CRISPY FRIED BACON, LETTUCE AND TOMATO. CHOOSE THE BREAD YOU PREFER AND TOAST IT IF YOU LIKE.

MAKES TWO

INGREDIENTS
  4 slices Granary (whole-wheat) bread
  15g/½oz/1 tbsp softened butter
  few crisp cos (Romano) or iceberg
    lettuce leaves
  1 large tomato, sliced
  8 rashers (strips) streaky (fatty)
    bacon
  30ml/2 tbsp mayonnaise

1 Spread two of the slices of bread with butter. Lay the lettuce over the bread and cover with sliced tomato.

2 Grill (broil) the bacon rashers until they begin to crisp, then arrange them over the sliced tomato.

3 Quickly spread the two remaining slices of bread with mayonnaise. Lay the bread over the bacon, press the sandwiches together gently and cut in half. Serve immediately.

Energy 587Kcal/2439kJ; Protein 17.5g; Carbohydrate 28.2g, of which sugars 3g; Fat 46.1g, of which saturates 8.5g; Cholesterol 414mg; Calcium 150mg; Fibre 2g; Sodium 587mg.

FRIED MOZZARELLA SANDWICH

THIS IS REASSURING SNACKING ITALIAN STYLE, WITH GLORIOUS MELTING MOZZARELLA IN CRISP FRIED EGG-SOAKED BREAD. THE RESULT IS A DELICIOUS SAVOURY SANDWICH.

MAKES TWO

INGREDIENTS
    115g/4oz mozzarella cheese,
      thickly sliced
    4 thick slices white bread
    1 egg
    30ml/2 tbsp milk
    vegetable oil, for frying
    salt and freshly ground black pepper
    tomato, to garnish

1 Place the cheese on two slices of bread and season to taste. Top with the remaining bread to make two cheese sandwiches.

2 Beat the egg with the milk. Season with salt and pepper to taste and pour into a shallow dish.

3 Carefully dip the sandwiches into the egg and milk mixture until thoroughly coated. Leave to soak while heating the oil in a large, heavy frying pan.

4 Fry the sandwiches, in batches if necessary, until golden brown and crisp on both sides. Remove from the frying pan and drain well on kitchen paper. Garnish with tomato.

VARIATION
Use any favourite cheese instead of mozzarella. Add some chopped spring onions (scallions) and sliced cooked ham or salami before sandwiching the bread together.

Energy 429Kcal/1789kJ; Protein 18.9g; Carbohydrate 30.5g, of which sugars 2.7g; Fat 26.6g, of which saturates 10.4g; Cholesterol 129mg; Calcium 331mg; Fibre 1.9g; Sodium 539mg.

TUNA MELT

THE COMBINATION OF TUNA AND GRILLED CHEESE OOZING OUT OF THE TOASTED BREAD MAKES THIS TOASTIE A HEAVENLY TREAT.

MAKES TWO

INGREDIENTS
    90g/3½oz can tuna, drained and
      flaked
    30ml/2 tbsp mayonnaise
    15ml/1 tbsp finely chopped celery
    15ml/1 tbsp finely chopped
      spring onion (scallion)
    15ml/1 tbsp chopped fresh parsley
    5ml/1 tsp lemon juice
    25g/1oz/2 tbsp softened butter
    4 slices wholemeal (whole-wheat)
      bread
    50g/2oz Gruyère or Emmenthal
      cheese, sliced
    salad leaves, tomatoes and corn,
      to garnish

1 Mix together the tuna, mayonnaise, celery, spring onion, parsley and lemon juice in a small bowl.

2 Butter the bread with half the butter and spread the tuna filling over two slices. Cover with the cheese, then sandwich with the remaining bread.

3 Butter the top of the bread and place under a moderate grill (broiler) for 1–2 minutes. Turn over, spread with butter and grill (broil) for a further 1–2 minutes until the cheese begins to melt. Garnish with salad leaves, tomatoes and corn.

Energy 567Kcal/2356kJ; Protein 22.3g; Carbohydrate 23.3g, of which sugars 1.6g; Fat 42.8g, of which saturates 15.5g; Cholesterol 96mg; Calcium 231mg; Fibre 3.2g; Sodium 832mg.

STEAK CIABATTA WITH HUMMUS AND SALAD

PACKED WITH GARLICKY HUMMUS AND A MUSTARD-SEASONED DRESSING ON THE CRUNCHY SALAD,
THESE STEAK SANDWICHES HAVE A FILLING TO BE RECKONED WITH.

SERVES FOUR

INGREDIENTS
3 garlic cloves, crushed to a paste
  with enough salt to season the
  steaks
30ml/2 tbsp extra virgin olive oil
4 sirloin steaks, 2.5cm/1in thick,
  total weight about 900g/2lb
2 romaine lettuce hearts
4 small ciabatta breads
salt and ground black pepper
For the dressing
10ml/2 tsp Dijon mustard
5ml/1 tsp cider or white wine vinegar
15ml/1 tbsp olive oil
For the hummus
400g/14oz can chickpeas, drained
  and rinsed
45ml/3 tbsp tahini
2 garlic cloves, crushed
juice of 1 lemon
30ml/2 tbsp water

1 To make the hummus, place the chickpeas in a food processor and pulse to a paste. Add the tahini, garlic, lemon juice, salt and pepper. Pour in the water and pulse to mix.

2 Make a dressing by mixing the mustard and vinegar in a jar. Add the oil and season to taste. Shake well.

3 Mix the garlic and oil in a dish. Add the steaks and rub the mixture into both surfaces.

4 Preheat the grill (broiler). Cook the steaks on a rack in a grill (broiling) pan. For rare meat, allow 2 minutes on one side and 3 minutes on the second side. For medium steaks, allow 4 minutes on each side. Transfer to a plate, cover and rest for 2 minutes.

5 Dress the lettuce. Split each ciabatta and heat on the grill rack for a minute. Fill with hummus, the steaks and leaves. Cut each in half to serve.

Energy 1060Kcal/4429kJ; Protein 75.9g; Carbohydrate 56.1g, of which sugars 3.5g; Fat 60.6g, of which saturates 11.6g; Cholesterol 115mg; Calcium 446mg; Fibre 9.6g; Sodium 791mg.

CORNISH PASTIES

THESE TRADITIONAL PASTIES ARE MADE WITH A RICH CRUMBLY SHORTCRUST THAT MELTS IN THE MOUTH. THE FILLING IS RAW WHEN ENCLOSED IN THE PASTRY, SO MUST BE COOKED THOROUGHLY.

MAKES SIX

INGREDIENTS
    450g/1lb chuck steak, diced
    1 potato, about 175g/6oz, diced
    175g/6oz swede (rutabaga), diced
    1 onion, chopped
    2.5ml/½ tsp dried mixed herbs
    1 egg, beaten
    salt and ground black pepper
    salad, to garnish
For the pastry
    350g/12oz/3 cups plain
      (all-purpose) flour
    pinch of salt
    115g/4oz/½ cup butter, diced
    50g/2oz/¼ cup lard (shortening) or
      white vegetable fat
    75–90ml/5–6 tbsp chilled water

1 To make the pastry, sift the flour and salt into a bowl. Using your fingertips or a pastry blender, lightly rub or cut in the butter and lard or vegetable fat, then sprinkle over most of the chilled water and mix to a soft dough, adding more water if necessary. Knead the pastry on a lightly floured surface for a few seconds until smooth. Wrap in clear film (plastic wrap) and chill for 30 minutes.

2 Preheat the oven to 220°C/425°F/ Gas 7. Divide the pastry into six pieces, then roll out each piece on a lightly floured surface to a 20cm/8in round.

3 Mix together the steak, vegetables, herbs and seasoning in a bowl, then spoon an equal amount on to one half of each pastry round.

4 Brush the pastry edges with water, then fold the free half of each round over the filling. Press the edges firmly together to seal, then use your fingertips to crimp the edges.

5 Brush the pasties with the beaten egg. Bake for 15 minutes, then reduce the temperature to 160°C/325°F/Gas 3 and bake for 1 hour more. Serve the pasties hot or cold with a salad garnish.

Energy 554Kcal/2317kJ; Protein 22.9g; Carbohydrate 53g, of which sugars 3.4g; Fat 29.2g, of which saturates 15.3g; Cholesterol 96mg; Calcium 110mg; Fibre 2.9g; Sodium 238mg.

CURRIED LAMB SAMOSAS

FILO PASTRY IS PERFECT FOR MAKING SAMOSAS AND IS SO LIGHT YOU'LL BE ABLE TO EAT LOTS OF THEM! YOU'LL BE AMAZED AT HOW QUICK AND EASY THEY ARE TO MAKE.

MAKES TWELVE

INGREDIENTS
  25g/1oz/2 tbsp butter
  225g/8oz/1 cup minced (ground)
    lamb
  30ml/2 tbsp mild curry paste
  12 filo pastry sheets
  salt and ground black pepper

1 Heat a little butter in a large pan and add the lamb. Fry for 5–6 minutes, stirring occasionally until browned. Stir in the curry paste and cook for 1–2 minutes. Season and set aside. Preheat the oven to 190°/375°C/Gas 5.

2 Melt the remaining butter in a small pan. Cut the pastry sheets in half lengthways. Brush one strip of pastry lightly with butter, then lay another strip on top and brush lightly and evenly with more butter.

3 Place a spoonful of lamb in the corner of the strip and fold over to form a triangle at one end. Keep folding over in the same way to form a triangular package. Brush with butter and place on a baking sheet. Repeat using the remaining pastry. Bake for 15–20 minutes until golden. Serve hot.

Energy 88Kcal/368kJ; Protein 4.6g; Carbohydrate 8.1g, of which sugars 0.2g; Fat 4.3g, of which saturates 2.3g; Cholesterol 19mg; Calcium 18mg; Fibre 0.3g; Sodium 26mg.

HUMMUS

THIS CLASSIC MIDDLE EASTERN DISH IS MADE FROM COOKED CHICKPEAS, GROUND TO A PASTE AND FLAVOURED WITH GARLIC, LEMON JUICE, TAHINI, OLIVE OIL AND CUMIN. IT IS DELICIOUS SERVED WITH WEDGES OF TOASTED PITTA BREAD OR CRUDITÉS.

SERVES FOUR TO SIX

INGREDIENTS
   400g/14oz can chickpeas, drained
   60ml/4 tbsp tahini
   2–3 garlic cloves, chopped
   juice of ½–1 lemon
   cayenne pepper
   small pinch to 1.5ml/¼ tsp ground
     cumin, to taste
   salt and ground black pepper

1 Using a potato masher or food processor coarsely mash the chickpeas. If you prefer a smoother purée, process them in a food processor or blender until smooth.

2 Mix the tahini into the chickpeas, then stir in the garlic, lemon juice, cayenne, cumin, and salt and pepper to taste. If needed, add a little water. Serve at room temperature.

Energy 461Kcal/1917kJ; Protein 17.8g; Carbohydrate 16.6g, of which sugars 0.6g; Fat 36.5g, of which saturates 5.1g; Cholesterol 0mg; Calcium 431mg; Fibre 8.7g; Sodium 232mg.

TARAMASALATA

THIS TASTY SPECIALITY MAKES AN EXCELLENT SNACK ON DULL DAYS, REVIVING MEMORIES OF HOLIDAYS IN THE SUN AND RELAXED EVENINGS SIPPING WELL-CHILLED WINE.

SERVES FOUR

INGREDIENTS
   115g/4oz smoked mullet roe
   2 garlic cloves, crushed
   30ml/2 tbsp grated onion

60ml/4 tbsp olive oil
4 slices white bread, crusts removed
juice of 2 lemons
30ml/2 tbsp milk or water
freshly ground black pepper
warm pitta bread, to serve

1 Place the smoked roe, garlic, onion, oil, bread and lemon juice in a blender or food processor and process until smooth. Add the milk or water and process again for a few seconds. (This will give the taramasalata a creamier texture.)

2 Pour the taramasalata into a bowl, cover with clear film (plastic wrap) and chill for 1–2 hours before serving. Sprinkle the dip with ground black pepper. Serve with warm pitta bread.

Energy 194Kcal/808kJ; Protein 8.6g; Carbohydrate 13.6g, of which sugars 1.6g; Fat 12.1g, of which saturates 1.7g; Cholesterol 95mg; Calcium 36mg; Fibre 0.6g; Sodium 1145mg.

POTATO SKINS WITH CAJUN DIP

DIVINELY CRISP AND NAUGHTY, THESE POTATO SKINS ARE GREAT ON THEIR OWN OR SERVED WITH THEIR PIQUANT DIP AS A DRIZZLED TOPPING OR ON THE SIDE.

SERVES TWO

INGREDIENTS
    2 large baking potatoes
    vegetable oil, for deep frying
For the dip
    120ml/4fl oz/½ cup natural (plain)
    yogurt
    1 garlic clove, crushed
    5ml/1 tsp tomato purée (paste)
    2.5ml/½ tsp green chilli purée or
    ½ small green chilli, chopped
    1.5ml/¼ tsp celery salt
    salt and ground black pepper

COOK'S TIP
If you prefer, you can microwave the potatoes to save time. This will take about 10 minutes.

1 Preheat the oven to 180°C/350°F/ Gas 4. Bake the potatoes for 45–50 minutes until tender. Cut them in half and scoop out the flesh, leaving a thin layer on the skins.

2 To make the dip, mix together all the ingredients and chill.

3 Heat a 1cm/½ in layer of oil in a large pan or deep-fat fryer. Cut each potato half in half again, then fry them until crisp and golden on both sides. Drain on kitchen paper, sprinkle with salt and black pepper and serve with a bowl of dip or a dollop of dip in each skin.

Energy 265Kcal/1095kJ; Protein 3.8g; Carbohydrate 12.2g, of which sugars 5g; Fat 22.8g, of which saturates 2.9g; Cholesterol 1mg; Calcium 121mg; Fibre 0.8g; Sodium 350mg.

CINNAMON RINGS

THESE SPICY LITTLE MEXICAN PUFFS ARE AUTHENTICALLY CALLED BUNUELOS. THEY RESEMBLE MINIATURE DOUGHNUTS AND TASTE SO GOOD IT IS HARD NOT TO OVER-INDULGE. MAKE THEM FOR A SNACK OR AS A PICK-ME-UP TO SERVE WITH COFFEE OR TEA.

MAKES TWELVE

INGREDIENTS
225g/8oz/2 cups plain (all-purpose)
   flour
pinch of salt
5ml/1 tsp baking powder
2.5ml/½ tsp ground anise
115g/4oz/½ cup caster (superfine)
   sugar
1 large (US extra large) egg
120ml/4fl oz/½ cup milk
50g/2oz/¼ cup butter
oil, for deep frying
10ml/2 tsp ground cinnamon
cinnamon sticks, to decorate

3 Pour the egg mixture and milk gradually into the flour, stirring all the time, until well blended, then add the melted butter. Mix first with a wooden spoon and then with your hands to make a soft dough.

6 Heat the oil for deep frying to a temperature of 190°C/375°F, or until a cube of dried bread, added to the oil, floats and then turns a golden colour in 30–60 seconds. Fry the *buñuelos* in small batches until they are puffy and golden brown, turning them once or twice during cooking. As soon as they are golden, lift them out of the oil using a slotted spoon and lie them on a double layer of kitchen paper to drain.

1 Sift the flour, salt, baking powder and ground anise into a mixing bowl. Add 30ml/2 tbsp of the caster sugar.

2 Place the egg and milk in a small jug (pitcher) and whisk well with a fork. Melt the butter in a small pan.

4 Lightly flour a work surface, tip the dough out on to it and knead for about 10 minutes, until smooth.

7 Mix the remaining caster sugar with the ground cinnamon in a small bowl. Add the *buñuelos*, one at a time, while they are still warm, toss them in the mixture until they are lightly coated and either serve at once or leave to cool. Decorate with cinnamon sticks.

COOK'S TIP
Buñuelos are sometimes served with syrup for dunking, which is just right when you need cheering up. For a syrup heat 175g/6oz/¾ cup soft dark brown sugar and 450ml/¾ pint/scant 2 cups water. Add a cinnamon stick and stir until the sugar dissolves, then boil and simmer for 15 minutes without stirring. Cool slightly before serving.

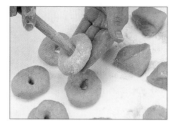

5 Divide the dough into 12 pieces and roll into balls. Slightly flatten each ball with your hand and then make a hole in the centre with the floured handle of a wooden spoon.

Energy 195Kcal/818kJ; Protein 2.6g; Carbohydrate 23.5g, of which sugars 10.8g; Fat 10.8g, of which saturates 3.2g; Cholesterol 29mg; Calcium 44mg; Fibre 0.5g; Sodium 38mg.

PAIN AU CHOCOLAT

A FRESHLY BAKED PAIN AU CHOCOLAT IS ALMOST IMPOSSIBLE TO RESIST, WITH ITS BUTTERY, FLAKY YET CRISP PASTRY CONCEALING A DELECTABLE CHOCOLATE FILLING. FOR A SPECIAL FINISH, DRIZZLE MELTED CHOCOLATE OVER THE TOPS OF THE FRESHLY BAKED AND COOKED PASTRIES.

MAKES NINE

INGREDIENTS
   250g/9oz/2¼ cups unbleached white
      bread flour
   30ml/2 tbsp skimmed milk powder
      (non fat dry milk)
   15ml/1 tbsp caster (superfine) sugar
   2.5ml/½ tsp salt
   7.5ml/1½ tsp easy-blend (rapid-rise)
      dried yeast
   140g/5oz/⅔ cup butter, softened
   125ml/4½fl oz/generous ½ cup hand-
      hot water
   225g/8oz plain (semisweet)
      chocolate, broken into pieces
For the glaze
   1 egg yolk
   15ml/1 tbsp milk

1 Mix the flour, milk powder, sugar and salt in a bowl. Stir in the yeast and make a well in the middle of these dry ingredients. Melt 25g/1oz/2 tbsp of the butter and add it to the dry ingredients, pouring it into the well in the middle of the mixture. Pour in the water and then mix to form a firm dough.

2 Turn the dough out on to a lightly floured surface and knead it thoroughly for about 10 minutes, until it is smooth and elastic. When pressed on the surface it should spring back rather than retain the dent.

3 Dust the bowl with flour and return the dough to it. Cover with clear film (plastic wrap) and leave in a warm place until doubled in size.

4 Meanwhile shape the remaining softened butter into an oblong block, about 2cm/¾in thick.

5 Lightly grease two baking sheets. When the dough has doubled in size, turn it out on to a floured surface. Knock back (punch down) and shape into a ball. Cut a cross halfway through the top of the dough.

6 Roll out around the cross, leaving a risen centre. Place the butter in the centre. Fold the rolled dough over the butter to enclose; seal the edges.

7 Roll to a rectangle 2cm/¾in thick, twice as long as wide. Fold the bottom third up and the top down; seal the edges with a rolling pin. Wrap in lightly oiled clear film. Place in the refrigerator and chill for 20 minutes.

8 Do the same again twice more, giving a quarter turn and chilling each time. Chill again for 30 minutes.

9 Roll out the dough to a rectangle measuring 52 x 30cm/21 x 12in. Using a sharp knife, cut the dough into three strips lengthways and widthways to make nine 18 x 10cm/7 x 4in rectangles.

10 Divide the chocolate among the three dough rectangles, placing the pieces lengthways at one short end.

11 Mix the egg yolk and milk for the glaze together. Brush the mixture over the edges of the dough.

12 Roll up each piece of dough to completely enclose the chocolate, then press the edges together to seal.

13 Place the pastries seam side down on the prepared baking sheets. Cover with oiled clear film and leave to rise in a warm place for about 30 minutes or until doubled in size.

14 Meanwhile, preheat the oven to 200°C/400°F/Gas 6. Brush the pastries with the remaining glaze and bake for about 15 minutes, or until golden. Turn out on to a wire rack to cool just slightly and serve warm.

VARIATION
Fill this flaky yeast pastry with a variety of sweet and savoury fillings. Try chopped nuts, tossed with a little brown sugar and cinnamon or, for a savoury filling, thin strips of cheese, wrapped in ham or mixed with chopped cooked bacon.

Energy 345Kcal/1441kJ; Protein 4g; Carbohydrate 39.3g, of which sugars 17.9g; Fat 20.1g, of which saturates 12.4g; Cholesterol 35mg; Calcium 51mg; Fibre 1.5g; Sodium 206mg

CHELSEA BUNS

SAID TO HAVE BEEN INVENTED BY THE OWNER OF THE CHELSEA BUN HOUSE IN LONDON AT THE END OF THE 17TH CENTURY, CHELSEA BUNS MAKE THE PERFECT ACCOMPANIMENT TO A CUP OF COFFEE OR TEA. THEY ARE SO DELICIOUS, IT IS DIFFICULT TO RESIST EATING SEVERAL IN ONE SITTING!

MAKES TWELVE

INGREDIENTS
  500g/1lb 2oz/4½ cups unbleached
    white bread flour
  2.5ml/½ tsp salt
  50g/2oz/¼ cup butter, softened
  75g/3oz/6 tbsp caster (superfine)
    sugar
  5ml.1tsp easy-blend dried yeast
  225ml/8fl oz/scant 1 cup hand-hot
    milk
  1 egg, beaten
For the glaze
  50g/2oz/¼ cup caster (superfine)
    sugar
  5ml/1 tsp orange flower water
For the filling
  25g/1oz/2 tbsp butter, melted
  115g/4oz/⅔ cup sultanas
    (golden raisins)
  25g/1oz/3 tbsp mixed chopped
    (candied) peel
  25g/1oz/2 tbsp currants
  25g/1oz/2 tbsp soft light brown sugar
  5ml/1 tsp mixed (apple pie) spice

1 Mix the flour and salt in a large bowl, then rub in the butter and stir in the sugar and yeast.

2 Make a well in the middle of the dry ingredients and add the milk and egg. Mix the liquids into the dry ingredients to make a firm dough.

3 Turn the dough out on to a floured surface and knead thoroughly for about 10 minutes, until it is smooth and elastic. Flour the mixing bowl, return the dough to it and cover with oiled clear film (plastic wrap). Leave in a warm place until doubled in size.

4 Lightly grease a 23cm/9in square cake tin (pan). When the dough has risen, turn it out on to a floured surface and knock it back (punch it down).

5 Roll out the dough on a lightly floured surface into a square that measures about 30cm/12in.

6 Brush the dough with the melted butter for the filling and sprinkle it with the sultanas, mixed peel, currants, brown sugar and mixed spice, leaving a 1cm/½in border along one edge.

7 Starting at a covered edge, roll the dough up, Swiss (jelly) roll fashion. Press the edges together to seal. Cut the roll into 12 slices and then place these cut side uppermost in the prepared tin.

8 Cover with oiled clear film. Leave the buns to rise in a warm place for about 30–45 minutes, or until the dough slices have doubled in size and are almost at the top of the tin.

9 Meanwhile, preheat the oven to 200°C/400°F/Gas 6. Bake the buns for 15–20 minutes, or until they have risen well and are evenly golden all over.

10 Once they are baked, leave the buns to cool slightly in the tin before lifting them out and transferring them to a wire rack to cool.

11 Gently heat the ingredients for the glaze in a small pan until the sugar is dissolved. Brush the mixture over the warm buns. Serve slightly warm.

COOK'S TIP
Use icing (confectioners') sugar instead of caster sugar and make a thin glaze icing to brush or trickle over the freshly baked buns.

Energy 283Kcal/1199kJ; Protein 5g; Carbohydrate 55.7g, of which sugars 23.9g; Fat 6.1g, of which saturates 3.5g; Cholesterol 14mg; Calcium 99mg; Fibre 1.6g; Sodium 138mg.

BLUEBERRY MUFFINS

LIGHT AND FRUITY, THESE WELL-KNOWN AMERICAN MUFFINS ARE DELICIOUS AT ANY TIME OF DAY.
THEY TASTE TERRIFIC AND THE BLUEBERRIES MAKE A USEFUL CONTRIBUTION TO A HEALTHY DIET.

MAKES TWELVE

INGREDIENTS
  180g/6¼oz/generous 1½ cups
    plain (all-purpose) flour
  60g/2¼ oz/generous ¼ cup sugar
  10ml/2 tsp baking powder
  1.5ml/¼ tsp salt
  2 eggs
  50g/2oz/4 tbsp butter, melted
  175ml/6fl oz/¾ cup milk
  5ml/1 tsp vanilla essence
  5ml/1 tsp grated lemon rind
  175g/6oz/1½ cups fresh blueberries

1 Preheat the oven to 200°C/400°F/
Gas 6. Grease a 12-cup patty tin
(muffin pan) or arrange 12 paper muffin
cases on a baking tray.

2 Sift the flour, sugar, baking powder
and salt into a large mixing bowl. In
another bowl, whisk the eggs until
blended. Add the melted butter, milk,
vanilla and lemon rind to the eggs, and
stir thoroughly to combine.

3 Make a well in the dry ingredients
and pour in the egg mixture. With a
large metal spoon, stir until the flour is
just moistened, but not smooth.

VARIATION
Muffins are delicious with all kinds of
different fruits. Try out some variations
using this basic muffin recipe. Replace
the blueberries with the same weight of
bilberries, blackcurrants, stoned (pitted)
cherries or raspberries.

4 Add the blueberries to the muffin
mixture and gently fold in, being careful
not to crush the berries.

5 Spoon the batter into the muffin tin
or paper cases, leaving enough room for
the muffins to rise.

6 Bake for 20–25 minutes, until the
tops spring back when touched lightly.
Leave the muffins in the tin, if using, for
5 minutes before turning out on to a
wire rack to cool a little before serving.

COOK'S TIP
If you want to serve these muffins for
breakfast, prepare the dry ingredients
the night before to save time.

Energy 127Kcal/536kJ; Protein 3.3g; Carbohydrate 18.6g, of which sugars 7.1g; Fat 5g, of which saturates 2.7g; Cholesterol 48mg; Calcium 56mg; Fibre 1g; Sodium 96mg.

PRETZELS

PRETZELS ARE A REAL OLD-FASHIONED EVERYDAY TREAT. THE SOFT CHEWY TEXTURE AND SALTY TASTE ARE PARTICULARLY APPEALING. CARAWAY SEEDS SPRINKLED ON TOP GIVE A SLIGHTLY ANISEED FLAVOUR TO THIS ALL-AMERICAN SNACK.

MAKES TWELVE

INGREDIENTS
7g/¼ oz fresh yeast
75ml/5 tbsp water
15ml/1 tbsp unbleached plain
  (all-purpose) flour
For the dough
7g/¼ oz fresh yeast
150ml/¼ pint/⅔ cup lukewarm water
75ml/5 tbsp lukewarm milk
400g/14oz/3½ cups unbleached
  white bread flour
7.5ml/1½ tsp salt
25g/1oz/2 tbsp butter, melted
For the topping
1 egg yolk
15ml/1 tbsp milk
sea salt or caraway seeds

3 Turn out on to a lightly floured surface and knock back (punch down) the dough. Knead into a ball, return to the bowl, re-cover and leave to rise for 30 minutes.

4 Turn out the dough on to a lightly floured surface. Divide the dough into 12 equal pieces and form into balls. Take one ball of dough and cover the remainder with a dishtowel. Roll into a thin stick 46cm/18in long and about 1cm/½ in thick in the middle and thinner at the ends. Bend each end of the dough stick into a horseshoe. Cross over and place the ends on top of the thick part of the pretzel. Repeat with the remaining dough balls.

5 Place on the floured baking sheet to rest for 10 minutes. Meanwhile, preheat the oven to 190°C/375°F/Gas 5. Bring a large pan of water to the boil, then reduce to a simmer. Add the pretzels to the simmering water in batches, about 2–3 at a time and poach for about 1 minute. Drain the pretzels on a dishtowel and place on the greased baking sheets, spaced well apart.

6 Mix the egg yolk and milk together and brush this glaze over the pretzels. Sprinkle with sea salt or caraway seeds and bake the pretzels for 25 minutes, or until they are deep golden. Transfer to a wire rack to cool.

1 Lightly flour a baking sheet. Also grease two baking sheets. Cream the yeast for the yeast sponge with the water, then mix in the flour, cover with clear film (plastic wrap) and leave to stand at room temperature for 2 hours.

2 Mix the yeast for the dough with the water until dissolved, then stir in the milk. Sift 350g/12oz/3 cups of the flour and the salt into a large bowl. Add the yeast sponge mixture and the butter; mix for 3–4 minutes. Turn out on to a lightly floured surface and knead in the remaining flour to make a medium firm dough. Place in a lightly oiled bowl, cover with lightly oiled clear film and leave to rise, in a warm place, for 30 minutes, or until almost doubled in bulk.

Energy 136Kcal/577kJ; Protein 3.5g; Carbohydrate 27.2g, of which sugars 0.8g; Fat 2.3g, of which saturates 1.2g; Cholesterol 5mg; Calcium 56mg; Fibre 1.1g; Sodium 262mg.

COMFORTING
DISHES

When you need something really tasty to eat,
the recipes in this chapter provide plenty of
options. Indisputably delicious, they are also
relatively simple to make without any need for
tricky techniques.

TOMATO AND FRESH BASIL SOUP

BASIL HAS AN UPLIFTING INFLUENCE, HELPING TO BRIGHTEN DULL MOODS, AND THIS SOUP IS FULL OF SUMMER SUNSHINE. IT IS QUICK AND HOT FOR COLD DAYS OR REFRESHING WHEN SERVED CHILLED.

SERVES FOUR TO SIX

INGREDIENTS
15ml/1 tbsp olive oil
25g/1oz/2 tbsp butter
1 medium onion, finely chopped
900g/2lb ripe Italian plum tomatoes,
  roughly chopped
1 garlic clove, roughly chopped
about 750ml/1¼ pints/3 cups
  chicken or vegetable stock
120ml/4fl oz/½ cup dry white wine
30ml/2 tbsp sun-dried tomato paste
30ml/2 tbsp shredded fresh basil,
  plus a few whole leaves, to garnish
150 ml/¼ pint/⅔ cup double (heavy)
  cream
salt and freshly ground black pepper

1 Heat the oil and butter in a large pan until foaming. Add the onion and cook gently for about 5 minutes, stirring frequently, until softened but not brown.

2 Stir in the tomatoes and garlic, then add the stock, white wine and sun-dried tomato paste. Season to taste. Bring to the boil, lower the heat and half cover the pan. Simmer the soup steadily for about 20 minutes, stirring occasionally, until the tomatoes are pulpy.

3 Process the soup with the basil in a blender or food processor, then press through a sieve into a clean pan.

4 Add the cream and heat through, stirring. Do not allow the soup to boil. Check the consistency and add more stock if necessary and then taste for seasoning. Pour into heated bowls and garnish with basil. Serve at once.

VARIATION
The soup can be served chilled. Pour it into a container after sieving and chill for at least 4 hours. Serve in chilled bowls.

Energy 326Kcal/1351kJ; Protein 2.7g; Carbohydrate 9.7g, of which sugars 9.1g; Fat 28.9g, of which saturates 16.4g; Cholesterol 65mg; Calcium 45mg; Fibre 2.6g; Sodium 272mg.

CREAM OF ONION SOUP

THIS WONDERFULLY SOOTHING SOUP HAS A DEEP, BUTTERY FLAVOUR THAT IS COMPLEMENTED BY CRISP CROÛTONS OR CHOPPED CHIVES, SPRINKLED OVER JUST BEFORE SERVING.

SERVES FOUR

INGREDIENTS
115g/4oz/½ cup unsalted (sweet)
  butter
1kg/2¼lb yellow onions, sliced
1 fresh bay leaf
105ml/7 tbsp dry white vermouth
1 litre/1¾ pints/4 cups good chicken
  or vegetable stock
150ml/¼ pint/⅔ cup double
  (heavy) cream
a little lemon juice (optional)
salt and ground black pepper
croûtons or chopped fresh chives,
  to garnish

1 Melt 75g/3oz/6 tbsp butter in a large pan. Set about 200g/7oz of the onions aside and add the rest to the pan with the bay leaf. Stir to coat in the butter, then cover and cook very gently for about 30 minutes. The onions should be soft and tender, but not browned.

COOK'S TIP
Adding the second batch of onions gives texture and a buttery flavour to this soup.

2 Add the vermouth, increase the heat and boil rapidly until the liquid has evaporated. Add the stock, 5ml/1 tsp salt and pepper to taste. Bring to the boil, lower the heat and simmer for 5 minutes, then remove from the heat.

3 Leave the soup to cool, then discard the bay leaf and process the soup in a blender or food processor. Return the soup to the rinsed pan.

4 Melt the remaining butter in another pan. Cook the remaining onions slowly, covered, until soft but not browned. Uncover and continue to cook gently until golden yellow.

5 Add the cream to the soup and reheat gently until hot. Season, adding a little lemon juice if liked. Add the buttery onions and stir for 1–2 minutes. Serve with croûtons or chopped chives.

Energy 522Kcal/2151kJ; Protein 4g; Carbohydrate 21.5g, of which sugars 15.6g; Fat 44.5g, of which saturates 27.5g; Cholesterol 113mg; Calcium 90mg; Fibre 3.5g; Sodium 397mg.

ROASTED GARLIC AND BUTTERNUT SQUASH SOUP WITH TOMATO SALSA

THIS IS A WONDERFUL, RICHLY FLAVOURED DISH. A SPOONFUL OF THE HOT AND SPICY TOMATO SALSA GIVES BITE TO THE SWEET-TASTING SQUASH AND GARLIC SOUP.

SERVES FOUR TO FIVE

INGREDIENTS
2 garlic bulbs, outer papery
  skin removed
75ml/5 tbsp olive oil
a few fresh thyme sprigs
1 large butternut squash, halved
  and seeded
2 onions, chopped
5ml/1 tsp ground coriander
1.2 litres/2 pints/5 cups vegetable or
  chicken stock
30–45ml/2–3 tbsp chopped fresh
  oregano or marjoram
salt and ground black pepper
For the salsa
4 large ripe tomatoes, halved
  and seeded
1 red (bell) pepper, halved and
  seeded
1 large fresh red chilli, halved
  and seeded
30–45ml/2–3 tbsp extra virgin
  olive oil
15ml/1 tbsp balsamic vinegar
pinch of caster (superfine) sugar

1 Preheat the oven to 220°C/425°F/ Gas 7. Place the garlic on a piece of foil and pour over half the olive oil. Add the thyme sprigs, then fold the foil around the garlic bulbs to enclose them. Place the foil parcel on a baking sheet with the butternut squash and brush the squash with 15ml/1 tbsp of the remaining olive oil. Add the tomatoes, red pepper and fresh chilli for the salsa.

2 Roast the vegetables for 25 minutes, then remove the tomatoes, pepper and chilli. Reduce the temperature to 190°C/375°F/Gas 5 and cook the squash and garlic for 20–25 minutes more, or until the squash is tender.

3 Heat the remaining oil in a large, heavy pan and cook the onions and ground coriander gently for about 10 minutes, or until softened.

4 Skin the pepper and chilli and process in a food processor or blender with the tomatoes and 30ml/2 tbsp olive oil. Stir in the vinegar and seasoning to taste, adding a pinch of caster sugar. Add the remaining oil if you think the salsa needs it.

5 Squeeze the roasted garlic out of its papery skin into the onions and scoop the squash out of its skin, adding it to the pan. Add the stock, 5ml/1 tsp salt and plenty of black pepper. Bring to the boil and simmer for 10 minutes.

6 Stir in half the oregano or marjoram and cool the soup slightly, then process it in a blender or food processor. Alternatively, press the soup through a fine sieve (strainer).

7 Reheat the soup without allowing it to boil, then taste for seasoning before ladling it into warmed bowls. Top each with a spoonful of salsa and sprinkle over the remaining chopped oregano or marjoram. Serve immediately.

Energy 298Kcal/1245kJ; Protein 4.2g; Carbohydrate 26.7g, of which sugars 18g; Fat 20.3g, of which saturates 2.9g; Cholesterol 0mg; Calcium 118mg; Fibre 5.7g; Sodium 225mg.

ROASTED ROOT VEGETABLE SOUP

ROASTING THE VEGETABLES GIVES THIS WINTER SOUP A WONDERFUL DEPTH OF FLAVOUR. YOU CAN USE OTHER VEGETABLES, IF YOU WISH, OR ADAPT THE QUANTITIES DEPENDING ON WHAT'S IN SEASON.

SERVES SIX

INGREDIENTS

50ml/2fl oz/¼ cup olive oil
1 small butternut squash, peeled,
  seeded and cubed
2 carrots, cut into thick rounds
1 large parsnip, cubed
1 small swede (rutabaga), cubed
2 leeks, thickly sliced
1 onion, quartered
3 bay leaves
4 thyme sprigs, plus extra to garnish
3 rosemary sprigs
1.2 litres/2 pints/5 cups
  vegetable stock
salt and freshly ground black pepper
soured cream, to serve

1 Preheat the oven to 200°C/400°F/ Gas 6. Put the olive oil into a large bowl. Add the prepared vegetables and toss until coated in the oil.

2 Spread out the vegetables in a single layer on one large or two small baking sheets. Tuck the herbs among the vegetables.

3 Roast for 50 minutes until tender, turning the vegetables occasionally to make sure they brown evenly. Remove from the oven, discard the herbs and transfer the vegetables to a large pan.

4 Pour the stock into the pan and bring to the boil. Reduce the heat, season to taste, then simmer for 10 minutes. Transfer the soup to a food processor or blender (or use a hand blender) and process for a few minutes until thick and smooth.

5 Return the soup to the pan to heat through. Season and serve with a swirl of sour cream. Garnish each serving with a sprig of thyme.

COOK'S TIP
Dried herbs can be used in place of fresh; sprinkle 2.5ml/½ tsp of each type over the vegetables in step 2.

Energy 134Kcal/563kJ; Protein 3g; Carbohydrate 17.2g, of which sugars 11.3g; Fat 6.5g, of which saturates 0.9g; Cholesterol 0mg; Calcium 96mg; Fibre 5.2g; Sodium 160mg.

MINESTRONE

*THIS CLASSIC ITALIAN SOUP IS PACKED FULL OF VEGETABLES TO GIVE THE SYSTEM A VITAMIN BOOST
AND HAS A FABULOUSLY STRONG FLAVOUR. IT'S HEARTY AND WARMING TOO.*

SERVES FOUR TO SIX

INGREDIENTS
1 onion
2 celery sticks
1 large carrot
45ml/3 tbsp olive oil
150g/5oz French (green) beans, cut
  into 5cm/2in pieces
1 courgette (zucchini), thinly sliced
1 potato, cut into 1cm/½in cubes
¼ Savoy cabbage, shredded
1 small aubergine (eggplant), cut into
  1cm/½in cubes
200g/7oz can cannellini beans,
  drained and rinsed
2 Italian plum tomatoes, chopped
1.2 litres/2 pints/5 cups stock
90g/3½oz dried vermicelli
salt and ground black pepper
For the pesto
  about 20 fresh basil leaves
  1 garlic clove
  10ml/2 tsp pine nuts
  15ml/1 tbsp grated Parmesan cheese
  15ml/1 tbsp grated Pecorino cheese
  30ml/2 tbsp olive oil

1 Chop the onion, celery and carrot
finely, either in a food processor or
by hand. Heat the oil in a large pan,
add the chopped mixture and cook over
a low heat, stirring frequently, for
5–7 minutes.

2 Mix in the French beans, courgette,
potato and cabbage. Stir-fry over a
medium heat for about 3 minutes. Add
the aubergine, cannellini beans and
tomatoes, and stir-fry for 2–3 minutes
more. Pour in the stock with salt and
pepper to taste. Bring to the boil. Stir
well, cover and lower the heat. Simmer
for 40 minutes, stirring occasionally.

3 Meanwhile, process all the pesto
ingredients in a food processor until the
mixture forms a smooth sauce, adding
15–45ml/1–3 tbsp water through the
feeder tube if necessary.

4 Break the pasta into small pieces
and add it to the soup. Simmer, stirring
frequently, for 5 minutes. Add the pesto
sauce and stir it in well, then simmer
for 2–3 minutes more, or until the pasta
is *al dente*. Taste for seasoning. Serve
hot, in warmed soup plates or bowls.

Energy 387Kcal/1618kJ; Protein 13.1g; Carbohydrate 40g, of which sugars 9.6g; Fat 20.6g, of which saturates 4g; Cholesterol 8mg; Calcium 173mg; Fibre 7.7g; Sodium 527mg.

LEEK AND POTATO SOUP

ROCKET ADDS ITS DISTINCTIVE, PEPPERY TASTE TO THIS WONDERFULLY SATISFYING SOUP.
SERVE IT HOT, GARNISHED WITH A GENEROUS SPRINKLING OF TASTY CIABATTA CROÛTONS.

SERVES FOUR TO SIX

INGREDIENTS
    50g/2oz/4 tbsp butter
    1 onion, chopped
    3 leeks, chopped
    2 medium floury potatoes, diced
    900ml/1½ pints/3¾ cups light
        chicken stock or water
    2 large handfuls rocket (arugula),
        roughly chopped
    150ml/¼ pint/⅔ cup double (heavy)
        cream
    salt and ground black pepper
    garlic-flavoured ciabatta croûtons,
        to serve

1 Melt the butter in a large heavy pan then add the onion, leeks and potatoes and stir until the vegetables are coated in butter. Heat the ingredients until sizzling then reduce the heat to low.

2 Cover and sweal the vegetables for 15 minutes. Pour in the stock or water and bring to the boil then reduce the heat, cover again and simmer for 20 minutes until the vegetables are tender.

3 Press the soup through a sieve or pass through a food mill and return to the rinsed-out pan. (When puréeing the soup, don't use a blender or food processor, as these will give the soup a gluey texture.) Add the chopped rocket to the pan and cook the soup gently, uncovered, for 5 minutes.

4 Stir in the cream, then season to taste and reheat gently. Ladle the soup into warmed soup bowls and serve with a scattering of garlic-flavoured ciabatta croûtons in each.

Energy 385Kcal/1596kJ; Protein 5.3g; Carbohydrate 21.3g, of which sugars 5.4g; Fat 31.5g, of which saturates 19.2g; Cholesterol 78mg; Calcium 91mg; Fibre 4.4g; Sodium 282mg.

CHICKEN SOUP WITH DUMPLINGS

A BOWL OF CHICKEN SOUP CAN HEAL THE SOUL AS WELL AS THE BODY, AS ANYONE WHO HAS EVER SUFFERED FROM A HEAVY COLD OR FLU AND BEEN COMFORTED WILL KNOW.

SERVES SIX TO EIGHT

INGREDIENTS

- 1–1.5kg/2¼–3¼lb chicken, cut into portions
- 2–3 onions
- 3–4 litres/5–7 pints/12–16 cups water
- 3–5 carrots, thickly sliced
- 3–5 celery sticks, thickly sliced
- 1 small parsnip, cut in half
- 30–45ml/2–3 tbsp roughly chopped fresh parsley
- 30–45ml/2–3 tbsp chopped fresh dill
- 1–2 pinches ground turmeric
- 2 chicken stock (bouillon) cubes
- 2 garlic cloves, finely chopped (optional)
- salt and ground black pepper

For the dumplings
- 175g/6oz/¾ cup medium matzo meal
- 2 eggs, lightly beaten
- 45ml/3 tbsp vegetable oil or rendered chicken fat
- 1 garlic clove, finely chopped (optional)
- 30ml/2 tbsp chopped fresh parsley, plus extra to garnish
- ½ onion, finely grated
- 1–2 pinches of chicken stock (bouillon) cube or powder (optional)
- about 90ml/6 tbsp water
- salt and ground black pepper

1 Put the chicken in a very large pan. Keeping them whole, cut a large cross in the stem end of each onion and add to the pan with the water, carrots, celery, parsnip, parsley, half the dill, the turmeric, and salt and black pepper.

2 Cover the pan and bring to the boil, then immediately lower the heat so that the liquid just simmers. Skim the soup and discard the scum that rises to the top. (Scum will continue to form but it is only the first scum that rises that will detract from the clarity and flavour of the soup.)

3 Add the crumbled stock cubes and simmer for 2–3 hours. When the chicken is cooked and the soup is well flavoured, remove the chicken pieces, and skim off the fat from the liquid surface. Alternatively, chill the soup and remove the layer of solid fat that forms.

4 To make the dumplings, in a large bowl combine the matzo meal with the eggs, oil or fat, chopped garlic, if using, parsley, onion, salt and pepper. Add only a little chicken stock cube or powder, if using, as these are salty. Add the water and mix together until the mixture is of the consistency of a thick, soft paste.

5 Cover the matzo batter and chill for 30 minutes, during which time the mixture will become firm.

6 Bring a pan of water to the boil and have a bowl of water next to the stove. Dip two tablespoons into the water, then take a spoonful of the matzo batter. With wet hands, roll it into a ball, then slip it into the boiling water and reduce the heat so that the water simmers. Continue with the remaining matzo batter, working relatively quickly, then cover the pan and cook for 15–20 minutes.

7 Remove the dumplings from the pan with a slotted spoon and transfer to a plate for about 20 minutes to firm up.

8 To serve, reheat the soup, adding the remaining dill and the garlic, if using. Put two to three dumplings in each bowl, pour over the hot soup and garnish.

VARIATIONS

- Instead of dumplings, the soup can be served over rice or noodles.
- To make lighter dumplings, separate the eggs and add the yolks to the matzo mixture. Whisk the whites until stiff then fold into the mixture.

Energy 449Kcal/1866kJ; Protein 27.4g; Carbohydrate 30g, of which sugars 6.2g; Fat 24.3g, of which saturates 5.4g; Cholesterol 186mg; Calcium 58mg; Fibre 2.9g; Sodium 399mg

FRENCH COUNTRY OMELETTE

ALL OMELETTES ARE DELICIOUS AND CAN BE AS SUBSTANTIAL AS YOU WISH TO MAKE THEM BY ADDING FAVOURITE INGREDIENTS. THEY ARE ALSO PERFECT FOR SHARING.

SERVES TWO

INGREDIENTS

45–75ml/3–5 tbsp sunflower oil
50g/2oz thick bacon rashers (strips)
   or pieces, rinds removed and
   chopped
2 thick slices of bread, cut into
   small cubes
1 small onion, chopped
1–2 celery sticks, thinly sliced
115g/4oz cooked potato, diced
5 eggs, beaten
2 garlic cloves, crushed
handful of young spinach or sorrel
   leaves, stalks removed, torn
   into pieces
few sprigs of parsley, chopped
salt and ground black pepper

1 Heat the oil in a large heavy frying pan, and fry the bacon and bread cubes until they are crisp and turning golden. Add the chopped onion, celery and diced potato, and continue cooking slowly, stirring frequently until all the vegetables are soft and beginning to turn golden brown.

2 Beat the eggs with the garlic and seasoning, and pour over the vegetables. When the underside is beginning to set, add the spinach or sorrel. Cook until they have wilted and the omelette is only just soft in the middle. Fold the omelette in half and slide it out of the pan. Serve topped with the parsley, if liked.

Energy 549Kcal/2286kJ; Protein 27.1g; Carbohydrate 27.3g, of which sugars 3g; Fat 38.1g, of which saturates 8.2g; Cholesterol 584mg; Calcium 140mg; Fibre 1.9g; Sodium 770mg.

SPANISH OMELETTE

THE TRADITIONAL SPANISH OMELETTE CONSISTS SIMPLY OF POTATOES, ONIONS AND EGGS. THIS ONE ALSO HAS OTHER VEGETABLES AND WHITE BEANS. IT IS USUALLY THICK AND SUBSTANTIAL, MAKING IT A FILLING MEAL. SERVE IT WITH A FRUITY RED WINE.

SERVES SIX

INGREDIENTS

30ml/2 tbsp olive oil, plus extra
   for drizzling
1 Spanish onion, chopped
1 small red (bell) pepper, seeded
   and diced
2 celery sticks, chopped
225g/8oz potatoes, peeled, diced
   and cooked
400g/14oz can cannellini
   beans, drained
8 eggs
salt and ground black pepper
sprigs of oregano, to garnish
green salad and olives, to serve

1 Heat the olive oil in a 30cm/12in non-stick or heavy frying pan until hot but not smoking. Add the onion, red pepper and celery, stir well and cook over medium heat for 3–5 minutes, stirring often, until the vegetables are soft, but not coloured.

2 Add the potatoes and beans, and cook, stirring or turning gently, for several minutes to heat through.

3 In a small bowl, beat the eggs with a fork, then season well and pour over the ingredients in the pan.

4 Stir until it begins to thicken, then allow it to cook over a low heat for about 8 minutes. The omelette should be firm, but still moist in the middle. Cool slightly then invert on to a serving plate.

5 Cut the omelette into thick wedges. Serve warm or cool with a green salad and olives and a little olive oil. Garnish with oregano.

COOK'S TIP
In Spain, this omelette is often served as a tapas dish or appetizer. It is delicious served cold, cut into bite-size pieces and accompanied with a chilli sauce or mayonnaise for dipping. Other sliced seasonal vegetables, baby artichoke hearts and chickpeas can also be used in this recipe.

Energy 253Kcal/1059kJ; Protein 15.5g; Carbohydrate 20g, of which sugars 4.8g; Fat 13.2g, of which saturates 3.1g; Cholesterol 304mg; Calcium 74mg; Fibre 4.6g; Sodium 403mg.

FRITTATA WITH SUN-DRIED TOMATOES

PERFECT FOR A FILLING TREAT FOR LUNCHTIME. THIS SIMPLE FRITATTA HAS LOTS OF FLAVOUR. SERVE IT WITH FRENCH BREAD AND SALAD DRIZZLED WITH A TASTY DRESSING.

SERVES THREE TO FOUR

INGREDIENTS

6 sun-dried tomatoes
60ml/4 tbsp olive oil
1 small onion, finely chopped
pinch of fresh thyme leaves
6 eggs
50g/2oz/⅔ cup freshly grated
 Parmesan cheese
salt and ground black pepper
sprigs of thyme, to garnish
shavings of Parmesan, to serve

1 Place the tomatoes in a small bowl and pour on enough hot water to just cover them. Leave to soak for about 15 minutes. Lift the tomatoes out of the water and pat dry on kitchen paper. Reserve the soaking water. Cut the tomatoes into thin strips.

2 Heat the oil in a large non-stick frying pan. Stir in the onion and cook for 5–6 minutes or until softened and golden. Stir in the sun-dried tomatoes and thyme, and cook over a moderate heat for a further 2–3 minutes, stirring from time to time. Season with salt and ground black pepper.

3 Break the eggs into a bowl and beat lightly. Stir in 45ml/3 tbsp of the tomato soaking water and the Parmesan. Raise the heat under the frying pan. When the oil is sizzling, add the eggs. Mix quickly into the other ingredients, then stop stirring. Lower the heat to moderate and cook for 4–5 minutes, or until the base is golden and the top puffed.

4 Take a large plate, place it upside down over the pan and, holding it firmly with oven gloves, turn the pan and the frittata over on to it. Slide the frittata back into the pan, and continue cooking for 3–4 minutes until golden brown on the second side. Remove from the heat. Cut the frittata into wedges, garnish with sprigs of thyme and serve.

Energy 515Kcal/2130kJ; Protein 22.6g; Carbohydrate 2.9g, of which sugars 1.8g; Fat 46.3g, of which saturates 10.9g; Cholesterol 473mg; Calcium 281mg; Fibre 0.3g; Sodium 600mg.

SPICY SAUSAGE AND CHEESE TORTILLA

CHORIZO SAUSAGE IMPARTS ITS OWN RICH FLAVOUR TO THIS SUBSTANTIAL OMELETTE. CUT INTO WEDGES AND SERVE WITH TAPAS FOR AN INDULGENT LUNCH.

SERVES FOUR TO SIX

INGREDIENTS
75ml/5 tbsp olive oil
175g/6oz chorizo or spicy sausages, thinly sliced
675g/1½lb potatoes, peeled and thinly sliced
275g/10oz onions, halved and thinly sliced
4 eggs, beaten
30ml/2 tbsp chopped fresh parsley, plus extra to garnish
115g/4oz/1 cup Cheddar cheese, grated
salt and ground black pepper

1 Heat 15ml/1 tbsp of the oil in a non-stick frying pan, about 20cm/8in in diameter, and fry the sausage until golden brown and cooked through. Lift out with a slotted spoon and drain on kitchen paper.

2 Add a further 30ml/2 tbsp oil to the pan and fry the potatoes and onions for 2–3 minutes, turning frequently (the pan will be very full). Cover tightly and cook over a gentle heat for about 30 minutes, turning occasionally, until softened and slightly golden.

3 In a mixing bowl, mix the beaten eggs with the parsley, cheese, sausage and plenty of seasoning. Gently stir in the potatoes and onions until well coated, taking care not to break up the potato slices too much.

4 Wipe out the pan with kitchen paper and heat the remaining 30ml/2 tbsp oil. Add the potato mixture and cook over a very low heat, until the egg begins to set. Use a palette knife to lift the edges of the mixture occasionally and prevent the tortilla from sticking to the sides of the pan.

5 Preheat the grill (broiler) to hot. When the base of the tortilla has set, which should take about 5 minutes, protect the pan handle with foil and place under the grill until the tortilla is set and golden. Cut into wedges and serve garnished with parsley.

Energy 610Kcal/2539kJ; Protein 23.7g; Carbohydrate 38.6g, of which sugars 5.6g; Fat 40.7g, of which saturates 14.2g; Cholesterol 275mg; Calcium 299mg; Fibre 3.5g; Sodium 708mg.

CHEESE AND ONION FLAN

BAKING SAVOURY TARTS IS JUST AS SATISFYING AS MAKING BUNS AND CAKES. MADE WITH YEAST DOUGH, THIS FRENCH CLASSIC IS GREAT FOR KNEADING OUT TENSIONS AND TROUBLES.

SERVES FOUR

INGREDIENTS
    15g/½oz/1 tbsp butter
    1 onion, halved and sliced
    2 eggs
    250ml/8fl oz/1 cup single (light)
        cream
    225g/8oz strong semi-soft cheese,
        rind removed (about 175g/6oz
        without rind), sliced
    salt and ground black pepper
    salad leaves, to serve
For the yeast dough
    10ml/2 tsp dried yeast
    120ml/4fl oz/½ cup milk
    5ml/1 tsp sugar
    1 egg yolk
    225g/8oz/2 cups plain (all-purpose)
        flour
    2.5ml/½ tsp salt
    50g/2oz/4 tbsp butter, softened

1 To make the dough, place the yeast in a bowl. Warm the milk in a small pan until it is at body temperature and stir into the yeast with the sugar. Continue stirring until the yeast has dissolved completely. Leave the yeast mixture to stand for about 3 minutes, then beat in the egg yolk.

COOK'S TIP
If you prefer to use easy-blend yeast, omit step 1. Beat the egg yolk and milk together in a jug. Add the dry yeast to the flour and salt in the food processor, and pulse to combine. Pour in the egg and milk mixture, and proceed with the recipe as normal.

2 Put the flour and salt in a food processor fitted with a metal blade, and pulse to combine. With the machine running, slowly pour in the yeast mixture. Scrape down the sides and continue processing for 2–3 minutes. Add the softened butter and process for another 30 seconds.

3 Transfer the dough to a lightly greased bowl. Cover the bowl with a dishtowel and allow to rise in a warm place for about 1 hour until the dough has doubled in bulk.

4 Remove the dough from the bowl and place on a lightly floured surface. Knock back (punch down) the dough. Sprinkle a little more flour on the work surface and roll out the dough to a 30cm/12in round.

5 Line a 23cm/9in flan tin (quiche pan) or dish with the dough. Gently press it into the tin or dish and trim off any overhanging pieces, leaving a 3mm/⅛in rim around the flan case. Cover with a dishtowel, set aside in a warm place and leave the dough to rise again for about 30 minutes, or until puffy.

6 Meanwhile, melt the butter in a heavy pan and add the onion. Cover the pan and cook over a medium-low heat for about 15 minutes, until softened, stirring occasionally. Remove the lid and continue cooking, stirring frequently, until the onion is very soft and caramelized.

7 Preheat the oven to 180°C/350°F/ Gas 4. Beat together the eggs and cream. Season and stir in the cooked onion.

8 Arrange the cheese on the base of the flan case. Pour over the egg mixture and bake for 30–35 minutes until the base is golden and the centre is just set. Cool slightly on a wire rack and serve warm with salad leaves.

Energy 717Kcal/2990kJ; Protein 24.8g; Carbohydrate 50.6g, of which sugars 6.9g; Fat 46.5g, of which saturates 28.1g; Cholesterol 288mg; Calcium 350mg; Fibre 2.3g; Sodium 735mg.

QUICHE LORRAINE

THIS FLAVOURED QUICHE IS A TRUE COMFORT CLASSIC: VERY THIN, MELT-IN-THE-MOUTH PASTRY, A CREAMY, LIGHT FILLING AND TASTY SMOKED BACON MORSELS.

SERVES FOUR TO SIX

INGREDIENTS
  6 rindless smoked streaky (fatty)
    bacon rashers (strips)
  300ml/½ pint/1¼ cups double
    (heavy) cream
  3 eggs, plus 2 yolks
  25g/1oz/2 tbsp butter
  salt and ground black pepper
For the pastry
  175g/6oz/1½ cups plain (all-purpose)
    flour, sifted
  pinch of salt
  115g/4oz/½ cup butter, at room
    temperature, diced
  1 egg yolk

1 To make the pastry, place the flour, salt, butter and egg yolk in a food processor and process until blended. Tip out on to a lightly floured surface and bring the mixture together into a ball. Leave to rest for 20 minutes.

2 Lightly flour a deep 20cm/8in round flan tin (quiche pan) and place it on a baking sheet. Roll out the pastry and use to line the flan tin, trimming off any overhanging pieces.

3 Gently press the pastry into the corners of the tin. If the pastry breaks, gently push it together again. Chill for 20 minutes. Preheat the oven to 200°C/400°F/Gas 6.

4 Meanwhile, snip the bacon into small pieces using kitchen scissors and grill (broil) until the fat runs. Arrange in the pastry case. Beat together the cream, the eggs and yolks and seasoning, and pour into the pastry case.

5 Bake the quiche for 15 minutes, then reduce the oven temperature to 180°C/350°F/Gas 4 and bake for 20 minutes more. When the filling is puffed up and golden brown and the pastry edge crisp, remove the quiche from the oven and top with small cubes of butter. Leave to stand for 5 minutes before serving. This allows the filling to settle and cool a little before serving, making it easier to cut the quiche.

COOK'S TIP
To prepare the quiche in advance, bake for 5–10 minutes less than the time stated, until the filling is just set. Reheat at 190°C/375°F/Gas 5 for 10 minutes.

Energy 976Kcal/4043kJ; Protein 18.1g; Carbohydrate 35.5g, of which sugars 2.2g; Fat 85.8g, of which saturates 48.4g; Cholesterol 519mg; Calcium 149mg; Fibre 1.4g; Sodium 678mg.

RED ONION TART <u>WITH A</u> CORN MEAL CRUST

RED ONIONS ARE WONDERFULLY MILD AND SWEET AND VERY MOREISH WHEN COOKED AND THEY GO WELL WITH FONTINA CHEESE AND THYME IN THIS TART. CORN MEAL GIVES THE PASTRY A CRUMBLY TEXTURE TO CONTRAST WITH THE JUICINESS OF THE ONION FILLING.

SERVES FIVE TO SIX

INGREDIENTS
60ml/4 tbsp olive oil
1kg/2¼lb red onions, thinly sliced
2–3 garlic cloves, thinly sliced
5ml/1 tsp chopped fresh thyme, plus
    a few whole sprigs
5ml/1 tsp soft dark brown sugar
10ml/2 tsp sherry vinegar
225g/8oz Fontina cheese,
    thinly sliced
salt and ground black pepper
For the pastry
115g/4oz/1 cup plain (all-purpose)
    flour
75g/3oz/¾ cup fine yellow corn meal
5ml/1 tsp soft dark brown sugar
5ml/1 tsp chopped fresh thyme
90g/3½oz/7 tbsp butter
1 egg yolk
30–45ml/2–3 tbsp iced water

1 To make the pastry, sift the plain flour and corn meal into a bowl with 5ml/1 tsp salt. Season with pepper and stir in the sugar and thyme. Rub in the butter until the mixture looks like breadcrumbs. Beat the egg yolk with 30ml/2 tbsp iced water and use to bind the pastry, adding another 15ml/1 tbsp iced water if necessary. Gather the dough into a ball, wrap in clear film (plastic wrap) and chill it for 30–40 minutes.

2 Heat 45ml/3 tbsp of the oil in a pan. Add the onions. Cover and cook slowly, stirring occasionally, for 20–30 minutes. They should collapse but not brown.

3 Add the garlic and chopped thyme, then cook, stirring occasionally, for another 10 minutes. Increase the heat slightly, then add the sugar and sherry vinegar. Cook, uncovered, for another 5–6 minutes, until the onions start to caramelize slightly. Season to taste with salt and pepper. Cool.

4 Preheat the oven to 190°C/375°F/Gas 5. Roll out the pastry thinly and use to line a 25cm/10in loose-based metal flan tin (quiche pan).

5 Prick the pastry all over with a fork and support the sides with foil. Bake for 12–15 minutes, until lightly coloured.

6 Remove the foil and spread the caramelized onions evenly over the base of the pastry case. Add the slices of Fontina and sprigs of thyme and season with pepper. Drizzle over the remaining oil, then bake for 15–20 minutes, until the filling is piping hot and the cheese is beginning to bubble. Garnish the tart with thyme and serve immediately.

Energy 592Kcal/2458kJ; Protein 15.8g; Carbohydrate 46.4g, of which sugars 13.3g; Fat 38g, of which saturates 19.2g; Cholesterol 121mg; Calcium 207mg; Fibre 3.8g; Sodium 368mg.

SMOKED SALMON QUICHE <u>WITH</u> POTATO PASTRY

THE INGREDIENTS IN THIS LIGHT BUT RICHLY-FLAVOURED QUICHE PERFECTLY COMPLEMENT THE MELT-IN-THE-MOUTH PASTRY MADE WITH POTATOES.

SERVES SIX

INGREDIENTS

For the pastry
115g/4oz floury maincrop
  potatoes, diced
225g/8oz/2 cups plain (all-purpose)
  flour, sifted
115g/4oz/8 tbsp butter, diced
½ egg, beaten
10ml/2 tsp chilled water

For the filling
275g/10oz smoked salmon
6 eggs, beaten
150ml/¼ pint/⅔ cup full cream milk
300ml/½ pint/1¼ cups double
  (heavy) cream
30–45ml/2–3 tbsp chopped
  fresh dill
30ml/2 tbsp capers, chopped
salt and ground black pepper

1 Boil the potatoes in a large pan of lightly salted water for 15 minutes or until tender. Drain well through a colander and return to the pan. Mash the potatoes until smooth and set aside to cool completely.

VARIATIONS
These quantities can also be used to make six individual quiches. Prepare as above, but reduce the cooking time by about 15 minutes. For extra piquancy, sprinkle some finely grated fresh Parmesan cheese over the top of each quiche before baking.

2 Place the flour in a bowl and rub in the butter to form fine crumbs. Beat in the potatoes and egg. Bring the mixture together, adding chilled water if needed.

3 Roll the pastry out on a floured surface and use to line a deep 23cm/9in round, loose-based, fluted flan tin (quiche pan). Chill for 1 hour.

4 Preheat the oven to 200°C/400°F/ Gas 6. Place a baking sheet in the oven to preheat it. Chop the salmon into bite-size pieces and set aside.

5 For the filling, beat the eggs, milk and cream together. Then stir in the dill and capers and season with pepper. Add the salmon and stir to combine.

6 Remove the pastry case from the fridge, prick the base well and pour the mixture into it. Bake on a baking sheet for 35–45 minutes until set and golden.

COOK'S TIPS
• To ensure the base cooks through it is vital to preheat a baking sheet in the oven first.
• Make the most of smoked salmon offcuts for this quiche, as they are much cheaper.
• Serve the quiche warm, when it is especially delicious with mixed salad leaves combined with some more dill.

Energy 698Kcal/2902kJ; Protein 24.8g; Carbohydrate 34.6g, of which sugars 2.8g; Fat 52.3g, of which saturates 29.3g; Cholesterol 355mg; Calcium 154mg; Fibre 1.4g; Sodium 1086mg.

BUBBLE AND SQUEAK

WHETHER YOU HAVE LEFTOVERS, OR COOK THIS OLD-FASHIONED CLASSIC FROM FRESH, BE SURE TO GIVE IT A REALLY GOOD "SQUEAK" (FRY) IN THE PAN SO IT TURNS A RICH HONEY BROWN AS ALL THE FLAVOURS CARAMELIZE TOGETHER.

SERVES FOUR

INGREDIENTS
   60ml/4 tbsp dripping, bacon fat or
      vegetable oil
   1 onion, finely chopped
   450g/1lb floury potatoes, cooked
      and mashed
   225g/8oz cooked cabbage or Brussels
      sprouts, finely chopped
   salt and ground black pepper

1 Heat 30ml/2 tbsp of the dripping, fat or oil in a heavy-based frying pan. Add the onion and cook, stirring frequently, until softened but not browned.

2 In a large bowl, mix together the potatoes and cooked cabbage or sprouts and season with salt and plenty of pepper to taste.

3 Add the vegetables to the pan with the cooked onions, stir well, then press the vegetable mixture into a large, even cake.

4 Cook over a medium heat for about 15 minutes until the cake is browned underneath.

5 Invert a large plate over the pan, and, holding it tightly against the pan, turn them both over together. Lift off the frying pan, return it to the heat and add the remaining dripping, fat or oil. When hot, slide the cake back into the pan, browned side uppermost.

6 Cook over a medium heat for 10 minutes or until the underside is golden brown. Serve hot, in wedges.

COOK'S TIP
If you don't have leftover cooked cabbage or Brussels sprouts, shred raw cabbage and cook with Brussels sprouts in boiling salted water until tender. Drain, then chop.

Energy 205Kcal/857kJ; Protein 3.5g; Carbohydrate 23.3g, of which sugars 4.2g; Fat 11.5g, of which saturates 1.2g; Cholesterol 0mg; Calcium 34mg; Fibre 3g; Sodium 15mg.

MUSHROOM PILAU

THIS DISH IS SIMPLICITY ITSELF. A HANDFUL OF HERBS IMPARTS AN AROMATIC FLAVOUR, AND THE RICE MAKES A SATISFYING MEAL THAT IS PERFECT FOR A QUICK AND EASY SUPPER.

SERVES FOUR

INGREDIENTS
    30ml/2 tbsp vegetable oil
    2 shallots, finely chopped
    1 garlic clove, crushed
    3 green cardamom pods
    25g/1oz/2 tbsp ghee or butter
    175g/6oz/2½ cups button (white)
      mushrooms, sliced
    225g/8oz/generous 1 cup basmati
      rice, soaked
    5ml/1 tsp grated fresh root ginger
    good pinch of garam masala
    450ml/¾ pint/scant 2 cups water
    15ml/1 tbsp chopped fresh coriander
      (cilantro)
    salt

1 Heat the oil in a flameproof casserole and fry the shallots, garlic and cardamoms for 3–4 minutes until the shallots are beginning to brown.

2 Add the ghee or butter, then the mushrooms and fry for 2–3 minutes.

3 Add the rice, ginger and garam masala. Stir-fry over a low heat for 2–3 minutes, then stir in the water and a little salt. Bring to the boil, then cover tightly and simmer over a very low heat for 10 minutes.

4 Remove the casserole from the heat. Leave the pilau to stand, covered, for 5 minutes to complete the cooking. Add the chopped coriander and fork it through the rice. Spoon into a serving bowl and serve at once.

Energy 306Kcal/1273kJ; Protein 5.2g; Carbohydrate 45.5g, of which sugars 0.5g; Fat 11.2g, of which saturates 4g; Cholesterol 13mg; Calcium 17mg; Fibre 0.7g; Sodium 41mg.

TWO CHEESE RISOTTO

THIS UNDENIABLY RICH AND CREAMY RISOTTO IS JUST THE THING TO SERVE ON COLD WINTER
EVENINGS WHEN EVERYONE NEEDS WARMING UP AND CHEERING UP.

SERVES THREE TO FOUR

INGREDIENTS
7.5ml/1½ tsp olive oil
50g/2oz/4 tbsp butter
1 onion, finely chopped
1 garlic clove, crushed
275g/10oz/1½ cups risotto rice,
  preferably Vialone Nano
175ml/6 fl oz/¾ cup dry white wine
1 litre/1¾ pints/4 cups simmering
  vegetable or chicken stock
75g/3oz/¾ cup Fontina cheese,
  cubed
50g/2oz/⅔ cup freshly grated
  Parmesan cheese, plus extra,
  to serve
salt and freshly ground black pepper

1 Heat the olive oil with half the butter in a pan and gently fry the onion and garlic for 5–6 minutes until soft. Add the rice and cook, stirring all the time, until the grains are coated in fat and have become slightly translucent around the edges.

2 Stir in the wine. Cook, stirring, until the liquid has been absorbed, then add a ladleful of hot stock. Stir until the stock has been absorbed, then add the remaining stock in the same way, waiting for each quantity of stock to be absorbed before adding more.

3 When the rice is half cooked, stir in the Fontina cheese, and continue cooking and adding stock. Keep stirring the rice all the time.

4 When the risotto is creamy and the grains are tender but still have a bit of "bite", stir in the remaining butter and the Parmesan. Season, then remove the pan from the heat, cover and leave to rest for 3–4 minutes before serving.

Energy 688Kcal/2863kJ; Protein 19.4g; Carbohydrate 77.7g, of which sugars 3.3g; Fat 28.2g, of which saturates 16.9g; Cholesterol 75mg; Calcium 304mg; Fibre 0.7g; Sodium 697mg.

QUICK RISOTTO

THIS IS RATHER A CHEAT'S RISOTTO AS IT DEFIES ALL THE RULES THAT INSIST THE STOCK IS ADDED
GRADUALLY. INSTEAD, THE RICE IS COOKED QUICKLY IN A CONVENTIONAL WAY, AND THE OTHER
INGREDIENTS ARE SIMPLY THROWN IN AT THE LAST MINUTE. IT TASTES GOOD FOR ALL THAT.

SERVES THREE TO FOUR

INGREDIENTS
275g/10oz/1½ cups risotto rice
1 litre/1¾ pints/4 cups simmering
  chicken stock
115g/4oz/1 cup mozzarella cheese,
  cut into small cubes
2 egg yolks
30ml/2 tbsp freshly grated Parmesan
  cheese
75g/3oz cooked ham, cut into
  small cubes
30ml/2 tbsp chopped fresh parsley
salt and freshly ground black pepper
fresh parsley sprigs, to garnish
freshly grated Parmesan cheese,
  to serve

1 Put the rice in a pan. Pour in the stock, bring to the boil and then cover and simmer for about 18–20 minutes until the rice is tender.

2 Remove the pan from the heat and quickly stir in the mozzarella, egg yolks, Parmesan, ham and parsley. Season well with salt and pepper.

3 Cover the pan and stand for 2–3 minutes to allow the cheese to melt, then stir again. Pile into warmed serving bowls, garnish and serve immediately, with extra Parmesan cheese.

Energy 544Kcal/2271kJ; Protein 24.6g; Carbohydrate 73.6g, of which sugars 0.3g; Fat 16.3g, of which saturates 8.6g; Cholesterol 181mg; Calcium 296mg; Fibre 0g; Sodium 838mg.

CHINESE FRIED RICE

THIS DISH IS QUICK, SIMPLE AND INEXPENSIVE; MOST IMPORTANTLY, IT IS ALSO EXTREMELY TASTY AND SATISFYING. ENJOY IT WITH A BOTTLE OF WINE.

SERVES FOUR

INGREDIENTS
  50g/2oz cooked ham
  50g/2oz cooked prawns (shrimp)
  3 eggs
  5ml/1 tsp salt
  2 spring onions (scallions), finely
    chopped
  60ml/4 tbsp vegetable oil
  115g/4oz/1 cup green peas, thawed
    if frozen
  15ml/1 tbsp light soy sauce
  15ml/1 tbsp Chinese rice wine or
    dry sherry
  450g/1lb/4 cups cooked white long
    grain rice

1 Dice the cooked ham finely. Pat the cooked prawns dry on kitchen paper.

2 In a bowl, beat the eggs with a pinch of salt and a few spring onion pieces.

VARIATIONS
Use cooked chicken or turkey instead of the ham, doubling the quantity if you omit the prawns.

3 Heat about half the oil in a wok, stir-fry the peas, prawns and ham for 1 minute, then add the soy sauce and rice wine or sherry. Transfer to a bowl and keep hot.

4 Heat the remaining oil in the wok and scramble the eggs lightly. Add the rice and stir to make sure that the grains are separate. Add the remaining salt, the remaining spring onions and the prawn mixture. Toss over the heat to mix. Serve hot or cold.

Energy 371Kcal/1552kJ; Protein 15.2g; Carbohydrate 38.9g, of which sugars 1.5g; Fat 18.4g, of which saturates 3.1g; Cholesterol 203mg; Calcium 71mg; Fibre 1.6g; Sodium 997mg.

THAI FRIED RICE

THIS SUBSTANTIAL DISH IS BASED ON THAI FRAGRANT RICE, WHICH IS SOMETIMES KNOWN AS JASMINE RICE. CHICKEN, RED PEPPER AND SWEETCORN ADD COLOUR AND EXTRA FLAVOUR.

SERVES FOUR

INGREDIENTS
   475ml/16fl oz/2 cups water
   50g/2oz/½ cup coconut milk powder
   350g/12oz/1¾ cups Thai fragrant
      rice, rinsed
   30ml/2 tbsp groundnut oil
   2 garlic cloves, chopped
   1 small onion, finely chopped
   2.5cm/1in piece of fresh root
      ginger, grated
   225g/8oz skinless, boneless chicken
      breasts, cut into 1cm/½in dice
   1 red (bell) pepper, seeded and
      sliced
   115g/4oz/1 cup corn
   5ml/1 tsp chilli oil
   5ml/1 tsp hot curry powder
   2 eggs, beaten
   salt
   spring onions (scallions), to garnish

3 Push the vegetables to the sides of the wok, add the chicken to the centre and stir-fry for 2 minutes until it is just cooked. Add the rice and stir-fry over a high heat for about 3 minutes more, until properly reheated.

4 Stir in the sliced red pepper, corn, chilli oil and curry powder, with salt to taste. Toss over the heat for 1 minute. Stir in the beaten eggs and cook for 1 minute more. Garnish with spring onion shreds and serve.

1 Pour the water into a pan and whisk in the coconut milk powder. Add the rice, bring to the boil. Lower the heat, cover and cook for 12 minutes or until the rice is tender and the liquid has been absorbed. Spread the rice on a baking sheet and leave until cold.

2 Heat the oil in a wok, add the garlic, onion and ginger and stir-fry over a medium heat for 2 minutes.

COOK'S TIP
It is important that the rice is completely cold before being fried and the oil is very hot, or the rice will absorb too much oil.

Energy 540Kcal/2282kJ; Protein 25.5g; Carbohydrate 84.7g, of which sugars 4.2g; Fat 13.5g, of which saturates 3.1g; Cholesterol 245mg; Calcium 73mg; Fibre 1.9g; Sodium 523mg.

SPICY FRIED NOODLES

THIS IS A WONDERFULLY VERSATILE DISH AS YOU CAN ADJUST IT TO INCLUDE YOUR FAVOURITE INGREDIENTS — JUST AS LONG AS YOU KEEP A BALANCE OF FLAVOURS, TEXTURES AND COLOURS.

SERVES FOUR

INGREDIENTS

225g/8oz egg thread noodles
60ml/4 tbsp vegetable oil
2 garlic cloves, finely chopped
175g/6oz pork fillet (tenderloin),
  sliced into thin strips
1 skinless, boneless chicken breast
  portion (about 175g/6oz), sliced
  into thin strips
115g/4oz/1 cup peeled cooked
  prawns (shrimp), rinsed if canned
45ml/3 tbsp fresh lemon juice
45ml/3 tbsp Thai fish sauce
30ml/2 tbsp soft light brown sugar
2 eggs, beaten
½ fresh red chilli, seeded and finely
  chopped
50g/2oz/⅔ cup beansprouts
60ml/4 tbsp roasted peanuts,
  chopped
3 spring onions (scallions), cut into
  5cm/2in lengths and shredded
45ml/3 tbsp chopped fresh coriander
  (cilantro)

1 Bring a large pan of water to the boil. Add the noodles, remove the pan from the heat and leave for 5 minutes

2 Meanwhile, heat 45ml/3 tbsp of the oil in a wok or large frying pan, add the garlic and cook for 30 seconds. Add the pork and chicken and stir-fry until lightly browned, then add the prawns and stir-fry for 2 minutes.

3 Stir in the lemon juice, then add the fish sauce and sugar. Stir-fry until the sugar has dissolved.

4 Drain the noodles and add to the wok or pan with the remaining 15ml/1 tbsp oil. Toss all the ingredients together.

5 Pour the beaten eggs over the noodles and stir fry until almost set, then add the chilli and bean sprouts.

6 Divide the roasted peanuts, spring onions and coriander leaves into two equal portions, add one portion to the pan and stir-fry for about 2 minutes.

7 Tip the noodles on to a serving platter. Sprinkle on the remaining roasted peanuts, spring onions and chopped coriander and serve immediately.

COOK'S TIP
Store beansprouts in the refrigerator and use within a day of purchase, as they tend to lose their crispness and become slimy and unpleasant quite quickly. The most commonly used beansprouts are sprouted mung beans, but you could use other types of beansprouts instead.

Energy 610Kcal/2560kJ; Protein 39.9g; Carbohydrate 52.4g, of which sugars 12g; Fat 28.3g, of which saturates 5.6g; Cholesterol 245mg; Calcium 78mg; Fibre 2.8g; Sodium 523mg

SICHUAN NOODLES

FLAVOUR IS AN ALL-IMPORTANT FEATURE OF COMFORT MEALS. THOSE THAT ARE NOT FAMILIAR FROM CHILDHOOD AT LEAST HAVE TO BE SUFFICIENTLY PUNCHY AND DELICIOUS TO FILL THE SENSES WITH THE JOY OF EATING. THIS IS ONE OF THOSE DISHES AND IT IS ALSO SUPER-QUICK TO MAKE.

SERVES FOUR

INGREDIENTS

450g/1lb fresh or 225g/8oz dried
  egg noodles
½ cucumber, sliced lengthways,
  seeded and diced
4–6 spring onions (scallions)
a bunch of radishes, about 115g/4oz
225g/8oz mooli (daikon), peeled
115g/4oz/2 cups beansprouts, rinsed,
  then left in iced water and drained
60ml/4 tbsp groundnut oil or
  sunflower oil
2 garlic cloves, crushed
45ml/3 tbsp toasted sesame paste
15ml/1 tbsp sesame oil
15ml/1 tbsp light soy sauce
5–10ml/1–2 tsp chilli sauce, to taste
15ml/1 tbsp rice vinegar
120ml/4 fl oz/½ cup chicken stock
  or water
5ml/1 tsp sugar, or to taste
salt and ground black pepper
roasted peanuts or cashew nuts,
  to garnish

1 If using fresh noodles, cook them in boiling water for 1 minute then drain well. Rinse the noodles in fresh water and drain again. Cook dried noodles according to the instructions on the packet, draining and rinsing them as for fresh noodles.

2 Place the cucumber in a colander or sieve, sprinkle with salt and leave to drain over a bowl for 15 minutes, rinse well, then drain and pat dry on kitchen paper. Place in a large salad bowl.

3 Cut the spring onions into fine shreds. Cut the radishes in half and slice finely. Coarsely grate the mooli using a mandolin or a food processor. Add all the vegetables to the cucumber and toss gently.

4 Heat half the oil in a wok or frying pan and stir-fry the noodles for about 1 minute. Using a slotted spoon, transfer the noodles to a large serving bowl and keep warm.

5 Add the remaining oil to the wok. When it is hot, fry the garlic to flavour the oil. Remove from the heat and stir in the sesame paste, with the sesame oil, soy and chilli sauces, vinegar and stock or water. Add a little sugar and season to taste. Warm through over a gentle heat. Do not overheat or the sauce will thicken too much. Pour the sauce over the noodles and toss well. Garnish with peanuts or cashew nuts and serve with the vegetables.

Energy 499Kcal/2088kJ; Protein 11.8g; Carbohydrate 60.3g, of which sugars 7.1g; Fat 25g, of which saturates 5.3g; Cholesterol 23mg; Calcium 85mg; Fibre 4.5g; Sodium 510mg.

PASTA WITH PESTO

BOTTLED PESTO IS A USEFUL STAND-BY, BUT IT BEARS NO RESEMBLANCE TO THE HEADY AROMA AND FLAVOUR OF THE FRESH PASTE. IT IS QUICK AND EASY TO MAKE IN A FOOD PROCESSOR.

SERVES FOUR

INGREDIENTS

50g/2oz/1⅓ cups fresh basil leaves,
  plus fresh basil leaves, to garnish
2–4 garlic cloves
60ml/4 tbsp pine nuts
120ml/4fl oz/½ cup extra virgin
  olive oil
115g/4oz/1⅓ cups freshly grated
  Parmesan cheese, plus extra
  to serve
25g/1oz/⅓ cup freshly grated
  Pecorino cheese
400g/14oz/3½ cups dried pasta
salt and ground black pepper

1 Put the basil leaves, garlic and pine nuts in a blender or food processor. Add 60ml/4 tbsp of the olive oil. Process until the ingredients are finely chopped, then stop the machine, remove the lid and scrape down the sides of the bowl.

2 Turn the machine on again and slowly pour the remaining oil in a thin, steady stream through the feeder tube. You may need to stop the machine and scrape down the sides of the bowl once or twice to make sure everything is evenly mixed.

3 Scrape the mixture into a large bowl and beat in the cheeses with a wooden spoon. Taste and add salt and pepper if necessary.

4 Cook the pasta according to the instructions on the packet. Drain it well, then add it to the bowl of pesto and toss well. Serve immediately, garnished with the fresh basil leaves. Hand shaved Parmesan around separately.

COOK'S TIP
Pesto can be made up to 2–3 days in advance. To store pesto, transfer it to a small bowl and pour a thin film of olive oil over the surface. Cover the bowl tightly with clear film and keep it in the fridge.

Energy 713Kcal/2969kJ; Protein 24.1g; Carbohydrate 43.2g, of which sugars 2.7g; Fat 50.5g, of which saturates 11.6g; Cholesterol 35mg; Calcium 468mg; Fibre 2.1g; Sodium 385mg.

CREAM FETTUCINE

THIS SIMPLE RECIPE WAS INVENTED BY A ROMAN RESTAURATEUR CALLED ALFREDO, WHO BECAME FAMOUS FOR SERVING IT WITH A GOLD FORK AND SPOON. TODAY'S BUSY COOKS WILL FIND CARTONS OF LONG-LIFE CREAM INVALUABLE FOR THIS SLIGHTLY NAUGHTY SUPPER-IN-A-HURRY RECIPE.

SERVES FOUR

INGREDIENTS
  50g/2oz/¼ cup butter
  200ml/7fl oz/scant 1 cup double
    (heavy) cream
  50g/2 oz/⅔ cup freshly grated
    Parmesan cheese, plus extra to serve
  350g/12oz fresh fettucine
  salt and freshly ground black pepper

COOK'S TIP
When you find a source of really good fresh pasta, buy some as an emergency ingredient and freeze it for future use. Spread it out thinly in a packet for freezing, if possible, so that it thaws quickly. Cook it from frozen and allow 1–2 minutes extra cooking time.

1 Melt the butter in a large pan. Add the cream and bring it to the boil. Simmer for 5 minutes, stirring constantly, then add the Parmesan cheese, with salt and freshly ground black pepper to taste, and turn off the heat under the pan.

2 Bring a large pan of salted water to the boil. Drop in the pasta all at once and quickly bring the water back to the boil, stirring occasionally. Cook for 2–3 minutes, or according to the instructions on the packet. Drain well.

3 Turn on the heat under the pan of cream to low, add the cooked pasta all at once and toss until it is thoroughly coated in the sauce. Taste the sauce for seasoning. Serve immediately, with extra grated Parmesan handed around separately.

Energy 697Kcal/2912kJ; Protein 16.3g; Carbohydrate 65.8g, of which sugars 3.8g; Fat 42.8g, of which saturates 26g; Cholesterol 108mg; Calcium 199mg; Fibre 2.6g; Sodium 226mg.

PENNE <u>WITH</u> CREAM <u>AND</u> SMOKED SALMON

NO SUPPER DISH COULD BE SIMPLER. FRESHLY COOKED PASTA IS TOSSED WITH CREAM, SMOKED SALMON AND THYME. FROM START TO FINISH IT TAKES UNDER 15 MINUTES TO MAKE.

SERVES FOUR

INGREDIENTS
 350g/12oz/3 cups dried penne
 115g/4oz thinly sliced smoked
  salmon
 2–3 fresh thyme sprigs
 25g/1oz/2 tbsp butter
 150ml/¼ pint/⅔ cup double
  (heavy) cream
 salt and ground black pepper

VARIATION
Substitute low-fat cream cheese for half
the cream in the sauce, for a less rich
mixture that still tastes very good.

1 Bring a large pan of lightly salted
water to the boil. Add the pasta and
cook for about 12 minutes, or according
to the instructions on the packet, until
the penne are tender but still firm
to the bite.

2 Meanwhile, using kitchen scissors or
a small, sharp knife, cut the smoked
salmon into thin strips, each about
5mm/¼in wide, and place on a plate.
Strip the leaves from the thyme sprigs.

3 Melt the butter in a large pan. Stir in
the cream with a quarter of the salmon
and thyme leaves, then season with
pepper. Heat gently for 3–4 minutes,
stirring constantly. Do not allow the
sauce to boil. Taste for seasoning.

4 Drain the pasta, return it to the pan,
and toss it in the cream and salmon
sauce. Divide among four warmed bowls
and top with the remaining salmon and
thyme leaves. Serve immediately.

Energy 496Kcal/2075kJ; Protein 17.9g; Carbohydrate 49.6g, of which sugars 2.4g; Fat 28.7g, of which saturates 14.7g; Cholesterol 72mg; Calcium 81mg; Fibre 0g; Sodium 617mg.

MACARONI CHEESE

*RICH AND CREAMY, THIS IS A DELUXE MACARONI CHEESE. IT GOES WELL WITH EITHER A TOMATO AND
BASIL SALAD OR A LEAFY GREEN SALAD.*

SERVES FOUR

INGREDIENTS

250g/9oz/2¼ cups short-cut
macaroni
50g/2oz/¼ cup butter
50g/2oz/½ cup plain (all-purpose)
flour
600ml/1 pint/2½ cups milk
100ml/3½ fl oz/scant ½ cup *panna
da cucina* or double (heavy) cream
100ml/3½ fl oz/scant ½ cup dry
white wine
50g/2oz/½ cup grated Gruyère or
Emmenthal cheese
50g/2oz Fontina cheese, diced small
50g/2oz Gorgonzola cheese, crumbled
75g/3oz/1 cup freshly grated
Parmesan cheese
salt and ground black pepper

COOK'S TIP
Fontina is a mountain cheese with a
slightly sweet, nutty flavour. If you can't
get it, use Taleggio or simply double the
quantity of Gruyère or Emmenthal.

1 Preheat the oven to 180°C/350°F/
Gas 4. Cook the pasta according to the
instructions on the packet.

2 Meanwhile, gently melt the butter in
a pan, add the flour and cook, stirring,
for 1–2 minutes. Add the milk a little at
a time, whisking vigorously after each
addition. Stir in the cream, then the dry
white wine. Bring to the boil. Cook,
stirring constantly, until the sauce
thickens. Remove from the heat.

3 Add the Gruyère or Emmenthal,
Fontina, Gorgonzola and about a third
of the grated Parmesan to the sauce.
Stir well to mix in the cheeses, then
taste for seasoning and add salt and
pepper if necessary.

4 Drain the pasta well and tip it into a
baking dish. Pour the sauce over the
pasta and mix well, then sprinkle the
remaining Parmesan over the top. Bake
for 25–30 minutes or until golden
brown. Serve hot.

Energy 743Kcal/3104kJ; Protein 30.3g; Carbohydrate 52.1g, of which sugars 8.9g; Fat 45.4g, of which saturates 27.8g; Cholesterol 123mg; Calcium 673mg; Fibre 0.4g; Sodium 593mg.

MIXED MEAT CANNELLONI

A CREAMY, RICH FILLING AND SAUCE MAKE THIS AN UNUSUAL CANNELLONI — IT IS SERIOUSLY GOOD.

SERVES FOUR

INGREDIENTS
60ml/4 tbsp olive oil
1 onion, finely chopped
1 carrot, finely chopped
2 garlic cloves, crushed
2 ripe Italian plum tomatoes, peeled
  and finely chopped
130g/4½oz minced (ground) beef
130g/4½oz minced pork
250g/9oz minced chicken
30ml/2 tbsp brandy
25g/1oz/2 tbsp butter
90ml/6 tbsp *panna da cucina* or
  double (heavy) cream
16 dried cannelloni tubes
75g/3oz/1 cup freshly grated
  Parmesan cheese
salt and ground black pepper
green salad, to serve
For the white sauce
50g/2oz/¼ cup butter
50g/2oz/½ cup plain (all-purpose)
  flour
900ml/1½ pints/3¾ cups milk
nutmeg

2 Add all the minced meats to the pan and cook gently for about 10 minutes, stirring frequently to break up any lumps of meat.

3 Pour in the brandy, increase the heat and boil, stirring, until it has reduced. Then add the butter and cream and cook gently, stirring occasionally, for about 10 minutes, until the mixture is rich and well cooked. Allow to cool.

4 Preheat the oven to 190°C/375°F/ Gas 5. Make the white sauce. Melt the butter in a medium pan, add the flour and cook, stirring, for 1–2 minutes. Add the milk a little at a time, whisking vigorously after each addition. Bring to the boil and cook, stirring, until the sauce is smooth and thick. Grate in nutmeg to taste, add salt and pepper and whisk. Remove from the heat.

5 Spoon a little of the white sauce into a baking dish. Fill the cannelloni tubes with the meat mixture and place in a single layer in the dish. Pour the remaining white sauce over them, then sprinkle with the Parmesan. Bake for 35–40 minutes or until the pasta feels tender when pierced with a skewer. Allow to stand for 10 minutes before serving with green salad.

1 Heat the oil in a medium skillet, add the onion, carrot, garlic and tomatoes and cook over a low heat, stirring, for about 10 minutes or until very soft.

COOK'S TIP
Sheets of fresh lasagne can be used instead of cannelloni tubes. Spoon some of the meat mixture at one end of a piece of lasagne and roll up, then place in the dish.

Energy 1029Kcal/4304kJ; Protein 52.7g; Carbohydrate 72.3g, of which sugars 17.6g; Fat 59.1g, of which saturates 28.9g; Cholesterol 188mg; Calcium 568mg; Fibre 3.6g; Sodium 521mg.

SPAGHETTI BOLOGNESE

THIS RECIPE WILL BRING BACK HAPPY MEMORIES OF FLAT-SHARING AND COMMUNAL EATING.

SERVES FOUR TO SIX

INGREDIENTS
30ml/2 tbsp olive oil
1 onion, finely chopped
1 garlic clove, crushed
5ml/1 tsp dried mixed herbs
1.25ml/¼ tsp cayenne pepper
350–450g/12oz–1lb minced
  (ground) beef
400g/14oz can chopped Italian
  plum tomatoes
45ml/3 tbsp tomato ketchup
15ml/1 tbsp sun-dried tomato paste
5ml/1 tsp Worcestershire sauce
5ml1 tsp dried oregano
450ml/¾ pint/1¾ cups beef or
  vegetable stock
45ml/3 tbsp red wine
400–450g/14oz–1lb dried spaghetti
salt and ground black pepper
freshly grated Parmesan cheese,
  to serve

1 Heat the oil in a medium pan, add the onion and garlic and cook over a low heat, stirring frequently, for about 5 minutes until softened. Stir in the mixed herbs and cayenne and cook for 2–3 minutes more. Add the minced beef and cook gently for about 5 minutes, stirring frequently and breaking up any lumps in the meat with a wooden spoon.

2 Stir in the canned tomatoes, ketchup, sun-dried tomato paste, Worcestershire sauce, oregano and plenty of black pepper. Pour in the stock and red wine and bring to the boil, stirring. Cover the pan, lower the heat and leave the sauce to simmer for 30 minutes, stirring occasionally.

3 Cook the pasta according to the instructions on the packet. Drain well and divide among warmed bowls. Taste the sauce and add a little salt if necessary, then spoon it on top of the pasta and sprinkle with a little grated Parmesan. Serve immediately, with grated Parmesan handed separately.

Energy 639Kcal/2692kJ; Protein 30.9g; Carbohydrate 83.5g, of which sugars 11.5g; Fat 21.7g, of which saturates 7.1g; Cholesterol 53mg; Calcium 59mg; Fibre 4.2g; Sodium 312mg.

RICOTTA AND FONTINA PIZZA

PIZZA IS ALWAYS COMFORTING. THE EARTHY FLAVOUR OF THE MUSHROOMS IS DELICIOUS WITH CHEESE.

MAKES FOUR

INGREDIENTS
  2.5ml/½ tsp active dried yeast
  pinch of granulated sugar
  450g/1lb/4 cups strong white
    bread flour
  5ml/1 tsp salt
  30ml/2 tbsp olive oil
For the tomato sauce
  400g/14oz can chopped tomatoes
  150ml/¼ pint/⅔ cup passata
  1 large garlic clove, finely chopped
  5ml/1 tsp dried oregano
  1 bay leaf
  10ml/2 tsp malt vinegar
  salt and freshly ground black pepper
For the topping
  30ml/2 tbsp olive oil
  1 garlic clove, finely chopped
  350g/12oz/4 cups mixed mushrooms
    (chestnut, flat or button), sliced
  30ml/2 tbsp chopped fresh oregano,
    plus whole leaves to garnish
  250g/9oz/generous 1 cup ricotta
    cheese
  225g/8oz Fontina cheese, sliced

1 Make the dough. Put 300ml/½ pint/ 1¼ cups warm water in a measuring jug. Add the yeast and the sugar and leave for 5–10 minutes until frothy. Sift the flour and salt into a large bowl and make a well in the centre. Gradually pour in the yeast mixture and the olive oil. Mix to make smooth dough.

2 Knead on a lightly floured surface for about 10 minutes until smooth, springy and elastic. Place the dough in a floured bowl, cover and leave to rise in a warm place for 1½ hours.

3 Meanwhile, make the tomato sauce. Place all the ingredients in a pan, cover and bring to the boil. Lower the heat, remove the lid and simmer for 20 minutes, stirring occasionally, until reduced.

4 Make the topping. Heat the oil in a frying pan. Add the garlic and mushrooms, with salt and pepper to taste. Cook, stirring, for about 5 minutes or until the mushrooms are tender and golden. Set aside.

5 Preheat the oven to 220°/425°F/ Gas 7. Brush four baking sheets with oil. Knead the dough for 2 minutes, then divide into four equal pieces. Roll out each piece to a 25cm/10in round and place on a baking sheet.

6 Spoon the tomato sauce over each dough round. Brush the edge with a little olive oil. Add the mushrooms, oregano and cheese. Bake for about 15 minutes until golden brown and crisp. Sprinkle the oregano leaves over.

Energy 749Kcal/3149kJ; Protein 30.8g; Carbohydrate 93.1g, of which sugars 7g; Fat 29.5g, of which saturates 15.7g; Cholesterol 84mg; Calcium 473mg; Fibre 5.4g; Sodium 1000mg.

HOT PEPPERONI PIZZA

THERE IS NOTHING MORE MOUTHWATERING THAN A FRESHLY BAKED PIZZA, ESPECIALLY WHEN THE TOPPING INCLUDES TOMATOES, PEPPERONI AND RED CHILLIES.

SERVES FOUR

INGREDIENTS
  225g/8oz/2 cups strong white
    bread flour
  10ml/2 tsp easy-blend (rapid-rise)
    dried yeast
  5ml/1 tsp granulated sugar
  2.5ml/½ tsp salt
  15ml/1 tbsp olive oil
  175ml/6fl oz/¾ cup mixed lukewarm
    milk and water
  400g/14oz can chopped tomatoes,
    strained
  2 garlic cloves, crushed
  5ml/1 tsp dried oregano
  225g/8oz mozzarella cheese, grated
  2 dried red chillies, crumbled
  225g/8oz pepperoni, sliced
  30ml/2 tbsp drained capers
  fresh oregano, to garnish

1 Sift the flour into a bowl. Stir in the yeast, sugar and salt. Make a well in the centre. Stir the olive oil into the milk and water, then stir the liquid into the flour. Mix to a soft dough.

2 Knead the dough on a lightly floured surface for 10 minutes until it is smooth and elastic. Cover and leave in a warm place for about 30 minutes or until the dough has doubled in bulk.

3 Preheat the oven to 220°C/425°F/ Gas 7. Turn the dough out on to a lightly floured surface and knead lightly for 1 minute. Divide it in half and roll each piece out to a 25cm/10in circle. Place on lightly oiled pizza trays or baking sheets.

4 To make the topping, mix the tomatoes, garlic and oregano in a bowl.

5 Spread half the tomato mixture over each base, leaving a border around the edge. Set half the mozzarella aside. Divide the rest between the pizzas.

6 Bake for 7–10 minutes until the dough rim on each pizza is pale golden.

7 Sprinkle the crumbled chillies over the pizzas, then arrange the pepperoni slices and capers on top. Sprinkle with the remaining mozzarella. Return the pizzas to the oven and bake for 7–10 minutes more. Sprinkle over the fresh oregano and serve at once.

Energy 556Kcal/2325kJ; Protein 24g; Carbohydrate 50.2g, of which sugars 5.2g; Fat 30.1g, of which saturates 12.7g; Cholesterol 136mg; Calcium 310mg; Fibre 2.7g; Sodium 992mg.

CLASSIC MARGHERITA PIZZA

THIS TOMATO, BASIL AND MOZZARELLA PIZZA IS SIMPLE TO PREPARE. THE SWEET FLAVOUR OF SUN-RIPE TOMATOES WORKS WONDERFULLY WITH THE BASIL AND MOZZARELLA.

SERVES TWO

INGREDIENTS
1 onion, finely chopped
1 garlic clove, crushed
30ml/2 tbsp olive oil
400g/14oz can chopped tomatoes
15ml/1 tbsp tomato purée (paste)
pinch of granulated sugar
15ml/1 tbsp chopped fresh basil
150g/5oz mozzarella cheese
4 ripe tomatoes
6–8 fresh basil leaves
30ml/2 tbsp grated Parmesan cheese
salt and ground black pepper
For the pizza base
225g/8oz/2 cups strong white
  bread flour
5ml/1 tsp salt
2.5ml/½ tsp easy-blend (rapid-rise)
  dried yeast
15ml/1 tbsp olive oil
150ml/¼ pint/⅔ cup warm water

1 Make the pizza base. Place the dry ingredients in a bowl. Add the oil and water. Mix to a soft dough and knead for 10 minutes. Cover and put in a warm place until doubled in bulk.

2 Preheat the oven to 220°C/425°F/ Gas 7. Make the topping. Fry the onion and garlic for 5 minutes in half the oil. Stir in the tomatoes, purée and sugar. Cook for 5 minutes. Stir in the basil and seasoning.

3 Knead the dough lightly for 5 minutes, then roll out to a round and place on a baking sheet.

4 Use a spoon to spread the tomato topping evenly over the base. Cut the mozzarella cheese and fresh tomatoes into thick slices. Arrange them in a circle, alternating the cheese with the tomato slices.

5 Roughly tear the basil leaves, add to the pizza and sprinkle with the Parmesan cheese. Drizzle over the remaining oil and season well with black pepper. Bake for 15–20 minutes until crisp and golden. Serve immediately.

Energy 881Kcal/3698kJ; Protein 34.5g; Carbohydrate 104.6g, of which sugars 16.8g; Fat 39g, of which saturates 16.2g; Cholesterol 59mg; Calcium 664mg; Fibre 7.7g; Sodium 559mg.

SUN-DRIED TOMATO CALZONE

CALZONE IS A TRADITIONAL FOLDED PIZZA. IN THIS TASTY VEGETARIAN VERSION, YOU CAN ADD MORE OR FEWER RED CHILLI FLAKES, DEPENDING ON TASTE AND HOW MUCH YOU NEED PEPPING UP.

SERVES TWO

INGREDIENTS

4 baby aubergines (eggplant)
3 shallots, chopped
45ml/3 tbsp olive oil
1 garlic clove, chopped
50g/2oz/⅓ cup sun-dried tomatoes
in oil, drained
1.5ml/¼ tsp dried red chilli flakes
10ml/2 tsp chopped fresh thyme
75g/3oz mozzarella cheese, cubed
salt and ground black pepper
15–30ml/1–2 tbsp freshly grated
Parmesan cheese, plus extra to serve
For the dough
225g/8oz/2 cups strong white
bread flour
5ml/1 tsp salt
2.5ml/½ tsp easy-blend (rapid-rise)
dried yeast
15ml/1 tbsp olive oil
150ml/¼ pint/⅔ cup warm water

1 Make the dough. Place the dry ingredients in a bowl and mix to form a soft dough with the oil and water. Knead for 10 minutes. Put in an oiled bowl, cover and leave in a warm place until doubled in size.

2 Preheat the oven to 220°C/425°F/ Gas 7. Dice the aubergines. Fry the shallots in a little oil until soft. Add the aubergines, garlic, sun-dried tomatoes, chilli, thyme and seasoning. Cook for 5 minutes. Divide the dough in half and roll out each piece on a lightly floured work surface to a circle measuring about 18cm/7in across.

3 Spread the aubergine mixture over half of each circle, leaving a 2.5cm/1in border, then scatter over the mozzarella. Dampen the edges with water, then fold over the dough to enclose the filling. Press the edges firmly together to seal. Place on greased baking sheets.

4 Brush with half the remaining oil and make a small hole in the top of each calzone to allow steam to escape. Bake for 15–20 minutes until golden. Remove from the oven and brush with the remaining oil. Sprinkle over the Parmesan and serve immediately.

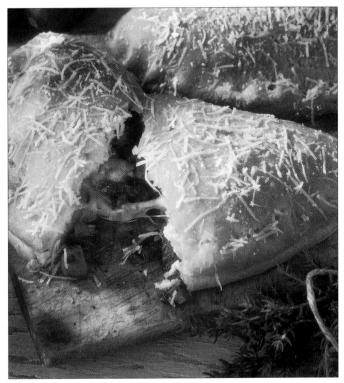

Energy 859Kcal/3596kJ; Protein 22.9g; Carbohydrate 92.4g, of which sugars 5.9g; Fat 46.8g, of which saturates 11.8g; Cholesterol 29mg; Calcium 413mg; Fibre 5.9g; Sodium 1474mg.

SALMON FISH CAKES

THE SECRET OF A GOOD FISH CAKE IS TO MAKE IT WITH FRESHLY PREPARED FISH AND POTATOES,
HOME-MADE BREADCRUMBS AND PLENTY OF INTERESTING SEASONING.

SERVES FOUR

INGREDIENTS

  450g/1lb cooked salmon fillet
  450g/1lb freshly cooked
    potatoes, mashed
  25g/1oz/2 tbsp butter, melted
  10ml/2 tsp wholegrain mustard
  15ml/1 tbsp each chopped fresh dill
    and chopped fresh parsley
  grated rind and juice of ½ lemon
  15ml/1 tbsp plain (all-purpose) flour
  1 egg, lightly beaten
  150g/5oz/1¼ cups dried breadcrumbs
  60ml/4 tbsp sunflower oil
  salt and ground black pepper
  rocket (arugula) and chives, to garnish
  lemon wedges, to serve

1 Flake the cooked salmon, discarding
any skin and bones. Put it in a bowl
with the mashed potato, melted butter
and wholegrain mustard, and mix well.
Stir in the dill and parsley and lemon
rind and juice. Season to taste with salt
and pepper.

2 Divide the mixture into 8 portions
and shape each into a ball, then flatten
into a thick disc. Dip the fish cakes first
in flour, then in egg and finally in
breadcrumbs, making sure that they are
evenly coated.

3 Heat the oil in a frying pan until it is
very hot. Fry the fish cakes in batches
until golden brown and crisp all over. As
each batch is ready, drain on kitchen
paper and keep hot. Garnish with rocket
leaves and chives and serve with lemon.

COOK'S TIP
Any fresh white or hot-smoked fish is
suitable; smoked cod and haddock are
particularly good.

Energy 602Kcal/2522kJ; Protein 31.7g; Carbohydrate 52.3g, of which sugars 1.8g; Fat 31g, of which saturates 7.2g; Cholesterol 122mg; Calcium 94mg; Fibre 2.5g; Sodium 401mg.

FRIED PLAICE WITH TOMATO SAUCE

THIS SIMPLE DISH IS PERENNIALLY POPULAR WITH CHILDREN. IT WORKS EQUALLY WELL WITH LEMON SOLE OR DABS (THESE DO NOT NEED SKINNING), OR FILLETS OF HADDOCK AND WHITING.

SERVES FOUR

INGREDIENTS

25g/1oz/¼ cup plain (all-purpose) flour
2 eggs, beaten
75g/3oz/¾ cup dried breadcrumbs,
  preferably home-made
4 small plaice or flounder, skinned
15g/½oz/1 tbsp butter
15ml/1 tbsp sunflower oil
salt and ground black pepper
1 lemon, quartered, to serve
fresh basil leaves, to garnish
For the tomato sauce
30ml/2 tbsp olive oil
1 red onion, finely chopped
1 garlic clove, finely chopped
400g/14oz can chopped tomatoes
15ml/1 tbsp tomato purée (paste)
15ml/1 tbsp torn fresh basil leaves

1 First make the tomato sauce. Heat the olive oil in a large pan, add the finely chopped onion and garlic and cook gently for about 5 minutes, until softened and pale golden. Stir in the chopped tomatoes and tomato purée and simmer for 20–30 minutes, stirring occasionally. Season with salt and pepper and stir in the basil.

2 Spread out the flour in a shallow dish, pour the beaten eggs into another and spread out the breadcrumbs in a third. Season the fish with salt and pepper.

3 Hold a fish in your left hand and dip it first in flour, then in egg and finally in the breadcrumbs, patting the crumbs on with your dry right hand.

4 Heat the butter and oil in a frying pan until foaming. Fry the fish one at a time in the hot fat for about 5 minutes on each side, until golden brown and cooked through, but still juicy in the middle. Drain on kitchen paper and keep hot while you fry the rest. Serve with lemon wedges and the tomato sauce, garnished with basil leaves.

Energy 323Kcal/1354kJ; Protein 20.5g; Carbohydrate 25.4g, of which sugars 5.5g; Fat 16.3g, of which saturates 4.2g; Cholesterol 154mg; Calcium 106mg; Fibre 1.8g; Sodium 338mg.

NO PLACE LIKE HOME

*Every country has its classic recipes and every
cook a favourite dish for nurturing their family
and sharing with friends. This chapter offers a
few examples of meals that have travelled far to
become internationally appreciated.*

VEGETABLE MOUSSAKA

THIS CLASSIC GREEK DISH IS REALLY FLAVOURSOME. IT CAN BE SERVED WITH WARM FRESH BREAD FOR A HEARTY, SATISFYING MEAL THAT GIVES A GREAT SENSE OF HEALTHY EATING AND WELL-BEING.

SERVES SIX

INGREDIENTS

450g/1lb aubergines (eggplant), sliced
115g/4oz/½ cup whole green lentils
600ml/1 pint/2½ cups vegetable stock
1 bay leaf
45ml/3 tbsp olive oil
1 onion, sliced
1 garlic clove, crushed
225g/8oz/3 cups mushrooms, sliced
400g/14oz can chickpeas, rinsed and drained
400g/14oz can chopped tomatoes
30ml/2 tbsp tomato purée (paste)
10ml/2 tsp dried *herbes de Provence*
300ml/½ pint/1¼ cups natural (plain) yogurt
3 eggs
50g/2oz mature Cheddar cheese, grated
salt and freshly ground black pepper
sprigs of fresh flat leaf parsley, to garnish

1 Sprinkle the aubergine slices with salt and place in a colander. Cover and place a weight on top. Leave for at least 30 minutes, to allow the bitter juices to be extracted.

2 Meanwhile, place the lentils, stock and bay leaf in a pan, cover, bring to the boil and simmer for about 20 minutes, until the lentils are just tender but not mushy. Add a little extra water if necessary. Drain thoroughly and keep warm.

3 Heat 15ml/1 tbsp of the oil in a large pan, add the onion and garlic and cook for 5 minutes, stirring. Stir in the lentils, mushrooms, chickpeas, tomatoes, tomato purée, herbs and 45ml/3 tbsp water. Bring to the boil, cover and simmer gently for 10–15 minutes, stirring from time to time.

4 Preheat the oven to 180°C/350°F/ Gas 4. Rinse the aubergine slices, drain and pat dry. Heat the remaining oil in a frying pan and fry the slices in batches for 3–4 minutes, turning once to brown both sides.

5 Season the lentil mixture with salt and pepper. Arrange a layer of aubergine slices in the bottom of a large, shallow, ovenproof dish or roasting tin, then spoon over a layer of the lentil mixture. Continue to build up the layers in this way until all the aubergine slices and lentil mixture are used up.

6 Beat the yogurt, eggs, salt and pepper together and pour the mixture over the dish. Sprinkle generously with the grated Cheddar cheese and bake for about 45 minutes, until the topping is golden brown and bubbling. Serve immediately, garnished with the flat leaf parsley.

VARIATION

Sliced and sautéed courgettes (zucchini) or potatoes can be used instead of the aubergines in this dish.

Energy 327Kcal/1373kJ; Protein 20.3g; Carbohydrate 29.7g, of which sugars 9.1g; Fat 15g, of which saturates 4.1g; Cholesterol 123mg; Calcium 240mg; Fibre 7.2g; Sodium 407mg.

VEGETABLE KORMA

THE CAREFUL BLENDING OF SPICES IS WARMING AND STIMULATING IN TRADITIONAL INDIAN COOKING.
THIS KORMA DISH IS RICH, CREAMY AND SUBTLY FLAVOURED.

SERVES FOUR

INGREDIENTS

50g/2oz/¼ cup butter
2 onions, sliced
2 garlic cloves, crushed
2.5cm/1in piece fresh root
  ginger, grated
5ml/1 tsp ground cumin
15ml/1 tbsp ground coriander
6 cardamom pods
5cm/2in piece of cinnamon stick
5ml/1 tsp ground turmeric
1 fresh red chilli, seeded and
  finely chopped
1 potato, peeled and cut into
  2.5cm/1in cubes
1 small aubergine (eggplant),
  chopped
115g/4oz/1½ cups mushrooms,
  thickly sliced
175ml/6fl oz/¾ cup water
115g/4oz/1 cup green beans, cut into
  2.5cm/1in lengths
60ml/4 tbsp natural (plain) yogurt
150ml/¼ pint/⅔ cup double
  (heavy) cream
5ml/1 tsp garam masala
salt and ground black pepper
fresh coriander (cilantro) sprigs,
  to garnish
boiled rice and poppadums, to serve

1 Melt the butter in a heavy pan. Add the onions and cook for 5 minutes until soft. Add the garlic and ginger and cook for 2 minutes, then stir in the cumin, coriander, cardamom pods, cinnamon stick, turmeric and finely chopped chilli. Cook, stirring constantly, for 30 seconds.

2 Add the potato cubes, aubergine and mushrooms and the water. Cover the pan, bring to the boil, then lower the heat and simmer for 15 minutes. Add the beans and cook, uncovered, for 5 minutes. With a slotted spoon, remove the vegetables to a warmed serving dish and keep hot.

3 Increase the heat and allow the cooking liquid to bubble up until it has reduced a little. Season with salt and pepper, then stir in the yogurt, cream and garam masala. Pour the sauce over the vegetables and garnish with fresh coriander. Serve with boiled rice and crisp poppadums.

Energy 363Kcal/1499kJ; Protein 4.8g; Carbohydrate 16.6g, of which sugars 8.2g; Fat 31.3g, of which saturates 19.2g; Cholesterol 78mg; Calcium 88mg; Fibre 3.7g; Sodium 104mg.

LENTIL DHAL

THIS LENTIL DHAL MAKES A SUSTAINING AND COMFORTING MEAL WHEN SERVED WITH RICE OR INDIAN BREADS AND ANY DRY-SPICED DISH, PARTICULARLY A CAULIFLOWER OR POTATO DISH.

SERVES FOUR TO SIX

INGREDIENTS
40g/1½oz/3 tbsp butter or ghee
1 onion, chopped
2 green chillies, seeded and chopped
15ml/1 tbsp chopped fresh root
  ginger
225g/8oz/1 cup yellow or red lentils
900ml/1½ pints/3¾ cups water
45ml/3 tbsp roasted garlic purée
5ml/1 tsp ground cumin
5ml/1 tsp ground coriander
200g/7oz tomatoes, peeled and
  diced
a little lemon juice
salt and ground black pepper
30–45ml/2–3 tbsp coriander
  (cilantro) sprigs, to garnish
For the spicy garnish
30ml/2 tbsp groundnut (peanut) oil
4–5 shallots, sliced
2 garlic cloves, thinly sliced
15g/½oz/1 tbsp butter or ghee
5ml/1 tsp cumin seeds
5ml/1 tsp mustard seeds
3–4 small dried red chillies
8–10 fresh curry leaves

COOK'S TIP
Ghee is a type of clarified butter that has had all the milk solids and water removed by heating – it was originally made to extend the keeping qualities of butter in India. It is the main cooking fat used in traditional Indian cooking. Because the milk solids have been removed, ghee has a high smoking point and can therefore be cooked at higher temperatures than ordinary butter. Look for it in Indian and Asian stores or with specialist ranges in the supermarket.

1 First begin the spicy garnish. Heat the oil in a large, heavy pan. Add the shallots and fry them over a medium heat, stirring occasionally, until they are crisp and browned. Add the garlic and cook, stirring frequently, for a moment or two until the garlic colours slightly. Use a slotted spoon to remove the mixture from the pan and set aside.

2 Melt the butter or ghee in the pan and cook the onion, chillies and ginger for 10 minutes, until golden.

3 Stir in the lentils and water, then bring to the boil, reduce the heat and part-cover the pan. Simmer, stirring occasionally, for 50–60 minutes, until similar to a very thick soup.

4 Stir in the roasted garlic purée, cumin and ground coriander, then season with salt and pepper to taste. Cook for a further 10–15 minutes, uncovered, stirring frequently.

5 Stir in the tomatoes and then adjust the seasoning, adding a little lemon juice to taste if necessary.

6 To make the spicy garnish: melt the butter or ghee in a frying pan. Add the cumin and mustard seeds and fry until the mustard seeds pop. Stir in the chillies, curry leaves and the shallot mixture, then immediately swirl the mixture into the cooked dhal. Garnish with coriander, spicy fried shallots and garlic and serve.

Energy 359Kcal/1502kJ; Protein 14.3g; Carbohydrate 36.3g, of which sugars 5.1g; Fat 18.4g, of which saturates 8.9g; Cholesterol 32mg; Calcium 43mg; Fibre 3.8g; Sodium 87mg.

CLASSIC FISH AND CHIPS

THIS TRADITIONAL BRITISH DISH IS DELICIOUS AND WHOLESOME WHEN WELL COOKED. THE FISH SHOULD BE THICK AND SUCCULENT IN FINE CRISP BATTER. THE OIL FOR FRYING MUST BE BEST QUALITY, AND VERY HOT TO COOK THE FOOD FAST WITHOUT MAKING IT GREASY.

SERVES FOUR

INGREDIENTS

    450g/1lb potatoes
    groundnut oil for deep fat frying
    4 x 175g/6oz cod fillets, skinned
      and any tiny bones removed
For the batter
    75g/3oz/⅔ cup plain (all-purpose)
      flour
    1 egg yolk
    10ml/2 tsp oil
    175ml/6fl oz/¾ cup water
    salt

3 To make the batter, sift the flour into a bowl. Add a pinch of salt. Make a well in the middle of the flour and place the egg yolk in this. Add the oil and a little of the water. Mix the yolk with the oil and water, then gradually add the remaining water, mixing in the flour. When the flour and liquids are combined, beat well until the batter is completely smooth. Cover and set aside until ready to use.

5 Dip the pieces of fish fillet into the batter and turn them to make sure they are evenly coated. Allow any excess batter to drip off before carefully lowering the fish into the hot oil.

6 Cook the fish for 5 minutes, turning once, if necessary, so that the batter browns evenly. The batter should be crisp and golden. Drain on kitchen paper. Serve at once, with lemon wedges and the chips.

1 To make the chips, cut the potatoes into 5mm/¼in thick slices. Then cut the slices into 5mm/¼in fingers or chips. Rinse the chips thoroughly in cold water, drain them well and then dry them thoroughly in a clean dishtowel.

4 Cook the chips again in the fat for about a further 5 minutes, until they are golden and crisp. Drain on kitchen paper and season with salt. Keep hot in a low oven while you cook the pieces of fish.

VARIATIONS

• Although cod is the traditional choice for fish and chips, other white fish can be used: haddock is a popular alternative. Rock salmon, sometimes sold as huss or dogfish, also has a good flavour. Pollock or hoki are also suitable. Thin fillets, such as plaice or sole, tend to be too thin and can be overpowered by the batter. Egg and breadcrumb coating is more suitable for thin fish.

• To coat fish with egg and breadcrumbs, dip the fillets in seasoned flour, then in beaten egg and finally in fine, dry white breadcrumbs. Repeat a second time if the fish is to be deep fried.

• Chunky chips are traditional with thick battered fish. Cut the potatoes into thick fingers to make chunky chips and allow slightly longer for the second frying.

2 Heat the oil in a deep fat fryer to 180°C/350°F. Add the chips to the fryer and cook for 3 minutes, then remove from the pan and shake off all fat. Set to one side.

COOK'S TIP

Use fresh rather than frozen fish for the very best texture and flavour. If you have to use frozen fish, defrost it thoroughly and make sure it is dry before coating with batter.

Energy 645Kcal/2700kJ; Protein 32.6g; Carbohydrate 54.3g, of which sugars 0.7g; Fat 34.5g, of which saturates 3.5g; Cholesterol 38mg; Calcium 130mg; Fibre 3.4g; Sodium 294mg.

BAKED FISH <u>WITH</u> POTATOES <u>AND</u> GARLIC

THIS SIMPLE BRITISH DISH CAN BE MADE WITH ANY WHITE FISH. TARTARE SAUCE OR A THICK VINAIGRETTE AND HARD-BOILED EGG ARE DELICIOUS ACCOMPANIMENTS.

SERVES FOUR

INGREDIENTS

1kg/2¼lb waxy potatoes, cut
  into chunks
50g/2oz/¼ cup butter
2 onions, thickly sliced
4 garlic cloves
few fresh thyme sprigs
2–3 fresh bay leaves
450ml/¾ pint/scant 2 cups
  vegetable or fish stock,
  plus 45ml/3 tbsp
900g/2lb monkfish tail in one piece,
  skin and membrane removed
30–45ml/2–3 tbsp white wine
50g/2oz/1 cup fresh
  white breadcrumbs
15g/½ oz fresh parsley, chopped
15ml/1 tbsp olive oil
salt and ground black pepper

1 Preheat the oven to 190°C/375°F/ Gas 5. Put the chunks of potato in an ovenproof dish. Melt half the butter in a large frying pan and cook the onions gently for 5–6 minutes. Add the onions to the potatoes and mix.

2 Slice 2–3 of the garlic cloves and add to the potatoes with the thyme and bay leaves, and season with salt and freshly ground black pepper.

3 Pour in the main batch of stock over the potatoes and bake, stirring once or twice, for 50–60 minutes, until the potatoes are just tender.

4 Nestle the monkfish into the potatoes and season with salt and pepper. Bake for 10–15 minutes. Mix the 45ml/3 tbsp stock with the wine and use to baste the monkfish 2–3 times during cooking.

5 Finely chop the remaining garlic. Melt the remaining butter and toss it with the breadcrumbs, chopped garlic, most of the chopped parsley and seasoning until the crumbs are evenly moistened. Spoon the breadcrumb mixture over the monkfish, pressing it down gently with the back of a spoon.

6 Drizzle the olive oil over the crumb-covered fish, return the dish to the oven and bake for a final 10–15 minutes, until the breadcrumbs are crisp and golden and all the liquid has been absorbed. Sprinkle the remaining parsley on to the potatoes and serve immediately.

Energy 519Kcal/2193kJ; Protein 42.1g; Carbohydrate 56.1g, of which sugars 7.9g; Fat 15.2g, of which saturates 7.4g; Cholesterol 58mg; Calcium 71mg; Fibre 3.8g; Sodium 367mg.

CLASSIC FISH PIE

*MASHED-POTATO TOPPED PIES INVARIABLY SCORE WELL AMONG COMFORT FOOD FAVOURITES. THIS
ENGLISH FISH PIE HAS A SATISFYING CREAMY SAUCE UNDER THE GOLDEN POTATO CRUST.*

SERVES FOUR

INGREDIENTS
  butter, for greasing
  450g/1lb mixed fish, such as
    cod or salmon fillets and
    peeled prawns (shrimp)
  finely grated rind of 1 lemon
  450g/1lb floury potatoes
  25g/1oz/2 tbsp butter
  1 egg, beaten
  salt and ground black pepper
For the sauce
  15g/½oz/1 tbsp butter
  15ml/1 tbsp plain (all-purpose) flour
  150ml/¼ pint/⅔ cup milk
  45ml/3 tbsp chopped fresh parsley

3 Meanwhile make the sauce. Melt the
butter in a pan, add the flour and cook,
stirring, for a few minutes. Remove from
the heat and gradually whisk in the
milk. Return to the heat and bring to
the boil then reduce the heat and
simmer, whisking all the time, until the
sauce has thickened and achieved a
smooth consistency. Add the parsley
and season to taste. Pour over the
fish mixture.

4 Drain the potatoes well and then
mash with the butter.

5 Pipe or spoon the potatoes on top of
the fish mixture. Brush the beaten egg
over the potatoes. Bake for 45 minutes
until the top is golden brown. Serve hot.

1 Preheat the oven to 220°C/425°F/
Gas 7. Grease an ovenproof dish and
set aside. Cut the fish into bite-sized
pieces. Season the fish, sprinkle over
the lemon rind and place in the base
of the prepared dish. Allow to sit while
you make the topping.

2 Cook the potatoes in boiling salted
water until tender.

Energy 301Kcal/1262kJ; Protein 26.5g; Carbohydrate 24.1g, of which sugars 2.6g; Fat 11.6g, of which saturates 6.2g; Cholesterol 132mg; Calcium 76mg; Fibre 1.6g; Sodium 173mg.

SEAFOOD CHOWDER

LIKE MOST CHOWDERS, THIS DISH FROM NEW ENGLAND IS A SUBSTANTIAL, HOMELY DISH, WHICH IS DELICIOUS WITH CHUNKS OF GOOD CRUSTY BREAD.

SERVES FOUR TO SIX

INGREDIENTS

200g/7oz/generous 1 cup drained canned corn
600ml/1 pint/2½ cups milk
15g/½oz/1 tbsp butter
1 small leek, sliced
1 small garlic clove, crushed
2 rindless smoked streaky (fatty) bacon rashers (strips), finely chopped
1 small green or red (bell) pepper, seeded and diced
1 celery stick, chopped
115g/4oz/generous ½ cup white long grain rice
5ml/1 tsp plain (all-purpose) flour
about 450ml/¾ pint/scant 2 cups hot chicken or vegetable stock
4 large scallops
115g/4oz white fish fillet, such as monkfish, plaice or flounder
15ml/1 tbsp finely chopped fresh flat leaf parsley
good pinch of cayenne pepper
30–45ml/2–3 tbsp single (light) cream (optional)
salt and ground black pepper
crusty bread, to serve

VARIATIONS

• You can use other shellfish in place of the scallops if you prefer – try fresh or frozen prawns (shrimp), or mussels or clams, which are equally good in or out of their shells.
• Allow frozen shellfish to thaw at room temperature before adding to the chowder.
• Undyed, naturally smoked haddock or cod would make a delicious alternative fish.

1 Place half the drained corn in a food processor or blender. Add a little of the milk and then process until the mixture is thick and creamy. Set aside.

2 Melt the butter in a large, heavy pan. Add the leek, garlic and bacon and gently fry for 4–5 minutes until the leek has softened but not browned.

3 Add the diced green or red pepper and the chopped celery and cook over a very gentle heat for 3–4 minutes more, stirring frequently, until the pepper and celery have softened slightly.

4 Stir in the rice and cook for a few minutes, stirring occasionally, until the grains begin to swell, then sprinkle the flour evenly over the top of the rice and vegetables. Cook for about 1 minute, stirring all the time, then gradually stir in the remaining milk and the hot stock.

5 Bring the mixture to the boil over a medium heat, then lower the heat and stir in the creamed corn mixture, with the whole corn. Season well.

6 Cover the pan and simmer very gently for about 20 minutes, or until the rice is tender, stirring occasionally. Add a little more chicken or vegetable stock or water to the pan if the mixture thickens too quickly or if the rice begins to stick to the base of the pan.

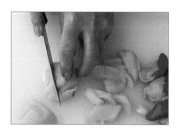

7 Cut the corals away from the scallops and set them aside; slice the white flesh into 5mm/¼in pieces. Cut the white fish fillet into bitesize chunks.

8 Add the scallops and chunks of fish to the chowder. Stir gently, then cook for 4 minutes.

9 Stir in the scallop corals, parsley and cayenne pepper. Cook for a few minutes until the scallops are just cooked and heated through, then stir in the cream, if using. Adjust the seasoning and serve

COOK'S TIP

Instead of using a food processor, chop the corn finely and transfer to a bowl. Beat in the milk a little at a time until the mixture is thick and creamy.

Energy 373Kcal/1569kJ; Protein 26g; Carbohydrate 45.1g, of which sugars 11.8g; Fat 10.4g, of which saturates 4.8g; Cholesterol 54mg; Calcium 217mg; Fibre 2.7g; Sodium 313mg.

STUFFED CHICKEN <u>IN</u> BACON COATS

*A SIMPLE CREAM CHEESE AND CHIVE FILLING FLAVOURS THESE CHICKEN BREASTS AND THEY ARE
BEAUTIFULLY MOIST WHEN COOKED IN THEIR BACON WRAPPING. SERVE JACKET POTATOES AND A
CRISP, FRESH GREEN SALAD AS ACCOMPANIMENTS.*

SERVES FOUR

INGREDIENTS
  4 skinless, boneless chicken breast
    portions, each weighing 175g/6oz
  115g/4oz/½ cup cream cheese
  15ml/1 tbsp chopped chives
  8 rindless unsmoked bacon
    rashers (strips)
  15ml/1 tbsp olive oil
  ground black pepper

1 Preheat the oven to 200°C/400°F/
Gas 6. Using a sharp knife, make a
horizontal slit from the side into each
chicken breast portion (the cheese
filling is stuffed into each slit).

2 To make the filling, beat together the
cream cheese and chives. Divide the
filling into four portions and, using a
teaspoon, fill each slit with some of the
cream cheese. Push the sides of the slit
together to keep the filling in.

3 Wrap each breast in two rashers of
bacon and place in an ovenproof dish.
Drizzle the oil over the chicken and
bake for 25–30 minutes, brushing
occasionally with the oil. Season with
black pepper and serve at once.

Energy 459Kcal/1913kJ; Protein 52.3g; Carbohydrate 0g, of which sugars 0g; Fat 27.7g, of which saturates 13g; Cholesterol 0mg; Calcium 40mg; Fibre 0g; Sodium 1070mg.

SOUTHERN FRIED CHICKEN

*FRIED CHICKEN IS NOW AN INTERNATIONAL FAST-FOOD FAVOURITE THAT ORIGINATED IN AMERICA.
THIS HOME-MADE VERSION IS SUBSTANTIAL AND TASTY. SERVE IT WITH POTATO WEDGES TO
COMPLETE THE MEAL.*

SERVES FOUR

INGREDIENTS
  15ml/1 tbsp paprika
  30ml/2 tbsp plain (all-purpose) flour
  4 skinless, boneless chicken breast
    portions, each weighing 175g/6oz
  30ml/2 tbsp sunflower oil
  salt and ground black pepper
For the corn cakes
  200g/7oz corn kernels
  350g/12oz mashed potato, cooled
  25g/1oz/2 tbsp butter
  150ml/¼ pint/⅔ cup sour cream,
    to serve
  15ml/1 tbsp chopped chives, to serve

COOK'S TIP
To make the mashed potato, cook the
potatoes in boiling salted water for about
20 minutes until tender, then drain well.
Add a little milk and mash until smooth.

1 Mix the paprika and flour together on
a plate. Coat each chicken breast
portion in the seasoned flour.

2 Heat the oil in a large frying pan and
add the floured chicken. Cook over a
high heat until a golden brown colour
on both sides. Reduce the heat and
continue cooking for 20 minutes more,
turning once or twice, or until the
chicken is cooked right through.

3 Meanwhile, make the corn cakes. Stir
the sweetcorn kernels into the cooled
mashed potato and season with plenty
of salt and pepper to taste. Using lightly
floured hands, shape the mixture into
12 even-size round cakes, each about
5cm/2in in diameter.

4 When the chicken breast portions are
cooked, use a slotted spoon to remove
them from the frying pan and keep hot.
Melt the butter in the pan and cook the
corn cakes for 3 minutes on each side,
or until golden and heated through.

5 Meanwhile, mix together the sour
cream with the chives in a bowl to make
a dip. Transfer the corn cakes from the
frying pan to serving plates and top with
the chicken breast portions. Serve at
once, offering the sour cream with
chives on the side.

Energy 505Kcal/2119kJ; Protein 47.8g; Carbohydrate 32.2g, of which sugars 3.3g; Fat 21.5g, of which saturates 9.3g; Cholesterol 158mg; Calcium 61mg; Fibre 2.5g; Sodium 172mg.

CHICKEN FLAUTAS

CRISP FRIED MEXICAN TORTILLAS WITH A CHICKEN AND CHEESE FILLING MAKE A DELICIOUS MEAL,
ESPECIALLY WHEN SERVED WITH A SPICY TOMATO SALSA. THE SECRET OF SUCCESS IS TO MAKE SURE
THAT THE OIL IS SUFFICIENTLY HOT TO PREVENT THE FLUTES FROM ABSORBING TOO MUCH OF IT.

MAKES TWELVE

INGREDIENTS
  2 skinless, boneless chicken breasts
  1 onion
  2 garlic cloves
  15ml/1 tbsp vegetable oil
  90g/3½oz feta cheese, crumbled
  12 corn tortillas, freshly made or a
    few days old
  oil, for frying
  salt and ground black pepper
For the salsa
  3 tomatoes, peeled, seeded
    and chopped
  juice of ½ lime
  small bunch of fresh coriander
    (cilantro), chopped
  ½ small onion, finely chopped
  3 fresh fresno chillies or similar
    fresh green chillies, seeded
    and chopped

1 Start by making the salsa. Mix the tomatoes, lime juice, coriander, onion and chillies in a bowl. Season with salt to taste and set aside.

COOK'S TIP
You might find it easier to keep the cocktail sticks in place until after the flutes have been fried, in which case remove them before serving.

2 Put the chicken breasts in a large pan, add water to cover and bring to the boil. Lower the heat and simmer for 15–20 minutes or until the chicken is cooked. Remove the chicken from the pan and let it cool a little. Using two forks, shred the chicken into small pieces. Set it aside.

3 Chop the onion finely and crush the garlic. Heat the oil in a frying pan, add the onion and garlic and fry over a low heat for about 5 minutes, or until the onion has softened but not coloured. Add the shredded chicken, with salt and pepper to taste. Mix well, remove from the heat and stir in the feta.

4 Before they can be rolled, soften the tortillas by steaming three or four at a time on a plate over boiling water for a few moments until they are pliable. Alternatively, wrap them in microwave-safe film and then heat them in a microwave oven on full power for about 30 seconds.

5 Place a spoonful of the chicken filling on one of the tortillas. Roll the tortilla tightly around the filling to make a neat cylinder. Secure with a cocktail stick (toothpick). Cover the roll with clear film (plastic wrap) to prevent the tortilla from drying out and splitting. Fill the remaining tortillas in the same way.

6 Pour oil into a frying pan to a depth of 2.5cm/1in. Heat it until a small cube of bread, added to the oil, rises to the surface and bubbles at the edges before turning golden. Remove the cocktail sticks, then add the flutes to the pan, a few at a time.

7 Fry the flutes for 2–3 minutes until golden, turning frequently. Drain on kitchen paper and serve at once, with the salsa.

Energy 89Kcal/374kJ; Protein 9.1g; Carbohydrate 6.9g, of which sugars 1.7g; Fat 2.9g, of which saturates 1.3g; Cholesterol 26mg; Calcium 43mg; Fibre 0.6g; Sodium 151mg.

CHICKEN FAJITAS

THE PERFECT DISH FOR CASUAL ENTERTAINING. IN MEXICO FAJITAS ARE FLOUR TORTILLAS THAT ARE BROUGHT TO THE TABLE FRESHLY COOKED. GUESTS ADD THEIR OWN FILLINGS BEFORE FOLDING THE TORTILLAS AND TUCKING IN. THIS IS DELICIOUSLY FUN FOOD FOR SOCIABLE DINING.

SERVES SIX

INGREDIENTS
3 skinless, boneless chicken breasts
finely grated rind and juice of
2 limes
30ml/2 tbsp caster (superfine) sugar
10ml/2 tsp dried oregano
2.5ml/½ tsp cayenne pepper
5ml/1 tsp ground cinnamon
2 onions
3 (bell) peppers (1 red, 1 yellow or
orange and 1 green)
45ml/3 tbsp vegetable oil
guacamole, salsa and sour cream,
to serve
For the tortillas
250g/9oz/2¼ cups plain (all-purpose)
flour, sifted
1.5ml/¼ tsp baking powder
pinch of salt
50g/2oz/¼ cup lard (shortening) or
white cooking fat
60ml/4 tbsp warm water

1 Slice the chicken breasts into 2cm/
¾in wide strips and place these in a
large bowl. Add the lime rind and juice,
caster sugar, oregano, cayenne and
cinnamon. Mix thoroughly. Set aside to
marinate for at least 30 minutes.

COOK'S TIP
Tortilla dough can be very difficult to roll
out thinly. If the dough is breaking up try
placing each ball between two sheets of
clean plastic (this can be cut from a new
sandwich bag). Roll out, turning over,
still inside the plastic, until the tortilla is
the right size.

2 Meanwhile, make the tortillas. Mix
the flour, baking powder and salt in a
large bowl. Rub in the lard, then add
the warm water, a little at a time, to
make a stiff dough. Knead this on a
lightly floured surface for 10–15
minutes until it is smooth and elastic.

3 Divide the dough into 12 small balls,
then roll each into a 15cm/6in round.
Cover the rounds with plastic or clear
film (plastic wrap) to stop them drying
out while you prepare the vegetables.

4 Cut the onions in half and slice them
thinly. Cut the peppers in half, remove
the cores and seeds, then slice the
flesh into 1cm/½in wide strips.

5 Heat a large frying pan or griddle and
cook each tortilla in turn for about
1 minute on each side, or until the
surface colours and begins to blister.
Keep the cooked tortillas warm and
pliable by wrapping them in a clean,
dry dishtowel.

6 Heat the oil in a large frying pan.
Stir-fry the marinated chicken for
5–6 minutes, then add the peppers
and onions and cook for 3–4 minutes
more, until the chicken strips are
cooked through and the vegetables
are soft and tender, but still juicy.

7 Spoon the chicken mixture into a
serving bowl and take it to the table
with the cooked tortillas, guacamole,
salsa and sour cream. Keep the tortillas
wrapped and warm.

8 To serve, each guest takes a warm
tortilla, spreads it with a little salsa, adds
a spoonful of guacamole and piles some
of the chicken mixture in the centre. The
final touch is to add a small dollop of
sour cream. The tortilla is then folded
over the filling and eaten in the hand.

Energy 405Kcal/1698kJ; Protein 26.4g; Carbohydrate 41.9g, of which sugars 8.8g; Fat 15.7g, of which saturates 4.5g; Cholesterol 69mg; Calcium 82mg; Fibre 3.4g; Sodium 157mg.

GREEN CHICKEN CURRY WITH COCONUT RICE

THERE IS SOMETHING SATISFYING ABOUT COOKING A ONE-POT MEAL. PERHAPS IT'S BECAUSE IT TAKES NO EFFORT TO MAKE, OR MAYBE IT'S THE BLEND OF FLAVOURS THAT MAKES IT SO APPEALING.

SERVES THREE TO FOUR

INGREDIENTS

4 spring onions (scallions), trimmed and roughly chopped

1–2 fresh green chillies, seeded and roughly chopped

2cm/¾in piece of fresh root ginger, peeled

2 garlic cloves

5ml/1 tsp Thai fish sauce

large bunch of fresh coriander (cilantro)

small handful of fresh parsley

30–45ml/2–3 tbsp water

30ml/2 tbsp sunflower oil

4 skinless, boneless chicken breasts, cubed

1 green (bell) pepper, seeded and finely sliced

75g/3oz piece of creamed coconut dissolved in 400ml/14fl oz/1⅔ cups boiling water

salt and freshly ground black pepper

For the rice

225g/8oz/generous 1 cup Thai fragrant rice, rinsed

75g/3oz piece of creamed coconut dissolved in 400ml/14fl oz/1⅔ cups boiling water

1 lemon grass stalk, quartered and bruised

2 Heat half the oil in large frying pan. Fry the chicken cubes until evenly browned. Transfer to a plate.

3 Heat the remaining oil. Stir-fry the green pepper for 3–4 minutes, then add the chilli and ginger paste. Fry, stirring, for 3–4 minutes until the mixture becomes fairly thick.

1 Process the spring onions, chillies, ginger, garlic, fish sauce, fresh herbs and water to a smooth paste in a food processor or blender.

4 Return the chicken to the pan and add the coconut liquid. Season. Bring to the boil, lower the heat; half cover the pan and simmer for 8–10 minutes.

5 When the chicken is cooked, transfer it with the peppers to a plate. Boil the cooking liquid remaining in the pan for 10–12 minutes until it is well reduced and fairly thick.

6 Meanwhile, put the rice in a large pan. Add the coconut liquid and the bruised pieces of lemon grass. Stir in a little salt, bring to the boil, then lower the heat, cover and simmer very gently for 10 minutes, or for the time recommended on the packet. When the rice is tender, discard the pieces of lemon grass and fork the rice on to a warmed serving plate.

7 Return the chicken and peppers to the green curry sauce, stir well and cook gently for a few minutes to heat through. Spoon the curry over the rice, and serve immediately.

COOK'S TIP

Lemon grass features in many Asian dishes, and makes the perfect partner for coconut, especially when used with chicken. In this recipe, bruise the tough, top end of the lemon grass stem in a pestle and mortar before use.

Energy 699Kcal/2963kJ; Protein 65.4g; Carbohydrate 82.9g, of which sugars 18.2g; Fat 14.2g, of which saturates 3g; Cholesterol 163mg; Calcium 184mg; Fibre 3.2g; Sodium 448mg.

COQ ᴬᵁ VIN

COOKING THIS FRENCH COUNTRY CASSEROLE FILLS THE HOUSE WITH AN ARRAY OF APPETITE-AROUSING AROMAS, FROM BACON COOKED WITH GARLIC, HERBS AND SHALLOTS, THROUGH TO THE HEADY SCENT OF THE RED WINE USED TO SIMMER THE CHICKEN TO PERFECT TENDERNESS.

SERVES SIX

INGREDIENTS
   45ml/3 tbsp light olive oil
   12 shallots
   225g/8oz rindless streaky (fatty)
      bacon rashers (strips), chopped
   3 garlic cloves, finely chopped
   225g/8oz small mushrooms, halved
   3 boneless chicken breast portions
   6 boneless chicken thighs
   1 bottle red wine
   salt and ground black pepper
   45ml/3 tbsp chopped fresh parsley,
      to garnish
For the bouquet garni
   3 sprigs each of fresh parsley, thyme
      and sage
   1 bay leaf
   4 peppercorns
For the *beurre manié*
   25g/1oz/2 tbsp butter, softened
   25g/1oz/¼ cup plain (all-purpose) flour

1 Heat the oil in a large, flameproof casserole, add the shallots and cook for 5 minutes, or until golden. Increase the heat, add the bacon, garlic and halved mushrooms and cook for 10 minutes more, stirring frequently.

2 Use a draining spoon to transfer the cooked ingredients to a plate. Halve the chicken breast portions, then brown, along with the thighs, in the oil remaining in the pan. As they cook, turn them to ensure they are golden brown all over. Return the shallots, garlic, mushrooms and bacon to the casserole and pour in the red wine.

3 Tie the ingredients for the bouquet garni in a bundle in a small piece of muslin (cheesecloth) and add to the casserole. Bring to the boil, reduce the heat and cover the casserole, then simmer for about 35 minutes.

4 To make the *beurre manié*, cream the butter and flour together in a small bowl using your fingers or a spoon to make a smooth paste.

5 Add small lumps of this paste to the bubbling casserole, stirring well until each piece has melted into the liquid before adding the next. When all the paste has been added, bring back to the boil and simmer for 5 minutes.

6 Season the casserole to taste with salt and pepper and serve garnished with chopped fresh parsley and accompanied by boiled potatoes.

Energy 496Kcal/2067kJ; Protein 39.2g; Carbohydrate 5g, of which sugars 1.8g; Fat 26.9g, of which saturates 8.5g; Cholesterol 153mg; Calcium 47mg; Fibre 1.1g; Sodium 600mg.

CHILLI CON CARNE

ORIGINALLY MADE WITH FINELY CHOPPED BEEF, CHILLIES AND KIDNEY BEANS BY HUNGRY LABOURERS WORKING ON THE TEXAN RAILROAD, THIS FAMOUS TEX-MEX STEW HAS BECOME AN INTERNATIONAL FAVOURITE. SERVE RICE OR BAKED POTATOES TO COMPLETE THIS HEARTY MEAL.

SERVES EIGHT

INGREDIENTS
 1.2kg/2½lb lean braising steak
 30ml/2 tbsp sunflower oil
 1 large onion, chopped
 2 garlic cloves, finely chopped
 15ml/1 tbsp plain (all-purpose) flour
 300ml/½ pint/1¼ cups red wine
 300ml/½ pint/1¼ cups beef stock
 30ml/2 tbsp tomato purée (paste)
 fresh coriander (cilantro) leaves,
  to garnish
 salt and ground black pepper
For the beans
 30ml/2 tbsp olive oil
 1 onion, chopped
 1 red chilli, seeded and chopped
 2 x 400g/14oz cans red kidney
  beans, drained and rinsed
 400g/14oz can chopped tomatoes
For the topping
 6 tomatoes, peeled and chopped
 1 green chilli, seeded and chopped
 30ml/2 tbsp chopped fresh chives
 30ml/2 tbsp chopped fresh
  coriander (cilantro)
 150ml/¼ pint/⅔ cup sour cream

2 Use a slotted spoon to remove the onion from the pan, then add the floured beef and cook over a high heat until browned on all sides. Remove from the pan and set aside, then flour and brown another batch of meat.

3 When the last batch of meat is browned, return the first batches with the onion to the pan. Stir in the wine, stock and tomato purée. Bring to the boil, reduce the heat and simmer for 45 minutes, or until tender.

4 Meanwhile, for the beans, heat the olive oil in a frying pan and cook the onion and chilli until softened. Add the kidney beans and tomatoes and simmer gently for 20–25 minutes, or until thickened and reduced.

5 Mix the tomatoes, chilli, chives and coriander for the topping. Ladle the meat mixture on to warmed plates. Add a layer of bean mixture and tomato topping. Finish with sour cream and garnish with coriander.

1 Cut the meat into thick strips and then cut it crossways into small cubes. Heat the oil in a large, flameproof casserole. Add the onion and garlic, and cook until softened but not coloured. Meanwhile, season the flour and toss a batch of meat in it.

VARIATION
This stew is equally good served with warm tortillas instead of rice.

Energy 469Kcal/1963kJ; Protein 42g; Carbohydrate 28.3g, of which sugars 11.2g; Fat 18.8g, of which saturates 6.8g; Cholesterol 106mg; Calcium 127mg; Fibre 8.1g; Sodium 523mg.

MEXICAN SPICY BEEF TORTILLA

THIS DISH IS NOT UNLIKE A LASAGNE, EXCEPT THAT THE SPICY MEAT IS MIXED WITH RICE AND IS LAYERED BETWEEN MEXICAN TORTILLAS, WITH A HOT SALSA SAUCE FOR AN EXTRA KICK.

SERVES FOUR

INGREDIENTS
1 onion, chopped
2 garlic cloves, crushed
1 fresh red chilli, seeded and sliced
350g/12oz rump (round) steak, cut
 into small cubes
15ml/1 tbsp oil
225g/8oz/2 cups cooked long
 grain rice
beef stock, to moisten
3 large wheat tortillas
For the salsa picante
 2 x 400g/14oz cans chopped tomatoes
 2 garlic cloves, halved
 1 onion, quartered
 1–2 fresh red chillies, seeded and
  roughly chopped
 5ml/1 tsp ground cumin
 2.5–5ml/½–1 tsp cayenne pepper
 5ml/1 tsp fresh oregano or 2.5ml/
  ½ tsp dried oregano
 tomato juice or water, if required
For the cheese sauce
 50g/2oz/4 tbsp butter
 50g/2oz/½ cup plain (all-purpose)
  flour
 600ml/1 pint/2½ cups milk
 115g/4oz/1 cup grated Cheddar cheese
 salt and freshly ground black pepper

1 Preheat the oven to 180°C/350°F/ Gas 4. Make the salsa picante. Place the tomatoes, garlic, onion and chillies in a food processor and process until smooth. Pour into a small pan, add the spices and oregano and season with salt. Gradually bring to the boil, stirring occasionally. Boil for 1–2 minutes, lower the heat, cover and simmer for 15 minutes. The sauce should be of a thick pouring consistency. Dilute with a little tomato juice or water as necessary.

2 Make the cheese sauce. Melt the butter in a pan and stir in the flour. Cook for 1 minute. Add the milk, stirring all the time until the sauce boils and thickens. Stir in all but 30ml/2 tbsp of the cheese and season to taste. Cover the pan closely and set aside.

3 Mix the onion, garlic and chilli in a large bowl. Add the steak cubes and mix well. Heat the oil in a frying pan and stir-fry the meat mixture for about 10 minutes, until the meat cubes have browned and the onion is soft. Stir in the rice and enough beef stock to moisten. Season to taste with salt and freshly ground black pepper.

4 Pour about a quarter of the cheese sauce into the bottom of a round ovenproof dish. Add a tortilla and then spread over half the salsa followed by half the meat mixture.

5 Repeat these layers, then add half the remaining cheese sauce and the final tortilla. Pour over the remaining cheese sauce and sprinkle the reserved cheese on top. Bake in the oven for 15–20 minutes until golden on top.

COOK'S TIP
You can use any type of beef for this dish. If braising or stewing steak are used, they should be very finely chopped or even minced and the bake should be cooked for an extra 10–15 minutes.

Energy 798Kcal/3360kJ; Protein 41.7g; Carbohydrate 92g, of which sugars 17.4g; Fat 31.4g, of which saturates 16.7g; Cholesterol 115mg; Calcium 515mg; Fibre 3.7g; Sodium 554mg.

MEXICAN TACOS

READY-MADE TACO SHELLS MAKE PERFECT EDIBLE CONTAINERS FOR SHREDDED SALAD, MEAT FILLINGS,
GRATED CHEESE AND SOUR CREAM. THIS IS AN EXCELLENT CHOICE OF SUPPER WHEN YOU FEEL LIKE
SOMETHING DELICIOUS BUT DO NOT WANT TO SPEND HOURS SLAVING OVER THE STOVE.

SERVES FOUR

INGREDIENTS
   15ml/1 tbsp olive oil
   250g/9oz lean minced (ground) beef
      or turkey
   2 garlic cloves, crushed
   5ml/1 tsp ground cumin
   5–10ml/1–2 tsp mild chilli powder
   8 ready-made taco shells
   ½ small iceberg lettuce, shredded
   1 small onion, thinly sliced
   2 tomatoes, chopped in chunks
   1 avocado, halved, stoned
      and sliced
   60ml/4 tbsp sour cream
   125g/4oz/1 cup crumbled *queso*
      blanco or *anejado*, or grated
      Cheddar or Monterey Jack cheese
   salt and ground black pepper

1 Heat the oil in a frying pan. Add the meat, with the garlic and spices, and brown over a medium heat, stirring frequently to break up any lumps. Season, cook for 5 minutes, then set aside to cool slightly.

2 Meanwhile, warm the taco shells according to the instructions on the packet. Do not let them get too crisp. Spoon the lettuce, onion, tomatoes and avocado slices into the taco shells. Top with the sour cream followed by the minced beef or turkey mixture.

COOK'S TIP
Stir-fried strips of turkey, chicken or pork are excellent instead of the minced beef.

3 Sprinkle the crumbled or grated cheese into the tacos and serve immediately. Tacos are eaten with the fingers, so have plenty of paper napkins handy.

Energy 497Kcal/2067kJ; Protein 25.4g; Carbohydrate 19.4g, of which sugars 3.8g; Fat 35.1g, of which saturates 14.3g; Cholesterol 74mg; Calcium 305mg; Fibre 3.6g; Sodium 511mg.

SHEPHERD'S PIE

THIS CLASSIC BRITISH PIE IS SO GOOD THAT IT IS DIFFICULT TO KNOW WHEN SECONDS OR THIRD
HELPINGS ARE ENOUGH. SERVE WITH A SELECTION OF FRESH VEGETABLES.

SERVES FOUR

INGREDIENTS
  30ml/2 tbsp oil
  1 onion, finely chopped
  1 carrot, finely chopped
  115g/4oz mushrooms, chopped
  500g/1¼lb lean chuck steak,
    minced (ground)
  300ml/½ pint/1¼ cups brown veal
    stock or water
  15ml/1 tbsp plain (all-purpose) flour
  bay leaf
  10–15ml/2–3 tsp Worcestershire
    sauce
  15ml/1 tbsp tomato purée (paste)
  675g/1½lb potatoes, boiled
  25g/1oz/2 tbsp butter
  45ml/3 tbsp hot milk
  15ml/1 tbsp chopped fresh tarragon
  salt and pepper

1 Heat the oil in a pan, add the onion, carrot and mushrooms and cook, stirring occasionally, until browned. Stir the beef into the pan and cook, stirring to break up the lumps, until lightly browned.

2 Blend a few spoonfuls of the stock or water with the flour, then stir this mixture into the pan. Stir in the remaining stock or water and bring to a simmer, stirring. Add the bay leaf, Worcestershire sauce and tomato purée, then cover and cook very gently for 1 hour, stirring occasionally. Uncover the pan towards the end of cooking to allow any excess water to evaporate, if necessary.

3 Preheat the oven to 190°C/375°F/ Gas 5. Gently heat the potatoes for a couple of minutes, then mash with the butter, milk and seasoning.

4 Add the tarragon and seasoning to the mince, then pour into a pie dish. Cover the mince with an even layer of potato and mark the top with the prongs of a fork. Bake for about 25 minutes, until golden brown.

Energy 426Kcal/1788kJ; Protein 33.9g; Carbohydrate 39.2g, of which sugars 6.3g; Fat 15.9g, of which saturates 5.9g; Cholesterol 0mg; Calcium 66mg; Fibre 3.7g; Sodium 240mg.

LANCASHIRE HOTPOT

THIS IS ONE OF THOSE SLOW, REASSURING RECIPES THAT HAS NURTURED GENERATIONS OF FAMILIES.

SERVES 4

INGREDIENTS
40g/1½oz/3 tbsp dripping, or 45ml/
   3 tbsp dripping, or 45ml/3 tbsp oil
8 middle neck lamb chops, about
   1kg/2¼lbs total weight
175g/6oz lambs' kidneys, cut into
   large pieces
1kg/2¼lbs potatoes, thinly sliced
3 carrots, thickly sliced
450g/1lb leeks, sliced
3 celery sticks, sliced
15ml/1 tbsp chopped fresh thyme
30ml/2 tbsp chopped fresh parsley
small sprig of rosemary
600ml/1 pint/2½ cups veal stock
salt and pepper

1 Preheat the oven to 170°C/325°F/
Gas 3. Heat the dripping or oil in a
frying pan and brown the chops and
kidneys in batches, then reserve the fat.

VARIATIONS
Pork chops can be used instead of lamb
to make a similar hotpot. Use thick loin
chops or boneless sparerib chops as
preferred. Pig's kidney is far stronger in
flavour than lambs' kidneys so 75g/3oz
chopped pig's kidney can be added or
this may be omitted. Add the shredded
leaves from a couple of sprigs of fresh
sage instead of the rosemary.

2 In a large casserole, make alternate
layers of lamb chops, kidneys,
three-quarters of the potatoes and the
carrots, leeks and celery, sprinkling
the herbs and seasoning over each
layer as you go. Tuck the rosemary
sprig down the side.

3 Arrange the remaining potatoes on
top. Pour over the stock, brush with the
reserved fat, then cover and bake for
2½ hours. Increase the oven
temperature to 220°C/425°F/Gas 7.
Uncover and cook for 30 minutes until
well browned on top.

Energy 724Kcal/3035kJ; Protein 51.6g; Carbohydrate 50g, of which sugars 8.7g; Fat 36.7g, of which saturates 13.6g; Cholesterol 278mg; Calcium 75mg; Fibre 7.3g; Sodium 233mg.

SAUSAGES WITH MUSTARD MASHED POTATO AND ONION GRAVY

BEAT THE WINTER BLUES WITH THIS SCRUMPTIOUS DISH. LONG, SLOW COOKING IS THE TRICK TO REMEMBER FOR GOOD ONION GRAVY AS THIS REDUCES AND CARAMELIZES THE ONIONS TO CREATE A WONDERFULLY SWEET FLAVOUR.

SERVES FOUR

INGREDIENTS
    12 pork and leek sausages
For the onion gravy
    30ml/2 tbsp olive oil
    25g/1oz/2 tbsp butter
    8 onions, sliced
    5ml/1 tsp caster (superfine) sugar
    15ml/1 tbsp plain (all-purpose) flour
    300ml/½ pint/1¼ cups beef stock
For the mashed potato
    1.5kg/3¼lb potatoes
    50g/2oz/¼ cup butter
    150ml/¼ pint/⅔ cup double
      (heavy) cream
    15ml/1 tbsp wholegrain mustard

1 To make the onion gravy, heat the oil and butter in a large pan until foaming. Add the onion slices and mix well to thoroughly coat them in the fat. Cover and cook gently for about 30 minutes, stirring frequently. Add the sugar and cook for a further 5 minutes, or until the onions are softened, reduced and slightly caramelized.

2 Remove the pan from the heat and stir in the flour, then gradually stir in the stock. Return the pan to the heat. Bring to the boil, stirring, then simmer for 3 minutes, or until thickened. Season.

VARIATION
For pesto mashed potato, omit the mustard and add 15ml/1 tbsp pesto, 2 crushed garlic cloves and olive oil.

3 Meanwhile, cook the potatoes and the pork and leek sausages. First, cook the potatoes in a pan of boiling salted water for 20 minutes, or until tender.

4 Drain the potatoes well and mash them with the butter, cream and wholegrain mustard. Season with salt and pepper to taste.

5 While the potatoes are cooking, preheat the grill (broiler) to medium. Arrange the sausages in a single layer in the grill (broiling) pan and cook for 15–20 minutes, or until cooked, turning frequently so that they brown evenly.

6 Serve the sausages with the creamy mashed potato and onion gravy.

Energy 1425Kcal/5921kJ; Protein 31.4g; Carbohydrate 106.1g, of which sugars 22.3g; Fat 100.3g, of which saturates 45.1g; Cholesterol 176mg; Calcium 190mg; Fibre 10g; Sodium 1634mg.

TOAD-IN-THE-HOLE

THIS IS ONE OF THOSE DISHES THAT IS CLASSIC COMFORT FOOD — REMEMBERED AS A CHILDHOOD
FAVOURITE AND PERFECT FOR LIFTING THE SPIRITS ON COLD DAYS. USE ONLY THE BEST SAUSAGES.

SERVES FOUR TO SIX

INGREDIENTS

175g/6oz/1½ cups plain
   (all-purpose) flour
30ml/2 tbsp chopped fresh chives
2 eggs
300ml/½ pint/1¼ cups milk
50g/2oz/¼ cup white vegetable
   fat or lard (shortening)
450g/1lb Cumberland sausages or
   good-quality pork sausages
salt and ground black pepper

VARIATION

For a young children's supper, omit the
chives and cook cocktail sausages in
patty tins (muffin pans) until golden.
Add the batter and cook for
10–15 minutes, until puffed and golden.

1 Preheat the oven to 220°C/425°F/
Gas 7. Sift the flour into a bowl with a
pinch of salt and pepper. Make a well
in the centre of the flour. Whisk the
chives with the eggs and milk, then
pour this into the well in the flour.
Gradually whisk the flour into the liquid
to make a smooth batter. Cover and
leave to stand for at least 30 minutes.

2 Put the fat into a roasting pan and
place in the oven for 3–5 minutes. Add
the sausages and cook for 15 minutes.
Turn the sausages twice during cooking.

3 Pour the batter over the sausages
and return to the oven. Cook for about
20 minutes, or until the batter is risen
and golden. Serve immediately.

Energy 752Kcal/3132kJ; Protein 22.3g; Carbohydrate 48.2g, of which sugars 5.8g; Fat 53.7g, of which saturates 20.6g; Cholesterol 183mg; Calcium 215mg; Fibre 1.9g; Sodium 931mg.

LASAGNE

THIS RICH ITALIAN LASAGNE IS MADE WITH GOOD HOME-MADE MEAT SAUCE AND A WHITE SAUCE LAYERED WITH FRESHLY GRATED PARMESAN CHEESE. KEEP THE LAYERS OF SAUCES THIN.

SERVES SIX

INGREDIENTS
  8–10 lasagne sheets, green or white
  75g/3oz/1 cup freshly grated
    Parmesan cheese
  salt and ground black pepper
  sprigs of flat leaf parsley, to garnish
For the meat sauce
  45ml/3 tbsp olive oil
  500g/1¼lb lean minced (ground)
    beef
  75g/3oz smoked bacon or
    pancetta, diced
  130g/4½oz chicken livers, trimmed
    and chopped (optional)
  1 onion, finely chopped
  2 garlic cloves, crushed
  150ml/¼ pint/⅔ cup dry white
    wine (optional)
  30–45ml/2–3 tbsp tomato purée
    (paste)
  2 x 400g/14oz cans chopped
    tomatoes
  45ml/3 tbsp single (light) cream
For the white sauce
  600ml/1 pint/2½ cups milk
  1 bay leaf
  1 small onion, sliced
  50g/2oz/¼ cup butter
  40g/1½oz/⅓ cup plain (all-purpose)
    flour
  freshly grated nutmeg

1 Bring a large pan of water to the boil and blanch the pasta sheets, a few at a time, for at least 2 minutes, taking care to keep them separate. Stir the pasta during cooking to stop it sticking. Drain the blanched sheets and set them aside in a bowl of cold water.

2 Make the meat sauce. Heat the oil in a large frying pan. Add the minced beef and cook, stirring, until it is evenly browned. Add the bacon or pancetta and chicken livers, if using, and cook for 3–4 minutes.

3 Add the onion and garlic. Cook for 5 minutes more, until the onion has softened slightly. Stir in the wine, if using. Bring to the boil and cook until well reduced.

4 Stir in the tomato purée and tomatoes, with salt and pepper to taste. Bring to the boil, then lower the heat and simmer for 15–20 minutes until thickened. Stir in the cream, if using, and set aside.

5 While the meat sauce is simmering, make the white sauce. Pour the milk into a pan and add the bay leaf and sliced onion. Heat gently until the milk is just below boiling point, then remove the pan from the heat and leave to infuse for 10 minutes. Strain the milk into a jug (pitcher) and discard the bay leaf and onion.

6 Melt the butter in a pan and stir in the flour. Cook for 1 minute, stirring, then gradually whisk in the milk until the mixture boils and thickens to a smooth sauce. Season and add nutmeg to taste.

7 Drain the pasta sheets and pat them dry on a clean dishtowel or with kitchen paper. Lay them out to prevent them from sticking together.

8 Spread some meat sauce on the base of a rectangular baking dish. Top with a single layer of pasta sheets. Trickle over some white sauce and sprinkle with Parmesan. Repeat the layers until all the ingredients have been used, finishing with a layer made by swirling the last of the two sauces together. Sprinkle liberally with Parmesan.

9 Preheat the oven to 190°C/375°F/ Gas 5 and bake the lasagne for about 30 minutes until bubbling and golden brown. Allow to stand for 10 minutes before cutting. Serve garnished with flat leaf parsley.

Energy 586Kcal/2457kJ; Protein 40.5g; Carbohydrate 39.8g, of which sugars 11.2g; Fat 30.7g, of which saturates 13.5g; Cholesterol 175mg; Calcium 343mg; Fibre 1.6g; Sodium 606mg.

MOUSSAKA

THIS CLASSIC GREEK DISH WITH LAMB, POTATOES AND AUBERGINES IS LAYERED WITH A RICH CHEESY TOPPING TO MAKE A SUBSTANTIAL MEAL THAT IS IRRESISTIBLY GOOD WITH A CRISP SIDE SALAD.

SERVES SIX

INGREDIENTS

30ml/2 tbsp olive oil
30ml/2 tbsp chopped fresh oregano
1 large onion, finely chopped
675g/1½lb lean lamb, minced
   (ground)
1 large aubergine (eggplant), sliced
2 x 400g/14oz cans chopped
   tomatoes
45ml/3 tbsp tomato purée (paste)
1 lamb stock cube, crumbled
2 floury main crop potatoes, halved
115g/4oz/1 cup Cheddar cheese,
   grated
150ml/¼ pint/⅔ cup single (light)
   cream
salt and ground black pepper
fresh bread, to serve

1 Preheat the oven to 180°C/350°F/ Gas 4. Heat the olive oil in a large deep-sided frying pan. Fry the oregano and onions over a low heat, stirring frequently, for about 5 minutes or until the onions have softened.

VARIATION

If you want to add more vegetables to the dish, use slices of courgette, grilled in the same way as the aubergines, instead of the sliced potato in the layers, then top the dish with a layer of well-seasoned mashed potatoes before pouring over the sauce. To make the dish even richer, add a sprinkling of freshly grated Parmesan cheese with each layer of aubergine.

2 Stir in the lamb and cook for 10 minutes until browned. Meanwhile, grill the aubergine slices for 5 minutes until browned, turning once.

3 Stir the tomatoes and purée into the mince mixture, and crumble the stock cube over it, stir well, season with salt and pepper and simmer uncovered for a further 15 minutes.

4 Meanwhile, cook the potatoes in lightly salted boiling water for 5–10 minutes until just tender. Drain, and when cool enough to handle, cut into thin slices.

5 Layer the aubergines, mince and potatoes in a 1.75 litre/3 pint/7½ cup oval ovenproof dish, finishing with a layer of potatoes.

6 Mix the cheese and cream together in a bowl and pour over the top of the other ingredients in the dish. Cook for 45–50 minutes until bubbling and golden on the top. Serve straight from the dish, while hot, with plenty of fresh, crusty bread.

COOK'S TIP

The larger the surface area of the dish, the quicker the moussaka will cook; however, the dish must be deep enough to hold the layers and allow the sauce to bubble up during baking without boiling over the rim.

Energy 465Kcal/1938kJ; Protein 30.5g; Carbohydrate 18.3g, of which sugars 7.4g; Fat 30.1g, of which saturates 14.7g; Cholesterol 119mg; Calcium 215mg; Fibre 2.8g; Sodium 281mg.

CORNED BEEF AND EGG HASH

THIS IS REAL NURSERY, OR COMFORT, FOOD AT ITS BEST! WHETHER YOU REMEMBER GRAN'S VERSION, OR PREFER THIS AMERICAN-STYLE HASH, IT TURNS CORNED BEEF INTO A SUPPER FIT FOR ANY GUEST.

SERVES FOUR

INGREDIENTS
  30ml/2 tbsp vegetable oil
  25g/1oz/2 tbsp butter
  1 onion, finely chopped
  1 green (bell) pepper, seeded
    and diced
  2 large firm boiled potatoes, diced
  350g/12oz can corned beef, cubed
  1.5ml/¼ tsp grated nutmeg
  1.5ml/¼ tsp paprika
  4 eggs
  salt and ground black pepper
  deep fried parsley, to garnish
  sweet chilli sauce or tomato sauce,
    to serve

COOK'S TIP
Put the can of corned beef into the fridge to chill for about half an hour before using – it will firm up and cut into cubes more easily.

1 Heat the oil and butter together in a large frying pan. Add the onion and fry for 5–6 minutes until softened.

2 In a bowl, mix together the green pepper, potatoes, corned beef, nutmeg and paprika and season well. Add to the pan and toss gently to distribute the cooked onion. Press down lightly and fry without stirring on a medium heat for about 3–4 minutes until a golden brown crust has formed on the underside.

3 Stir the mixture through to distribute the crust, then repeat the frying twice, until the mixture is well browned.

4 Make four wells in the hash and carefully crack an egg into each. Cover and cook gently for about 4–5 minutes until the egg whites are set.

5 Sprinkle with deep fried parsley and cut into quarters. Serve hot with sweet chilli sauce or tomato sauce.

Energy 419Kcal/1748kJ; Protein 32g; Carbohydrate 13.6g, of which sugars 4.4g; Fat 27g, of which saturates 10.7g; Cholesterol 321mg; Calcium 74mg; Fibre 1.9g; Sodium 881mg.

LAMB MEATBALLS WITH CHILLI TOMATO SAUCE

SERVE THESE PIQUANT ITALIAN-STYLE MEATBALLS WITH PASTA AND A LEAFY SALAD. SPRINKLE WITH A LITTLE GRATED PARMESAN CHEESE FOR THAT EXTRA ITALIAN TOUCH.

SERVES FOUR

INGREDIENTS
   450g/1lb lean minced (ground) lamb
   50g/2oz/1 cup fresh white breadcrumbs
   1 large onion, grated
   1 garlic clove, crushed
   15ml/1 tbsp chopped fresh parsley
   1 small egg, lightly beaten
   30ml/2 tbsp olive oil
   salt and ground black pepper
   60ml/4 tbsp finely grated Parmesan
     cheese and rocket (arugula) leaves,
     to serve
For the sauce
   1 onion, finely chopped
   400g/14oz can chopped tomatoes
   200ml/7fl oz/scant 1 cup passata
     (bottled strained tomatoes)
   5ml/1 tsp granulated sugar
   2 green chillies, seeded and
     finely chopped
   30ml/2 tbsp chopped fresh oregano
   salt and ground black pepper

3 Meanwhile, to make the sauce, mix together the chopped onion, tomatoes, passata, sugar, seeded and chopped chillies and oregano. Season well and pour the sauce into the clay pot.

4 Place the meatballs in the sauce, then cover and place in an unheated oven. Set the oven to 200°C/400°F/ Gas 6 and cook for 1 hour, stirring after 30 minutes. Serve with Parmesan cheese and rocket.

1 Soak a small clay pot in cold water for 15 minutes, then drain. Alternatively, the meatballs may be cooked in a lidded ovenproof dish or casserole. Place the minced lamb, breadcrumbs, onion, garlic, parsley and seasoning in a bowl and mix well. Add the beaten egg and mix by hand to bind the meatball mixture together thoroughly.

2 Shape the mixture into 20 small even-size balls. Heat the olive oil in a frying pan, add the meatballs and cook over a high heat, stirring occasionally, until they are browned all over.

Energy 389Kcal/1626kJ; Protein 26.9g; Carbohydrate 21.9g, of which sugars 10.1g; Fat 22.3g, of which saturates 8.1g; Cholesterol 129mg; Calcium 83mg; Fibre 2.7g; Sodium 345mg.

BLUES BUSTERS

*When the pace of life brings on a session of
singing the blues, kick-start a positive new
attitude with a real meal. This chapter is full of
fabulous dishes that make food worth eating and
life worth living. There are classic casseroles,
such as Fisherman's Stew and Traditional Beef
Stew with Dumplings; aromatic roast lamb or
chicken and steaming hot pies.*

TOMATO BREAD AND BUTTER PUDDING

THIS IS A GREAT FAMILY DISH AND IS IDEAL WHEN YOU DON'T HAVE TIME TO COOK ON THE DAY BECAUSE IT CAN BE PREPARED IN ADVANCE. IT MAKES A WONDERFULLY HEARTWARMING SUPPER.

SERVES FOUR

INGREDIENTS

50g/2oz/4 tbsp butter, softened
15ml/1 tbsp red pesto sauce
1 garlic and herb foccacia
150g/5oz mozzarella cheese,
  thinly sliced
2 large ripe tomatoes, sliced
300ml/½ pint/1¼ cups milk
3 large eggs
5ml/1 tsp fresh chopped oregano,
  plus extra to garnish
50g/2oz Pecorino Romano or Fontina
  cheese, grated
salt and ground black pepper

COOK'S TIP

If you like, you could use other cheeses, such as Beaufort, Bel Paese or Taleggio, in this dish.

1 Preheat the oven to 180°C/350°F/Gas 4. Blend together the butter and pesto sauce in a small bowl. Slice the herb bread and spread one side of each slice with the pesto mixture.

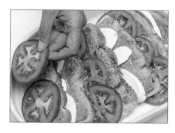

2 In an oval ovenproof dish, layer the bread slices with the mozzarella and tomatoes, overlapping each new layer with the next.

3 Beat together the milk, eggs and oregano, season well and pour over the bread. Leave to stand for 5 minutes.

4 Sprinkle over the grated cheese and bake the pudding in the oven for about 40 minutes or until golden brown and just set. Serve immediately, straight from the dish, sprinkled with more coarsely chopped oregano.

Energy 621Kcal/2601kJ; Protein 30.7g; Carbohydrate 52.2g, of which sugars 6.6g; Fat 33.8g, of which saturates 17.9g; Cholesterol 240mg; Calcium 618mg; Fibre 2.1g; Sodium 1082mg.

SWEET AND SOUR MIXED BEAN HOT-POT

GOLDEN POTATOES OVER AROMATIC BEANS AND VEGETABLES MAKE A COMFORT-FOOD CLASSIC.

SERVES SIX

INGREDIENTS

    450g/1lb unpeeled potatoes
    15ml/1 tbsp olive oil
    40g/1½oz/3 tbsp butter
    40g/1½oz/⅓ cup plain wholemeal
      (whole-wheat) flour
    300ml/½ pint/1¼ cups passata
      (bottled strained tomatoes)
    150ml/¼ pint/⅔ cup unsweetened
      apple juice
    60ml/4 tbsp each light soft brown
      sugar, tomato ketchup, dry sherry,
      cider vinegar and light soy sauce
    400g/14oz can butter beans
    400g/14oz can flageolet or
      cannellini beans
    400g/14oz can chickpeas
    175g/6oz/1 cup green beans,
      chopped and blanched
    225g/8oz/1 cup shallots, sliced
      and blanched
    225g/8oz/3 cups mushrooms, sliced
    15ml/1 tbsp each chopped fresh
      thyme and marjoram
    salt and freshly ground black pepper
    sprigs of fresh herbs, to garnish

1 Preheat the oven to 200°C/400°F/ Gas 6. Thinly slice the potatoes and par-boil them for 4 minutes. Drain thoroughly, then toss them in the oil so they are lightly coated. Set aside.

2 Place the butter, flour, passata, apple juice, sugar, ketchup, sherry, vinegar and soy sauce in a pan. Heat gently, whisking continuously, until the sauce comes to the boil and thickens. Simmer gently for 3 minutes, stirring constantly.

3 Rinse and drain the beans and chickpeas and add to the sauce with all the remaining ingredients, except the herb garnish. Stir well to mix all the ingredients thoroughly. Taste the mixture and add a little salt with freshly ground black pepper to taste.

4 Spoon the bean mixture into a casserole.

5 Arrange the potato slices over the top, overlapping them slightly so that they completely cover the bean mixture.

6 Cover the casserole with foil and bake for about 1 hour, until the potatoes are cooked and tender. Remove the foil for the last 20 minutes of the cooking time, to lightly brown the potatoes. Serve garnished with fresh herb sprigs.

COOK'S TIP
You can vary the proportions of beans used in this recipe, depending on what ingredients you have in your store cupboard.

Energy 427Kcal/1805kJ; Protein 17.7g; Carbohydrate 66.8g, of which sugars 22.4g; Fat 10.6g, of which saturates 4.2g; Cholesterol 14mg; Calcium 101mg; Fibre 12g; Sodium 1750mg.

FISHERMAN'S STEW

LIGHT SEAFOOD IN A CREAMY SAUCE MAKES AN IRRESISTIBLE CASSEROLE TO CHEER DREARY DAYS. THIS IS ESPECIALLY GOOD WITH LOTS OF WARM CRUSTY BREAD TO MOP UP EVERY LAST DROP.

SERVES SIX

INGREDIENTS
500g/1¼lb mussels
3 onions
2 garlic cloves, sliced
300ml/½ pint/1¼ cups fish stock
12 scallops
450g/1lb cod fillet
30ml/2 tbsp olive oil
1 large potato, about 200g/7oz
few sprigs of fresh thyme, chopped
1 red and 1 green (bell) pepper
120ml/4fl oz/½ cup dry white wine
250ml/8fl oz/1 cup crème fraîche
275g/10oz raw peeled prawns
  (shrimp)
75g/3oz/¾ cup grated mature
  Cheddar cheese
salt and ground black pepper
fresh thyme sprigs, to garnish

1 Clean the mussels, removing any beards. Discard any that stay open when tapped. Rinse in cold water.

2 Pour water into a large, frying pan to 2.5cm/1in. Chop an onion and add it to the pan, with the garlic. Bring to the boil, add the mussels and cover.

3 Cook the mussels for 5–6 minutes, shaking the pan occasionally. Remove them as they open, discarding any that remain shut. Remove the mussels from their shells and set them aside.

4 Strain the cooking liquid from the mussels through a muslin- (cheese-cloth-) lined sieve (strainer) to remove any sand. Make up the liquid with fish stock to 300ml/½ pint/1¼ cups.

5 If you have bought scallops in their shells, open them: hold a scallop shell in the palm of your hand, with the flat side uppermost. Insert the blade of a knife close to the hinge that joins the shells and prise apart. Run the blade of the knife across the inside of the flat shell to cut away the scallop. Only the white adductor muscle and the orange coral are eaten, so pull away and discard all other parts. Rinse the scallops under cold running water to remove any grit or sand, then put them in a bowl and set them aside.

6 Cut the cod into large cubes and put it in a bowl. Season with salt and pepper and set aside.

7 Cut the remaining onions into small wedges. Heat the olive oil in a large pan and fry the onion wedges for 2–3 minutes. Slice the potato about 1cm/½in thick and add to the pan, with the fresh chopped thyme. Cover and cook for about 15 minutes, until the potato has softened.

8 Core the peppers, remove the cores and seeds, then dice the flesh. Add to the onion and potato mixture and cook for a few minutes. Stir in the mixed mussel and fish stock, with the wine and crème fraîche.

9 Bring to just below boiling point, then add the cod and scallops. Lower the heat and simmer for 5 minutes, then add the prawns. Simmer for a further 3–4 minutes more, until all the seafood is cooked. Stir in the mussels and warm through for 1–2 minutes. Season the sauce if necessary. Spoon into bowls, garnish with the thyme sprigs and sprinkle with the cheese. Crusty bread is an ideal accompaniment.

Energy 502Kcal/2096kJ; Protein 45.8g; Carbohydrate 16.1g, of which sugars 7g; Fat 27g, of which saturates 15g; Cholesterol 220mg; Calcium 249mg; Fibre 2.2g; Sodium 480mg.

CHICKEN AND MUSHROOM PIE

THIS IS A CLASSIC PIE TO BRING A SMILE TO THE FACES OF DINERS OF ALL AGES. PORCINI MUSHROOMS INTENSIFY THE FLAVOUR OF THE CHICKEN AND VEGETABLES UNDER THE MELT-IN-THE-MOUTH CRUST.

SERVES SIX

INGREDIENTS

15g/½oz/¼ cup dried
  porcini mushrooms
50g/2oz/¼ cup butter
30ml/2 tbsp plain (all-purpose) flour
250ml/8fl oz/1 cup hot chicken stock
60ml/4 tbsp single (light) cream
1 onion, coarsely chopped
2 carrots, sliced
2 celery sticks, coarsely chopped
50g/2oz/¾ cup fresh mushrooms,
  quartered
450g/1lb cooked chicken
  meat, cubed
50g/2oz/½ cup fresh or frozen peas
salt and ground black pepper
beaten egg, to glaze

For the pastry
225g/8oz/2 cups plain
  (all-purpose) flour
1.5ml/¼ tsp salt
115g/4oz/½ cup cold butter, diced
65g/2½oz/⅓ cup white vegetable
  fat, diced
60–120ml/4–8 tbsp chilled water

1 To make the pastry, sift the flour and salt into a bowl. Cut or rub in the butter and white vegetable fat until the mixture resembles breadcrumbs. Sprinkle with 90ml/6 tbsp chilled water and mix until the dough holds together. If the dough is too crumbly, add a little more water, 15ml/1 tbsp at a time.

2 Gather the dough into a ball and flatten it into a round. Wrap and chill for at least 30 minutes.

3 To make the filling, put the mushrooms in a bowl. Cover with hot water and soak for 30 minutes. Drain in a muslin- (cheesecloth-) lined sieve (strainer), then dry on kitchen paper. Preheat the oven to 190°C/375°F/Gas 5.

4 Melt half of the butter in a heavy pan. Whisk in the flour and cook until bubbling, whisking constantly. Add the hot stock and whisk over a medium heat until the mixture boils. Cook for 2–3 minutes, then whisk in the cream. Season to taste, and set aside.

5 Heat the remaining butter in a large, non-stick frying pan and cook the onion and carrots over a low heat for about 5 minutes. Add the celery and fresh mushrooms and cook for 5 minutes more. Stir in the cooked chicken, peas and drained porcini mushrooms.

6 Add the chicken mixture to the hot cream sauce and stir to mix. Adjust the seasoning if necessary. Spoon the mixture into a 2.5 litre/4 pint/2½ quart oval baking dish.

7 Roll out the pastry to a thickness of about 3mm/⅛in. Cut out an oval 2.5cm/ 1in larger all around than the dish. Lay the pastry over the filling. Gently press around the edge of the dish to seal, then trim off the excess pastry. Crimp the edge of the pastry by pushing the forefinger of one hand into the edge and, using the thumb and forefinger of the other hand, pinch the pastry. Continue all round the pastry edge.

8 Press together the pastry trimmings and roll out again. Cut out mushroom shapes with a sharp knife and stick them on to the pastry lid with beaten egg. Glaze the lid with beaten egg and cut several slits in the pastry to allow the steam to escape.

9 Bake the pie for about 30 minutes, until the pastry has browned. Serve the pie hot.

Energy 576Kcal/2403kJ; Protein 23.8g; Carbohydrate 39.6g, of which sugars 4.7g; Fat 36.9g, of which saturates 20.3g; Cholesterol 127mg; Calcium 104mg; Fibre 3.1g; Sodium 334mg.

ROAST CHICKEN WITH MADEIRA GRAVY AND BREAD SAUCE

THIS IS A SIMPLE, TRADITIONAL DISH WHICH TASTES WONDERFUL AND MAKES A MEMORABLE FAMILY MEAL — PERFECT FOR SHARING AND CARING. ROAST POTATOES AND SEASONAL GREEN VEGETABLES, SUCH AS BRUSSELS SPROUTS STIR-FRIED WITH CHESTNUTS, ARE DELICIOUS WITH ROAST CHICKEN.

SERVES FOUR

INGREDIENTS
   50g/2oz/¼ cup butter
   1 onion, chopped
   75g/3oz/1½ cups fresh white
     breadcrumbs
   grated rind of 1 lemon
   30ml/2 tbsp chopped fresh parsley
   30ml/2 tbsp chopped fresh tarragon
   1 egg yolk
   1.5kg/3¼lb oven-ready chicken
   175g/6oz rindless streaky (fatty)
     bacon rashers (strips)
   salt and ground black pepper
For the bread sauce
   1 onion, studded with 6 cloves
   1 bay leaf
   300ml/½ pint/1¼ cups milk
   150ml/¼ pint/⅔ cup single
     (light) cream
   115g/4oz/2 cups fresh white
     breadcrumbs
   knob of butter
For the gravy
   10ml/2 tsp plain (all-purpose) flour
   300ml/½ pint/1¼ cups well-
     flavoured chicken stock
   dash of Madeira or sherry

1 Preheat the oven to 200°C/400°F/ Gas 6. To make the stuffing, melt half the butter in a pan and fry the onion for 5 minutes, or until softened.

2 Remove the pan from the heat and add the breadcrumbs, lemon rind, parsley and half the chopped tarragon. Season with salt and pepper, then mix in the egg yolk to bind the ingredients into a moist stuffing.

VARIATION
Cocktail sausages which have been wrapped in thin streaky bacon rashers make a delicious accompaniment to roast chicken. Roast them alongside the chicken for the final 25–30 minutes of the cooking time.

3 Fill the neck end of the chicken with stuffing, then truss the chicken neatly and weigh it. To calculate the cooking time, allow 20 minutes per 450g/1lb, plus 20 minutes.

4 Put the chicken in a roasting pan and season it well with salt and pepper. Beat together the remaining butter and tarragon, then smear this over the bird.

5 Lay the bacon rashers over the top of the chicken (this helps stop the light breast meat from drying out) and roast for the calculated time. Baste the bird every 30 minutes during cooking and cover with buttered foil if the bacon begins to over-brown.

6 Meanwhile, make the bread sauce. Put the clove-studded onion, bay leaf and milk in a small, heavy pan and bring slowly to the boil. Remove the pan from the heat and leave the milk to stand for at least 30 minutes so that it is gently infused with the flavouring ingredients.

7 Strain the milk into a clean pan (discard the flavouring ingredients) and add the cream and breadcrumbs. Bring slowly to the boil, stirring continuously, then reduce the heat and simmer gently for 5 minutes. Keep warm while you make the gravy and carve the chicken, then stir in the butter and season to taste just before serving.

8 Transfer the chicken to a warmed serving dish, cover tightly with foil and leave to stand for 10 minutes.

9 To make the gravy, pour off all but 15ml/1 tbsp fat from the roasting pan. Place the pan on the hob (stovetop) and stir in the flour. Cook the flour for 1 minute, or until golden brown, then stir in the stock and Madeira or sherry. Bring to the boil, stirring all the time, then simmer for about 3 minutes until thickened. Add seasoning to taste and strain the gravy into a warm sauceboat.

10 Carve the chicken and serve it at once, with the stuffing, gravy and hot bread sauce.

COOK'S TIP
To keep chicken moist during roasting, some recipes suggest cooking the bird on its sides, turning it halfway through cooking, and others place the breast down. Covering the top of the chicken breast with rashers of bacon and adding foil to prevent this from overcooking is the easiest and most effective method.

Energy 845Kcal/3523kJ; Protein 48.5g; Carbohydrate 44.2g, of which sugars 7.8g; Fat 53.9g, of which saturates 22.1g; Cholesterol 296mg; Calcium 215mg; Fibre 1.6g; Sodium 1147mg.

LAMB'S LIVER AND BACON CASSEROLE

LIVER AND BACON ARE BRILLIANT PARTNERS AND BOILED NEW POTATOES IN BUTTER GO WELL WITH THIS OLD FAVOURITE. THE TRICK WHEN COOKING LIVER IS TO SEAL IT QUICKLY, THEN SIMMER IT GENTLY AND BRIEFLY. PROLONGED AND/OR FIERCE COOKING MAKES LIVER HARD AND GRAINY.

SERVES FOUR

INGREDIENTS

   30ml/2 tbsp sunflower oil
   225g/8oz rindless unsmoked back
   (lean) bacon rashers (strips)
   2 onions, halved and sliced
   175g/6oz/2⅓ cups chestnut
   mushrooms or button (white)
   mushrooms, halved
   450g/1lb lamb's liver, trimmed
   and sliced
   25g/1oz/2 tbsp butter
   15ml/1 tbsp soy sauce
   30ml/2 tbsp plain (all-purpose) flour
   150ml/¼ pint/⅔ cup chicken stock
   salt and ground black pepper

1 Heat the oil in a frying pan. Chop the bacon and fry until crisp. Add the onions to the pan and cook for about 10 minutes, stirring frequently, or until softened. Add the mushrooms to the pan and fry for a further 1 minute.

2 Use a slotted spoon to remove the bacon and vegetables from the pan and set aside. Add the liver to the pan and cook over a high heat for 3–4 minutes, turning once to seal the slices on both sides. Remove the liver from the pan and keep warm.

3 Melt the butter in the pan, add the soy sauce and flour and blend together. Stir in the stock and bring to the boil, stirring until thickened. Return the liver and vegetables to the pan and heat through for 1 minute. Season with salt and pepper to taste, and serve at once with new potatoes and lightly cooked green beans.

Energy 440Kcal/1831kJ; Protein 34.9g; Carbohydrate 14.2g, of which sugars 4.8g; Fat 27.4g, of which saturates 9.4g; Cholesterol 527mg; Calcium 47mg; Fibre 1.9g; Sodium 1258mg.

LAMB PIE <u>AND</u> MUSTARD THATCH

SHEPHERD'S PIE WITH A TWIST: THE MUSTARD GIVES A REAL TANG TO THE POTATO TOPPING. ONE SERVING IS NEVER ENOUGH, SO ALLOW PLENTY FOR SECOND HELPINGS ALL ROUND.

SERVES FOUR

INGREDIENTS
800g/1¾lb floury potatoes, diced
60ml/4 tbsp milk
15ml/1 tbsp wholegrain or
    French mustard
a little butter
450g/1lb lean lamb, minced
1 onion, chopped
2 celery sticks, thinly sliced
2 carrots, diced
30ml/2 tbsp cornflour (cornstarch)
    blended into 150ml/¼ pint/⅔ cup
    lamb stock
15ml/1 tbsp Worcestershire sauce
30ml/2 tbsp chopped fresh rosemary,
    or 10ml/2 tsp dried
salt and ground black pepper
fresh vegetables, to serve

2 Fry the lamb in a non-stick pan, breaking it up with a fork, until browned all over. Add the onion, celery and carrots and cook for 2–3 minutes, stirring. Stir in the stock and cornflour. Bring to the boil, stirring all the while, then remove from the heat.

3 Stir in the Worcestershire sauce and rosemary and season to taste. Turn the lamb mixture into a 1.75 litre/3 pint/ 7 cup ovenproof dish and spread over the potato topping evenly. Bake for 30–35 minutes until golden. Serve hot with a selection of fresh vegetables.

1 Cook the potatoes in a large pan of boiling lightly salted water until tender. Drain well and mash until smooth, then stir in the milk, mustard, butter and seasoning to taste. Meanwhile preheat the oven to 200°C/400°F/Gas 6.

VARIATION
Although the original shepherd's pie is made with lamb, most people make it with minced beef as well. To vary the potato topping slightly, try adding horseradish – either creamed or for an even stronger flavour, freshly grated.

Energy 437Kcal/1841kJ; Protein 27.6g; Carbohydrate 54.6g, of which sugars 6.6g; Fat 13.6g, of which saturates 6.1g; Cholesterol 86mg; Calcium 68mg; Fibre 3.9g; Sodium 187mg.

LAMB STEW WITH VEGETABLES

THIS FARMHOUSE STEW IS COLOURFUL AND UPLIFTING, WITH LAMB AND YOUNG SPRING VEGETABLES
SUCH AS CARROTS, NEW POTATOES, BABY ONIONS, PEAS, FRENCH (GREEN) BEANS AND TURNIPS.

SERVES SIX

INGREDIENTS

60ml/4 tbsp vegetable oil
1.5kg/3–3½lb lamb shoulder,
  trimmed and cut into
  5cm/2in pieces
120ml/4fl oz/½ cup water
45–60ml/3–4 tbsp plain
  (all-purpose) flour
1 litre/1¾ pints/4 cups lamb stock
1 large bouquet garni
3 garlic cloves, lightly crushed
3 ripe tomatoes, skinned, seeded
  and chopped
5ml/1 tsp tomato purée (paste)
675g/1½lb small potatoes, peeled
  or scrubbed
12 baby carrots, scrubbed
115g/4oz French (green) beans, cut
  into 5cm/2in pieces
25g/1 oz/2 tbsp butter
12–18 baby onions
6 medium turnips, quartered
30ml/2 tbsp granulated sugar
¼ tsp dried thyme
175g/6oz/1¼ cups peas
50g/2oz/½ cup mangetouts
  (snowpeas)
salt and freshly ground pepper
45ml/3 tbsp chopped fresh parsley or
  coriander (cilantro), to garnish

1 Heat the oil in a large heavy frying
pan. Brown the lamb in batches, adding
more oil if needed, and place it in a
large, flameproof casserole. Add 45ml/
3 tbsp of the water to the pan and boil
for about 1 minute, stirring and
scraping the base of the pan, then pour
the liquid into the casserole.

2 Sprinkle the flour over the browned
meat in the casserole and set it over a
medium heat. Cook for 3–5 minutes until
browned. Stir in the stock, the bouquet
garni, garlic, tomatoes and tomato purée.
Season with salt and pepper.

3 Bring to the boil over a high heat.
Skim the surface, reduce the heat and
simmer, stirring occasionally, for about
1 hour until the meat is tender. Cool the
stew to room temperature, cover and
chill overnight.

4 About 1½ hours before serving, take
the casserole from the refrigerator, lift off
the solid fat and blot the surface with
kitchen paper to remove all traces of fat.
Set the casserole over a medium heat
and bring to a simmer. Cook the potatoes
in a pan of boiling salted water for
15–20 minutes, then transfer to a bowl
and add the carrots to the same water.
Cook for 4–5 minutes and transfer to the
same bowl. Add the French beans and
boil for 2–3 minutes. Transfer to the bowl
with the other vegetables.

5 Melt the butter in a heavy frying pan
and add the onions and turnips with a
further 45ml/3 tbsp water. Cover and
cook for 4–5 minutes. Stir in the sugar
and thyme and cook until the
vegetables are caramelized. Transfer
them to the bowl of vegetables. Add the
remaining water to the pan. Boil for
1 minute, incorporating the sediment,
then add to the lamb.

6 When the lamb and gravy are hot,
add the cooked vegetables to the stew
and stir gently to distribute. Stir in the
peas and mangetouts and cook for
5 minutes until they turn a bright green,
then stir in 30ml/2 tbsp of the parsley
or coriander.

7 Pour the stew into a large, warmed
serving dish. Scatter over the remaining
parsley or coriander and serve at once.

VARIATIONS
A wide variety of vegetables can be
used in the stew but the trick for
success is to avoid overcooking tender
young produce. For example, baby
broad beans can be added instead of
the French beans.
• Young red radishes are delicious
instead of, or as well as, the turnips.
• Mint is uplifting and refreshing with
the lamb and vegetables – add some
instead of the parsley or coriander to
garnish, or chop a large handful of fresh
mint leaves and add them with the
other herbs.

Energy 560Kcal/2346kJ; Protein 39.2g; Carbohydrate 41.9g, of which sugars 14.4g; Fat 27.4g, of which saturates 9.9g; Cholesterol 127mg; Calcium 90mg; Fibre 6.2g; Sodium 181mg.

ROAST LEG OF LAMB

WHEN YOUNG LAMB WAS SEASONAL TO SPRINGTIME, A ROAST LEG WAS AN EASTER SPECIALITY, SERVED WITH A SAUCE USING THE FIRST SPRIGS OF MINT OF THE YEAR AND EARLY NEW POTATOES. ROAST LAMB IS NOW WELL ESTABLISHED AS A YEAR-ROUND FAMILY FAVOURITE FOR SUNDAY LUNCH, OFTEN SERVED WITH CRISP ROAST POTATOES. THE AROMA OF LAMB ROASTING ENLIVENS BOTH APPETITE AND SPIRITS.

SERVES SIX

INGREDIENTS
    1.5kg/3¼lb leg of lamb
    4 garlic cloves, sliced
    2 fresh rosemary sprigs
    30ml/2 tbsp light olive oil
    300ml/½ pint/1¼ cups red wine
    5ml/1 tsp clear honey
    45ml/3 tbsp redcurrant jelly
    salt and ground black pepper
For the roast potatoes
    45ml/3 tbsp white vegetable fat or
    lard (shortening)
    1.3kg/3lb potatoes, such as Desirée,
    cut into chunks
For the mint sauce
    about 15g/½oz/½ cup fresh mint
    10ml/2 tsp caster (superfine) sugar
    15ml/1 tbsp boiling water
    30ml/2 tbsp white wine vinegar

1 Preheat the oven to 220°C/425°F/ Gas 7. Make small slits into the lamb all over the skin. Press a slice of garlic and a few rosemary leaves into each slit, then place the lamb in a roasting pan and season well. Drizzle the oil over the lamb and roast it for about 1 hour, or until it is cooked to taste.

COOK'S TIP
To make a quick and tasty gravy from the pan juices, add about 300ml/½ pint/ 1¼ cups red wine, stock or water and boil, stirring occasionally, until reduced and well-flavoured. Season to taste, then strain into a sauce boat to serve.

2 Meanwhile, mix the wine, honey and redcurrant jelly in a small pan and heat, stirring, until the jelly melts. Bring to the boil, then reduce the heat and simmer until reduced by half. Spoon this glaze over the lamb and return it to the oven for 30–45 minutes.

3 To prepare the potatoes, put the fat in a roasting pan on the oven shelf above the meat. Boil the potatoes for 5–10 minutes, then drain them and fluff up the surface of each with a fork.

4 Add the prepared potatoes to the hot fat and baste well, then roast them for 40–50 minutes, or until they are crisp.

5 Make the mint sauce while the potatoes are roasting. Place the mint on a chopping board and sprinkle the sugar over the top. Chop finely, then transfer the mint and sugar to a bowl.

6 Add the boiling water and stir until the sugar has dissolved. Add 15ml/ 1 tbsp vinegar and taste the sauce before adding the remaining vinegar. You may want to add slightly less or more than the suggested quantity. Leave the mint sauce to stand until you are ready to serve the meal.

7 Cover the lamb with foil and set it aside in a warm place to rest for 10–15 minutes before carving. Serve with the crisp roast potatoes, mint sauce and a selection of seasonal vegetables.

Energy 569Kcal/2376kJ; Protein 51.7g; Carbohydrate 45.2g, of which sugars 10.3g; Fat 35.2g, of which saturates 13.4g; Cholesterol 174mg; Calcium 29mg; Fibre 2.8g; Sodium 130mg.

PORK CASSEROLE WITH ONIONS, CHILLI AND DRIED FRUIT

INSPIRED BY SOUTH AMERICAN COOKING, A MOLE — PASTE — OF CHILLI, SHALLOTS AND NUTS IS ADDED TO THIS CASSEROLE OF PORK AND ONIONS. PART OF THE MOLE IS ADDED AT THE END OF COOKING TO RETAIN ITS FRESH FLAVOUR. SERVE WITH RICE AND A GREEN SALAD.

SERVES SIX

INGREDIENTS

25ml/1½ tbsp plain (all-purpose) flour
1kg/2¼lb shoulder or leg of pork, cut into 5cm/2in cubes
45–60ml/3–4 tbsp olive oil
2 large onions, chopped
2 garlic cloves, finely chopped
600ml/1 pint/2½ cups fruity white wine
105ml/7 tbsp water
115g/4oz ready-to-eat prunes
115g/4oz ready-to-eat dried apricots
grated rind and juice of 1 orange
pinch of muscovado (molasses) sugar (optional)
30ml/2 tbsp chopped fresh parsley
½–1 fresh green chilli, seeded and finely chopped (optional)
salt and ground black pepper

For the mole
3 *ancho* chillies and 2 *pasilla* chillies (or other varieties of large, medium-hot dried red chillies)
30ml/2 tbsp olive oil
2 shallots, chopped
2 garlic cloves, chopped
1 fresh green chilli, seeded and chopped
10ml/2 tsp ground coriander (cilantro)
5ml/1 tsp mild Spanish paprika or *pimentón*
50g/2oz/½ cup blanched almonds, toasted
15ml/1 tbsp chopped fresh oregano or 2.5ml/½ tsp dried oregano

1 Make the mole paste. Toast the chillies in a dry pan over a low heat for 1–2 minutes, until they are aromatic, then soak them in warm water for 30 minutes. Drain, reserving the soaking water, and discard the stalks and seeds.

2 Preheat the oven to 160°C/ 325°F/Gas 3.

3 Heat the oil in a small frying pan and fry the shallots, garlic, fresh green chilli and ground coriander over a very low heat for 5 minutes.

4 Transfer the shallot mixture to a food processor or blender and add the drained chillies, paprika or *pimentón*, almonds and oregano. Process the mixture, adding 45–60ml/3–4 tbsp of the chilli soaking liquid to make a workable paste.

5 Season the flour with salt and black pepper, then use to coat the pork. Heat 45ml/3 tbsp of the olive oil in a large, heavy frying pan and fry the pork, stirring frequently, until sealed on all sides. Transfer the pork cubes to a flameproof casserole.

6 If necessary, add the remaining oil to the frying pan and cook the onions and garlic gently for 8–10 minutes, stirring occasionally.

7 Add the wine and water to the frying pan. Cook for 2 minutes. Stir in half the mole paste, bring back to the boil and bubble for a few seconds before pouring over the pork.

8 Season lightly with salt and pepper and stir to mix, then cover and cook in the oven for 1½ hours.

9 Increase the oven temperature to 180°C/350°F/Gas 4. Stir in the prunes, apricots and orange juice. Taste the casserole for seasoning, adding the muscovado sugar if necessary, and more salt and pepper. Then cover and cook for another 30–45 minutes until the meat is succulent and delicious.

10 Place the casserole over a direct heat and stir in the remaining mole paste. Simmer, stirring once or twice, for 5 minutes. Serve sprinkled with the orange rind, chopped parsley and fresh chilli, if using.

Energy 468Kcal/1956kJ; Protein 38.8g; Carbohydrate 17.1g, of which sugars 16.9g; Fat 20.7g, of which saturates 4g; Cholesterol 105mg; Calcium 64mg; Fibre 2.9g; Sodium 134mg.

BRAISED PORK CHOPS <u>WITH</u> ONION <u>AND</u> MUSTARD SAUCE

THE PIQUANT SAUCE ADDS PUNCH AND FLAVOUR TO THIS SIMPLE SUPPER DISH. SERVE FAVOURITE CREAMY POTATO MASH AND BUTTERY BROCCOLI OR CABBAGE FOR THE PERFECT FEEL-BETTER MEAL.

SERVES FOUR

INGREDIENTS

4 pork loin chops, 2cm/¾in thick
30ml/2 tbsp plain (all-purpose) flour
45ml/3 tbsp olive oil
2 Spanish onions, thinly sliced
2 garlic cloves, finely chopped
250ml/8fl oz/1 cup dry cider
150ml/¼ pint/⅔ cup vegetable, chicken or pork stock
generous pinch of brown sugar
2 fresh bay leaves
6 fresh thyme sprigs
2 strips lemon rind
120ml/4fl oz/½ cup double (heavy) cream
30–45ml/2–3 tbsp wholegrain mustard
30ml/2 tbsp chopped fresh parsley
salt and ground black pepper

1 Preheat the oven to 200°C/400°F/Gas 6. Trim the chops of excess fat. Season the flour with salt and pepper and use to coat the chops. Heat 30ml/2 tbsp of the oil in a frying pan and brown the chops on both sides, then transfer them to an ovenproof dish.

2 Add the remaining oil to the pan and cook the onions over a fairly gentle heat until they soften and begin to brown at the edges. Add the garlic and cook for 2 minutes more.

3 Stir in any left-over flour, then gradually stir in the cider and stock. Season well with salt and pepper and add the brown sugar, bay leaves, thyme sprigs and lemon rind. Bring the sauce to the boil, stirring constantly, then pour over the chops.

4 Cover and cook in the oven for 20 minutes. Reduce the heat to 180°C/350°F/Gas 4 and continue cooking for another 30–40 minutes. Remove the foil for the last 10 minutes of the cooking time. Remove the chops from the dish and keep warm, covered with foil.

5 Tip the remaining contents of the dish into a pan or, if the dish is flameproof, place it over a direct heat. Discard the herbs and lemon rind, then bring to the boil.

6 Add the cream and continue to boil, stirring constantly. Taste for seasoning, adding a pinch more sugar if necessary. Finally, stir in the mustard to taste and pour the sauce over the braised chops. Sprinkle with the chopped parsley and serve immediately.

VARIATION
For a less rich sauce, omit the cream and purée the sauce in a blender. Reheat, thinning with a little extra stock if necessary, then adjust the seasoning and add mustard to taste. This will produce a sharper tasting sauce that will need less mustard.

Energy 541Kcal/2253kJ; Protein 39g; Carbohydrate 19.4g, of which sugars 9g; Fat 32.9g, of which saturates 14.1g; Cholesterol 135mg; Calcium 78mg; Fibre 2g; Sodium 88mg.

ROAST PORK WITH SAGE AND ONION STUFFING

SAGE AND ONION STUFFING IS GLORIOUS WITH ROAST PORK AND THERE'S SOMETHING EVER SO CHEERING ABOUT SNEAKING A SAMPLE OF CRACKLING BEFORE SERVING THE MEAT.

SERVES SIX TO EIGHT

INGREDIENTS
  1.3–1.6kg/3–3½lb boneless loin
    of pork
  60ml/4 tbsp fine, dry breadcrumbs
  10ml/2 tsp chopped fresh sage
  25ml/1½ tbsp plain (all-purpose)
    flour
  300ml/½ pint/1¼ cups cider
  150ml/¼ pint/⅔ cup water
  5–10ml/1–2 tsp crab apple or
    redcurrant jelly
  salt and ground black pepper
  sprigs of thyme, to garnish
For the stuffing
  25g/1oz/2 tbsp butter
  50g/2oz bacon, finely chopped
  2 large onions, finely chopped
  75g/3oz/1½ cups fresh
    white breadcrumbs
  30ml/2 tbsp chopped fresh sage
  5ml/1 tsp chopped fresh thyme
  10ml/2 tsp finely grated lemon rind
  1 small egg, beaten

1 Preheat the oven to 220°C/425°F/ Gas 7. Make the stuffing first. Melt the butter in a heavy pan and fry the bacon until it begins to brown, then add the onions and cook gently until they soften, but do not allow to brown. Mix with the breadcrumbs, sage, thyme, lemon rind and egg, then season well with salt and pepper.

2 Cut the rind off the joint of pork in one piece and score it well. Cooking the rind separately makes crisper crackling than leaving it on the pork.

3 Place the pork fat-side down and season. Add a layer of stuffing, then roll up and tie neatly.

4 Lay the rind over the pork and rub in 5ml/1 tsp salt. Roast for 2–2½ hours, basting with the pork fat once or twice. Reduce the temperature to 190°C/375°F/ Gas 5 after 20 minutes. Shape the remaining stuffing into balls and add to the roasting tin for the last 30 minutes.

5 Remove the rind from the pork. Increase the oven temperature to 220°C/425°F/Gas 7 and roast the rind for a further 20–25 minutes, until crisp.

6 Mix the dry breadcrumbs and sage and press them into the fat. Cook the pork for 10 minutes, then cover and set aside in a warm place for 15–20 minutes.

7 Remove all but 30–45ml/2–3 tbsp of the fat from the roasting tin and place it on the hob to make gravy. Stir in the flour, followed by the cider and water. Bring to the boil and then cook gently for 10 minutes. Strain the gravy into a clean pan, add the crab apple or redcurrant jelly, and cook for another 5 minutes. Adjust the seasoning.

8 Serve the pork cut into thick slices and the crisp crackling cut into strips with the cider gravy, garnished with thyme.

Energy 446Kcal/1874kJ; Protein 52.8g; Carbohydrate 26.4g, of which sugars 5.1g; Fat 15.1g, of which saturates 6g; Cholesterol 185mg; Calcium 76mg; Fibre 1.7g; Sodium 479mg.

CIDER-GLAZED HAM

WHEN THE BLUES STRIKE, FIGHT BACK BY ENTERTAINING RATHER THAN BEING ALONE AND MISERABLE.
THERE'S PLENTY OF FABULOUS FLAVOUR AND FOOD VALUE TO SHARE WITH FAMILY AND FRIENDS IN
THIS SUBSTANTIAL HAM, PREPARED WITH OLD-FASHIONED ENGLISH INGREDIENTS AND STYLE.

SERVES EIGHT TO TEN

INGREDIENTS
- 2kg/4½lb middle gammon (cured ham) joint
- 1 large or 2 small onions
- about 30 whole cloves
- 3 bay leaves
- 10 black peppercorns
- 1.3 litres/2¼ pints/5⅔ cups medium-dry (hard) cider
- 45ml/3 tbsp soft light brown sugar
- bunch of flat leaf parsley, to garnish

For the cranberry sauce
- 350g/12oz/3 cups cranberries
- 175g/6oz/¾ cup soft light brown sugar
- grated rind and juice of 2 clementines
- 30ml/2 tbsp port

1 Weigh the gammon and calculate the cooking time at 20 minutes per 450g/1lb, then place it in a large flameproof casserole or pan. Stud the onion or onions with 5–10 of the cloves and add to the casserole or pan with the bay leaves and peppercorns. (A large stockpot is ideal for cooking a big piece of meat but a deep roasting tin or pan will do in an emergency, with foil as a cover and turning the meat often for even cooking.)

2 Add 1.2 litres/2 pints/5 cups of the cider and enough water just to cover the gammon. Heat until simmering and then carefully skim off the scum that rises to the surface using a large spoon or ladle. Start timing the cooking from the moment the stock begins to simmer.

3 Cover with a lid or foil and simmer gently for the calculated time. Towards the end of the cooking time, preheat the oven to 220°C/425°F/Gas 7.

4 Heat the sugar and remaining cider in a pan; stir until the sugar has dissolved.

5 Simmer for 5 minutes to make a dark, sticky glaze. Remove the pan from the heat and leave to cool for 5 minutes.

6 Lift the gammon out of the casserole or pan. Carefully and evenly, cut the rind from the meat, then score the fat into a diamond pattern. Place the gammon in a large roasting pan or ovenproof dish.

7 Press a clove into the centre of each diamond, then carefully spoon over the glaze. Bake for 20–25 minutes, or until the fat is brown, glistening and crisp.

8 To make the cranberry sauce, simmer all the ingredients in a heavy pan for 15–20 minutes, stirring frequently. Transfer the sauce to a jug (pitcher). Serve the gammon hot or cold, garnished with parsley and with the cranberry sauce.

COOK'S TIP
Leave the gammon until it is just cool enough to handle before removing the rind. Snip off the string using a sharp knife or scissors, then carefully slice off the rind, leaving a thin, even layer of fat. Use a narrow-bladed, sharp knife for the best results.

VARIATION
Use honey in place of the soft light brown sugar for the glaze and serve the meat with redcurrant sauce or jelly.

Energy 447Kcal/1873kJ; Protein 44.1g; Carbohydrate 25.6g, of which sugars 25.6g; Fat 18.8g, of which saturates 6.3g; Cholesterol 58mg; Calcium 35mg; Fibre 1.3g; Sodium 2203mg.

STEAK AND KIDNEY PIE WITH MUSTARD GRAVY

FRAGRANT MUSTARD, BAY AND PARSLEY GRAVY COMPLEMENT THE BEEF BEAUTIFULLY IN THIS FABULOUS PIE THAT IS A PLEASURE TO PREPARE AS WELL AS TO EAT — A DEFINITE SPIRIT-LIFTER.

SERVES FOUR

INGREDIENTS
  450g/1lb puff pastry
  40ml/2½ tbsp plain
    (all-purpose) flour
  675g/1½lb rump (round)
    steak, cubed
  175g/6oz lamb's kidneys
  25g/1oz/2 tbsp butter
  1 onion, chopped
  15ml/1 tbsp English (hot) mustard
  2 bay leaves
  15ml/1 tbsp chopped fresh parsley
  150ml/¼ pint/⅔ cup beef stock
  1 egg, beaten
  salt and ground black pepper

1 Roll out two-thirds of the pastry on a floured surface to a thickness of 3mm/⅛in. Use to line the base and sides of a 1.5 litre/2½ pint/6¼ cup pie dish. Place a pie funnel in the centre of the dish.

2 Put the flour, salt and pepper in a bowl and toss the steak in the mixture.

3 Remove the fat, skin and tough central core from the kidneys, and slice them thickly. Add the slices to the steak and toss well.

4 Melt the butter in a pan, add the onion and fry over a low heat, stirring occasionally, until soft and translucent. Add the mustard, bay leaves, parsley and stock and stir well.

5 Preheat the oven to 190°C/375°F/ Gas 5. Place the steak and kidney in the pie dish and add the stock mixture.

6 Roll out the remaining puff pastry to a thickness of 3mm/⅛in to use for the pie lid. Brush the edges of the pastry case with beaten egg and cover with the lid. Press the edges firmly together to seal, then trim. Use the trimmings to decorate the top with pastry leaves.

7 Brush the pie with a little beaten egg and make a small hole in the pastry lid for the funnel. Bake for about 1 hour until the pastry is well risen and golden brown. Serve the pie hot, straight from the pie dish.

Energy 773Kcal/3238kJ; Protein 52.7g; Carbohydrate 54.3g, of which sugars 3.8g; Fat 41g, of which saturates 6.6g; Cholesterol 251mg; Calcium 104mg; Fibre 0.9g; Sodium 555mg.

BOEUF BOURGUIGNONNE

THE CLASSIC FRENCH DISH OF BEEF COOKED IN BURGUNDY STYLE, WITH RED WINE, SMALL PIECES OF
BACON, SHALLOTS AND MUSHROOMS, IS COOKED FOR SEVERAL HOURS AT A LOW TEMPERATURE. USING
TOP RUMP OR BRAISING STEAK REDUCES THE COOKING TIME WITHOUT FORFEITING FLAVOUR.

SERVES SIX

INGREDIENTS
   175g/6oz rindless streaky (fatty)
      bacon rashers (strips), chopped
   900g/2lb lean braising steak, such
      as top rump (rump roast) of beef or
      braising steak
   30ml/2 tbsp plain (all-purpose) flour
   45ml/3 tbsp sunflower oil
   25g/1oz/2 tbsp butter
   12 shallots
   2 garlic cloves, crushed
   175g/6oz/2⅓ cups mushrooms, sliced
   450ml/¾ pint/scant 2 cups robust
      red wine
   150ml/¼ pint/⅔ cup beef stock
      or consommé
   1 bay leaf
   2 sprigs each of fresh thyme, parsley
      and marjoram
   salt and ground black pepper

1 Preheat the oven to 160°C/325°F/
Gas 3. Heat a large flameproof
casserole, then add the bacon and
cook, stirring occasionally, until the
pieces are crisp and golden brown.

2 Meanwhile, cut the meat into 2.5cm/
1in cubes. Season the flour and use to
coat the meat. Use a slotted spoon to
remove the bacon from the casserole
and set aside. Add and heat the oil,
then brown the beef in batches and set
aside with the bacon.

VARIATION
Use lardons, which are available from
large supermarkets, instead of the bacon.

3 Add the butter to the fat remaining in
the casserole. Cook the shallots and
garlic until just starting to colour, then
add the mushrooms and cook for a
further 5 minutes. Replace the bacon
and meat, and stir in the wine and stock
or consommé. Tie the bay leaf, thyme,
parsley and marjoram together into a
bouquet garni and add to the casserole.

4 Cover and cook in the oven for
1½ hours, or until the meat is tender,
stirring once or twice. Season to taste
and serve the casserole with creamy
mashed root vegetables, such as
celeriac and potatoes.

COOK'S TIP
Boeuf Bourguignonne freezes very well.
Transfer the mixture to a dish so that it
cools quickly, then pour it into a rigid
plastic container. Push all the cubes of
meat down into the sauce or they will dry
out. Freeze for up to 2 months. Thaw
overnight in the refrigerator, then transfer
to a flameproof casserole and add
150ml/¼ pint/⅔ cup water. Stir well,
bring to the boil, stirring occasionally,
and simmer steadily for at least
10 minutes, or until the meat is hot.

Energy 455Kcal/1898kJ; Protein 39.2g; Carbohydrate 6.9g, of which sugars 1.7g; Fat 24.7g, of which saturates 8.9g; Cholesterol 122mg; Calcium 36mg; Fibre 1.1g; Sodium 500mg.

STEAK WITH STOUT AND POTATOES

THE IRISH WAY TO BRAISE BEEF IS IN STOUT OF COURSE AND TOPPED WITH THICKLY SLICED POTATOES. BAKE IT IN A MODERATE OVEN FOR LONG, SLOW TENDERIZING IF YOU PREFER.

SERVES FOUR

INGREDIENTS
675g/1½lb stewing beef
15ml/1 tbsp vegetable oil
25g/1oz/2 tbsp butter
225g/8oz tiny white onions
175ml/6fl oz/¾ cup stout or dark beer
300ml/½ pint/1¼ cups beef stock
bouquet garni
675g/1½lb firm, waxy potatoes, cut into thick slices
225g/8oz/3 cups large mushrooms, sliced
15ml/1 tbsp plain (all-purpose) flour
2.5ml/½ tsp mild mustard
salt and ground black pepper
chopped thyme sprigs, to garnish

3 Add the tiny white onions to the pan and cook for 3–4 minutes until lightly browned all over. Return the steak to the pan with the onions. Pour on the stout or beer and stock and season the whole mixture to taste.

5 Add the sliced mushrooms over the potatoes. Cover again and simmer for a further 30 minutes or so. Remove the steak and vegetables with a slotted spoon and arrange on a platter.

1 Trim any excess fat from the steak and cut into four pieces. Season both sides of the meat. Heat the oil and 10g/¼oz/1½ tsp of the butter in a large heavy pan.

4 Next add the bouquet garni to the pan and top with the potato slices distributing them evenly over the surface to cover the steak. Bring the ingredients to a boil then reduce the heat, cover with a tight-fitting lid and simmer gently for 1 hour.

6 Mix the remaining butter with the flour to make a roux. Whisk a little at a time into the cooking liquid in the pan. Stir in the mustard. Cook over a medium heat for 2–3 minutes, stirring all the while, until thickened.

7 Season the sauce and pour over the steak. Garnish with plenty of thyme sprigs and serve the dish at once.

2 Add the steak and brown on both sides, taking care not to burn the butter. Remove from the pan and set aside.

COOK'S TIP
To make onion peeling easier, first put the onions in a bowl and cover with boiling water. Allow them to soak for about 5 minutes and drain. The skins should now peel away easily.

VARIATION
For a dish that is lighter, but just as tasty, substitute four lamb leg steaks for the beef, and use dry (hard) cider instead of the stout or beer, and lamb or chicken stock instead of beef.

Energy 468Kcal/1968kJ; Protein 43.4g; Carbohydrate 38.9g, of which sugars 8.7g; Fat 14.8g, of which saturates 6.2g; Cholesterol 126mg; Calcium 50mg; Fibre 3.3g; Sodium 195mg.

TRADITIONAL BEEF STEW AND DUMPLINGS

THIS DISH CAN COOK IN THE OVEN WHILE YOU GO FOR A LONG WALK TO WORK UP AN APPETITE.

SERVES SIX

INGREDIENTS
   25g/1oz/1 tbsp plain (all-purpose)
      flour
   1.2kg/2½lb stewing steak, cubed
   30ml/2 tbsp olive oil
   2 large onions, sliced
   450g/1lb carrots, sliced
   300ml/½ pint/1¼ cups stout
      or dark beer
   3 bay leaves
   10ml/2 tsp brown sugar
   3 fresh thyme sprigs
   5ml/1 tsp cider vinegar
   salt and freshly ground black pepper
For the dumplings
   115g/4oz/1½ cups grated hard
      white fat
   225g/8oz/2 cups self-raising (self-
      rising) flour
   30ml/2 tbsp chopped mixed
      fresh herbs
   about 150ml/¼ pint/⅔ cup water

1 Preheat the oven to 160°C/325°F/
Gas 3. Season the flour and sprinkle
over the meat, tossing to coat.

2 Heat the oil in large casserole and
lightly sauté the onions and carrots.
Remove the vegetables with a slotted
spoon and reserve them.

3 Brown the meat well in batches in
the casserole.

4 Return all the vegetables to the
casserole and add any leftover
seasoned flour. Add the stout or beer,
bay leaves, sugar and thyme. Bring the
liquid to the boil, cover and then
transfer to the oven. Leave the meat to
cook for 1 hour and 40 minutes, before
making the dumplings.

5 Mix the grated fat, flour and herbs
together. Add enough water to make a
soft sticky dough.

6 Form the dough into small balls with
floured hands. Add the cider vinegar to
the meat and spoon the dumplings on
top. Cook for a further 20 minutes, until
the dumplings have cooked through,
and serve hot.

COOK'S TIPS
Suet pastry is one of the easiest pastries
to make. Remember always to use self-
raising flour for a light and fluffy result.
Traditionally, shredded beef suet is used
but vegetable suet is also available.
Alternatively, as in this recipe, white
cooking fat can be coarsely grated and
used. Thoroughly chill the fat, placing it
in the freezer for 10 minutes if
necessary, and chill the grater. This way
the fat will not melt as it is grated.
Then, when mixing and shaping the
pastry, handle it as lightly as possible
and avoid over-mixing. When cooked
uncovered, the dough turns golden
brown and slightly crusty on the
surface. When covered, it is soft, white
and fluffy. If the casserole is not big
enough to hold the stew and dumplings,
the dumplings can be simmered in a
pan of stock or water for about 15
minutes, until risen and fluffy. Drain
well on a slotted spoon and place on
top of the meat or on the plates.

Energy 648Kcal/2714kJ; Protein 50.3g; Carbohydrate 42.9g, of which sugars 10.6g; Fat 30.5g, of which saturates 11.2g; Cholesterol 152mg; Calcium 184mg; Fibre 4g; Sodium 297mg.

BEEF WELLINGTON

THIS ELEGANT DISH IS JUST THE CHOICE FOR A STYLISH, UPLIFTING DINNER WITH FRIENDS.

SERVES FOUR

INGREDIENTS
   675g/1½lb fillet steak, tied
   15ml/1 tbsp vegetable oil
   350g/12oz puff pastry
   1 egg, beaten, to glaze
   salt and ground black pepper
For the parsley pancakes
   50g/2oz/½ cup plain (all-purpose)
     flour
   150ml/¼ pint/⅔ cup milk
   1 egg
   30ml/2 tbsp chopped fresh parsley
For the mushroom pâté
   25g/1oz/2 tbsp butter
   2 shallots or 1 small onion,
     chopped
   450g/1lb/4 cups assorted wild and
     cultivated mushrooms, chopped
   50g/2oz/1 cup fresh white
     breadcrumbs
   75ml/5 tbsp double (heavy) cream
   2 egg yolks

2 To make the pancakes, beat the flour, a pinch of salt, half the milk, the egg and parsley together until smooth, then stir in the remaining milk. Heat a greased, non-stick pan and pour in enough batter to coat the bottom. When set, turn the pancake over and cook the other side briefly until lightly browned. Continue with the remaining batter – the recipe makes three or four pancakes.

4 Roll out the pastry to a 36 x 30cm/14 x 12in rectangle. Place two pancakes on the pastry and spread with mushroom pâté. Place the beef on top and spread over any remaining pâté, then the remaining pancakes. Cut out and reserve four squares from the corners of the pastry, then moisten the pastry with egg and wrap the meat. Decorate with the reserved pastry trimmings.

1 Preheat the oven to 220°/425°F/Gas 7. Season the fillet steak with several twists of black pepper. Heat the oil in a roasting tin, add the steak and quickly sear to brown all sides. Transfer to the oven and roast for 15 minutes for rare, 20 minutes for medium-rare or 25 minutes for well-done meat. Set aside to cool. Reduce the oven temperature to 190°C/375°F/ Gas 5.

3 To make the mushroom pâté, melt the butter in a frying pan and fry the shallots or onion for 7–10 minutes to soften without colouring. Add the mushrooms and cook until the juices run. Increase the heat so that the juices evaporate. Combine the breadcrumbs, cream and egg yolks. Add to the mushroom mixture and mix to a smooth paste. Allow to cool.

5 Put the beef Wellington on a baking sheet and brush evenly with beaten egg. Bake for about 40 minutes until golden brown. To ensure that the meat is heated through, test with a meat thermometer. It should read 52–54°C/125–130°F for rare, 57°C/135°F for medium-rare and 71°C/160°F for well-done meat. Serve cut into thick slices.

ROAST RIB OF BEEF

THIS BEATS ALL OTHER CUTS ON FLAVOUR. WITH YORKSHIRE PUDDINGS AND HORSERADISH SAUCE, IT IS IDEAL FOR A SUNDAY LUNCH GATHERING. WHAT BETTER WAY TO JOLLY UP A DISMAL WINTRY WEEK?

SERVES EIGHT TO TEN

INGREDIENTS
   45ml/3 tbsp mixed peppercorns
   15ml/1 tbsp juniper berries
   2.75kg/6lb rolled rib of beef
   30ml/2 tbsp Dijon mustard
   15ml/1 tbsp olive oil
For the Yorkshire puddings
   150ml/¼ pint/⅔ cup water
   150ml/¼ pint/⅔ cup milk
   115g/4oz/1 cup plain
      (all-purpose) flour
   pinch of salt
   2 eggs, beaten
   60ml/4 tbsp lard (shortening),
      melted, or sunflower oil (optional)
For the caramelized shallots
   20 shallots
   5 garlic cloves, peeled
   60ml/4 tbsp light olive oil
   15ml/1 tbsp caster (superfine) sugar
For the gravy
   150ml/¼ pint/⅔ cup red wine
   600ml/1 pint/2½ cups beef stock
   salt and ground black pepper

1 Preheat the oven to 230°C/450°F/ Gas 8. Crush the peppercorns and juniper berries. Sprinkle half the spices over the meat. Transfer to a roasting pan and roast for 30 minutes.

COOK'S TIP
If you prefer to cook beef on the bone, buy a 3.6kg/8lb forerib. Trim off the excess fat, scatter over the spices, then follow the instructions in steps 1 and 2. Roast at the lower temperature for 2 hours for rare beef, 2½ hours for medium rare, and 3 hours for well done.

2 Reduce the oven temperature to 180°C/350°F/Gas 4. Mix the mustard and oil into the remaining crushed spices and spread the resulting paste over the meat. Roast the meat for a further 1¼ hours if you like your meat rare, 1 hour 50 minutes for a medium-rare result or 2 hours 25 minutes for a joint that is medium to well done. Baste the joint frequently during cooking.

3 Make the Yorkshire puddings as soon as the beef is in the oven. Stir the water into the milk. Sift the flour and salt into a bowl. Make a well in the middle and gradually whisk in the eggs, followed by the milk and water to make a smooth batter. Cover and leave to stand for about 1 hour. (The batter can be made well in advance and chilled overnight in the refrigerator if convenient.)

4 An hour before the beef is due to be ready, mix the shallots and garlic cloves with the light olive oil and spoon into the roasting pan around the beef. After about 30 minutes, lightly sprinkle the sugar over the shallots and garlic, and stir the shallots and garlic 2–3 times during cooking.

5 Transfer the meat to a serving platter, cover tightly with foil and set aside in a warm place for 20–30 minutes. (This resting time makes carving easier.) Increase the oven temperature to 230°C/450°F/Gas 8. Divide 60ml/4 tbsp dripping from the meat or the lard or oil, if using, among 10 individual Yorkshire pudding pans or 16 large patty tins (muffin pans), and heat in the oven for about 5 minutes.

6 Spoon the Yorkshire pudding batter into the hot fat in the tins and bake for 20–30 minutes, or until risen, firm and golden brown. The time depends on the size of the tins: larger Yorkshire puddings will take longer than those in patty tins.

7 Make the gravy while the Yorkshire puddings are cooking. Simmer the red wine and beef stock together in a pan for about 5 minutes to intensify the flavour of the gravy.

8 Skim the fat from the meat juices in the roasting pan, then pour in the wine mixture and simmer until the gravy is reduced and thickened slightly to a syrupy consistency. Stir frequently with a wooden spoon to remove all of the roasting residue from the roasting pan. Season to taste.

9 Serve the beef with the individual Yorkshire puddings, caramelized shallots and gravy. Offer roast potatoes or game chips as accompaniments along with a selection of lightly cooked, seasonal vegetables.

Energy 741Kcal/3098kJ; Protein 78.5g; Carbohydrate 13.5g, of which sugars 2.6g; Fat 40.5g, of which saturates 15.8g; Cholesterol 245mg; Calcium 83mg; Fibre 1.1g; Sodium 216mg.

CHILL-OUT
DESSERTS

If there is one consolation to feeling slightly low,
then it must be the excuse to indulge in an
irresistible sweet. Luscious ice cream, mysterious
chocolate mousse or gooey chilled pies are all here
along with energizing fruit creations.

CLASSIC VANILLA ICE CREAM

NOTHING BEATS THE COMFORTING SIMPLICITY OF VANILLA ICE CREAM FOR EVOKING CHILDHOOD MEMORIES. VANILLA PODS ARE WELL WORTH BUYING FOR THE SUPERB FLAVOUR THEY IMPART.

SERVES FOUR

INGREDIENTS

1 vanilla pod
300ml/½ pint/1¼ cups semi-
   skimmed milk
4 egg yolks
75g/3oz/6 tbsp caster (superfine)
   sugar
5ml/1 tsp cornflour (cornstarch)
300ml/½ pint/1¼ cups double
   (heavy) cream

COOK'S TIP
Don't throw the vanilla pod away after
use. Instead, rinse it in cold water, dry
and store in the sugar jar. After a week or
so the sugar will take on the wonderful
aroma and flavour of the vanilla and will
be delicious sprinkled over summer
fruits. Use it to sweeten whipped cream,
custard, biscuits and shortbread.

1 Using a small knife slit the vanilla
pod lengthways. Pour the milk into a
heavy pan, add the vanilla pod and
bring to the boil. Remove from the heat
and leave for 15 minutes to allow the
flavours to infuse.

2 Lift the vanilla pod up. Holding it
over the pan, scrape the black seeds
out of the pod with a small knife so that
they fall back into the milk. Set the
vanilla pod aside and bring the milk
back to the boil.

3 Whisk the egg yolks, sugar and
cornflour in a bowl until the mixture is
thick and foamy. Gradually pour on the
hot milk, whisking constantly. Return
the mixture to the pan and cook over
a gentle heat, stirring all the time.

VARIATION
If you are using an ice cream maker: Stir
the cream into the custard and churn the
mixture until thick.

4 When the custard thickens and is
smooth, pour it back into the bowl. Cool
it, then chill.

5 Whip the cream until it has thickened
but still falls from a spoon. Fold it into
the custard and pour into a plastic tub
or similar freezerproof container. Freeze
for 6 hours or until firm enough to
scoop, beating twice with a fork, or in a
food processor.

6 Scoop into dishes, bowls or bought
cones – or eat straight from the tub.

Energy 542Kcal/2245kJ; Protein 6.8g; Carbohydrate 24.4g, of which sugars 24.4g; Fat 47.1g, of which saturates 27.4g; Cholesterol 309mg; Calcium 160mg; Fibre 0g, Sodium 59mg.

CHOCOLATE RIPPLE ICE CREAM

THIS CREAMY, DARK CHOCOLATE ICE CREAM, UNEVENLY RIPPLED WITH WONDERFUL SWIRLS OF RICH CHOCOLATE SAUCE, WILL STAY DELICIOUSLY SOFT EVEN AFTER FREEZING. NOT THAT IT WILL REMAIN IN THE FREEZER FOR LONG — IT IS PERFECT FOR CELEBRATIONS AS WELL AS TIMES OF GREATEST NEED!

SERVES FOUR TO SIX

INGREDIENTS
    4 egg yolks
    75g/3oz/6 tbsp caster (superfine)
      sugar
    5ml/1 tsp cornflour (cornstarch)
    300ml/½ pint/1¼ cups
      semi-skimmed milk
    250g/9oz dark (bittersweet)
      chocolate, broken
      into squares
    25g/1oz/2 tbsp butter, diced
    30ml/2 tbsp golden (light corn) syrup
    90ml/6 tbsp single (light) cream or
      cream and milk mixed
    300ml/½ pint/1¼ cups whipping
      cream
    wafer biscuits, to serve

1 Put the yolks, sugar and cornflour in a bowl and whisk until thick and foamy. Pour the milk into a pan, bring it just to the boil, then gradually pour it on to the yolk mixture, whisking constantly.

2 Return the mixture to the pan and cook over a gentle heat, stirring constantly until the custard thickens and is smooth. Pour it back into the bowl and stir in 150g/5oz of the chocolate until melted. Cover the chocolate custard closely, leave it to cool, then chill.

3 Put the remaining chocolate into a pan and add the butter. Spoon in the golden syrup. Heat gently, stirring, until the chocolate and butter have melted.

4 Stir in the single cream or cream and milk mixture. Heat gently, stirring continuously, until the mixture is smooth, then leave this chocolate sauce to cool, stirring occasionally.

5 Whip the cream until it has thickened, but is still soft enough to fall from a spoon. Fold it into the custard, pour into a plastic tub or similar freezerproof container and freeze for 5 hours until thick, beating once with a fork or electric whisk or in a food processor. Beat the ice cream in the tub one more time.

6 Add alternate spoonfuls of ice cream and chocolate sauce to a 1.5 litre/2½ pint/6¼ cup plastic container. Freeze for 5–6 hours until firm. Serve with wafers. Using an ice cream maker: Stir the cream into the custard and churn for 20–25 minutes until thick.

Energy 900Kcal/3749kJ; Protein 11g; Carbohydrate 74.9g, of which sugars 74.3g; Fat 63.9g, of which saturates 37.8g; Cholesterol 314mg; Calcium 211mg; Fibre 1.6g; Sodium 142mg

ICED RASPBERRY AND ALMOND TRIFLE

THIS DELICIOUS COMBINATION OF ALMONDY SPONGE, SHERRIED FRUIT, ICE CREAM AND MASCARPONE TOPPING IS SHEER INDULGENCE FOR TRIFLE LOVERS. THE SPONGE AND TOPPING CAN BE MADE A DAY IN ADVANCE AND THE ASSEMBLED TRIFLE WILL SIT HAPPILY IN THE FRIDGE FOR AN HOUR BEFORE SERVING.

SERVES EIGHT TO TEN

INGREDIENTS

115g/4oz/½ cup unsalted (sweet) butter, softened
115g/4oz/½ cup light muscovado (brown) sugar
2 eggs
75g/3oz/⅔ cup self-raising (self-rising) flour
2.5ml/½ tsp baking powder
115g/4oz/1 cup ground almonds
5ml/1 tsp almond essence
15ml/1 tbsp milk

To finish
300g/11oz/scant 2 cups raspberries
50g/2oz/½ cup flaked (sliced) almonds, toasted
90ml/6 tbsp fresh orange juice
200ml/7fl oz/scant 1 cup medium sherry
500g/1¼lb/2½ cups mascarpone cheese
150g/5oz/⅔ cup Greek (US strained plain) yogurt
30ml/2 tbsp icing (confectioners') sugar
about 250ml/8fl oz/1 cup vanilla ice cream
about 250ml/8fl oz/1 cup raspberry ice cream or sorbet

COOK'S TIP
The trifle will set better if all the ingredients are thoroughly chilled in the fridge before assembling. Chill again before serving.

1 Preheat the oven to 180°C/350°F/Gas 4. Grease and line a 20cm/8in round cake tin. Put the butter, sugar, eggs, flour, baking powder, almonds and almond essence in a large bowl and beat with an electric whisk for 2 minutes until creamy. Stir in the milk.

2 Spoon the mixture into the prepared tin, level the surface and bake for about 30 minutes or until just firm in the centre. Transfer to a wire rack and leave to cool.

3 Cut the sponge into chunky pieces and place these in the base of a 1.75 litre/3 pint/7½ cup glass serving dish. Scatter with half the raspberries and almonds. Mix the orange juice with 90ml/6 tbsp of the sherry.

4 Spoon over the orange and sherry mixture. Beat the mascarpone in a bowl with the yogurt, icing sugar and remaining sherry. Put the trifle dish and the mascarpone in the fridge until you are ready to assemble the trifle.

5 To serve, scoop the ice cream and sorbet into the trifle dish. Reserve a few of the remaining raspberries and almonds for the decoration, then scatter the rest over the ice cream. Spoon over the mascarpone mixture and scatter with the reserved raspberries and almonds. Chill the trifle for up to 1 hour before serving.

Energy 608Kcal/2537kJ; Protein 17.2g; Carbohydrate 41.9g, of which sugars 33.7g; Fat 39.4g, of which saturates 18.1g; Cholesterol 134mg; Calcium 357mg; Fibre 2.8g; Sodium 269mg.

CHOCOLATE, RUM AND RAISIN ROULADE

THIS RICH DESSERT TREAT CAN BE MADE AND FROZEN WELL IN ADVANCE. IF IT IS SLICED BEFORE FREEZING, SINGLE SLICES MAKE EXCELLENT IMPROMPTU PICK-ME-UPS. USE VANILLA, CHOCOLATE OR COFFEE ICE CREAM IF YOU PREFER, THOUGH ALL VERSIONS WILL BE JUST AS ENJOYABLY INDULGENT.

SERVES SIX

INGREDIENTS
  115g/4oz plain (semisweet)
    chocolate, broken into pieces
  4 eggs, separated
  115g/4oz/generous ½ cup
    caster (superfine) sugar
  cocoa powder and icing
    (confectioners') sugar, for dusting
For the filling
  150ml/¼ pint/⅔ cup double (heavy)
    cream
  15ml/1 tbsp icing (confectioners')
    sugar
  30ml/2 tbsp rum
  300ml/½ pint/1¼ cups rum and
    raisin ice cream

1 Make the roulade. Preheat the oven to 180°C/350°F/Gas 4. Grease a 33 x 23cm/13 x 9in Swiss roll tin (jelly roll pan) and line with non-stick baking parchment. Grease the parchment. Melt the chocolate in a heatproof bowl set over a pan of simmering water.

2 In a separate bowl, whisk the egg yolks with the caster sugar until thick and pale. Stir the melted chocolate into the yolk mixture. Whisk the egg whites in a grease-free bowl until stiff. Stir a quarter of the whites into the yolk mixture to lighten it, then fold in the remainder.

3 Pour the mixture into the prepared tin and spread it gently into the corners. Bake for about 20 minutes until the cake has risen and is just firm. Turn it out on to a sheet of greaseproof paper which has been supported on a baking sheet and generously dusted with caster sugar. Leave to cool, then peel away the lining paper.

4 Make the filling. Whip the cream with the icing sugar and rum until it forms soft peaks, then spread the mixture to within 1cm/½in of the edges of the sponge. Freeze for 1 hour.

5 Using a dessertspoon, scoop up long curls of the ice cream and lay an even layer over the cream.

6 Starting from a narrow end, carefully roll up the sponge, using the paper to help. Slide the roulade off the paper-lined baking sheet and on to a long plate that is freezerproof. Cover and freeze overnight. Transfer to the fridge 30 minutes before serving. Serve dusted with cocoa powder and icing sugar.

Energy 474Kcal/1982kJ; Protein 8.3g; Carbohydrate 47.5g, of which sugars 46.1g; Fat 27.5g, of which saturates 16g; Cholesterol 203mg; Calcium 117mg; Fibre 0.5g; Sodium 99mg.

ZABAGLIONE ICE CREAM TORTE

FOR ANYONE WHO LIKES ZABAGLIONE, THE FAMOUS, WHISKED ITALIAN DESSERT, THIS SIMPLE ICED VERSION IS AN ABSOLUTE MUST! ITS TASTE AND TEXTURE ARE JUST AS GOOD, AND THERE'S NO LAST-MINUTE WHISKING TO WORRY ABOUT.

SERVES TEN

INGREDIENTS

175g/6oz amaretti biscuits
115g/4oz/½ cup ready-to-eat dried
    apricots, finely chopped
65g/2½oz/5 tbsp unsalted (sweet)
    butter, melted
For the ice cream
65g/2½oz/5 tbsp light muscovado
    (brown) sugar
75ml/5 tbsp water
5 egg yolks
250ml/8fl oz/1 cup double (heavy)
    cream
75ml/5 tbsp Madeira or cream sherry
For the apricot compote
150g/5oz/generous ½ cup ready-to-
    eat dried apricots
25g/1oz/2 tbsp light muscovado sugar
150ml/½ pint/⅔ cup water

1 Put the biscuits in a strong plastic bag and crush with a rolling pin. Tip into a bowl and stir in the apricots and melted butter until evenly combined.

2 Using a dampened dessertspoon, pack the mixture evenly on to the bottom and up the sides of a 24cm/9½in loose-based flan tin (tart pan) about 4cm/1½in deep. Chill.

3 Make the ice cream. Put the sugar and water in a small, heavy pan and heat, stirring, until the sugar dissolves. Bring to the boil and boil for 2 minutes without stirring. Heat a large pan of water to simmering. Put the egg yolks in a large bowl that fits on the pan.

4 Off the heat, whisk the egg yolks until pale, then gradually whisk in the sugar syrup. Put the bowl over the pan of simmering water and continue to whisk for about 10 minutes or until the mixture is thick and pale, and holds the trail of the whisk when it is lifted out of the mixture.

5 Remove the bowl from the heat and carry on whisking for a further 5 minutes or until the mixture is cold. In a separate bowl, whip the cream with the Madeira or sherry until it stands in peaks.

6 Using a large metal spoon, fold the cream into the whisked mixture. Spoon it into the biscuit case, level the surface, cover and freeze overnight.

7 To make the compote, simmer the apricots and sugar in the water until the apricots are plump and the juices are syrupy, adding a little more water if necessary. Leave to cool and then chill.

8 Serve the torte in slices with a little of the compote spooned over, or to one side of, each portion.

Energy 367Kcal/1530kJ; Protein 4g; Carbohydrate 33.9g, of which sugars 26.3g; Fat 24g, of which saturates 13.6g; Cholesterol 149mg; Calcium 73mg; Fibre 1.9g; Sodium 112mg

ICED TIRAMISU

THE TITLE OF THIS FAVOURITE ITALIAN DESSERT MEANS "PICK-ME-UP", WHICH IS PROBABLY LARGELY TO DO WITH THE GENEROUS QUANTITY OF ALCOHOL THAT IS SO OFTEN THROWN IN. THE TRADITIONAL DESSERT IS NOT FROZEN BUT IT IS FABULOUS IN THIS GUISE, EVEN MADE WITH LIGHT FROMAGE FRAIS.

SERVES FOUR

INGREDIENTS
  150g/5oz/¾ cup caster (superfine)
    sugar
  150ml/¼ pint/⅔ cup water
  250g/9oz/generous 1 cup mascarpone
  200g/7oz/scant 1 cup virtually
    fat-free fromage frais
  5ml/1 tsp vanilla essence (extract)
  10ml/2 tsp instant coffee, dissolved
    in 30ml/2 tbsp boiling water
  30ml/2 tbsp coffee liqueur or brandy
  75g/3oz sponge finger biscuits
  cocoa powder, for dusting
  chocolate curls, to decorate

1 Put 115g/4oz/½ cup of the sugar into a small pan. Add the water and bring to the boil, stirring until the sugar has dissolved. Leave the syrup to cool, then chill it.

4 Meanwhile, put the instant coffee mixture in a small bowl, sweeten with the remaining sugar, then add the liqueur or brandy. Stir well and leave to cool.

5 Crumble the biscuits into small pieces and toss them in the coffee mixture. If you have made the ice cream by hand, beat it again.

6 Spoon a third of the ice cream into a 900ml/1½ pint/3¾ cup plastic container, spoon over half the biscuits then top with half the remaining ice cream.

7 Sprinkle over the last of the coffee-soaked biscuits, then cover with the remaining ice cream. Freeze for 2–3 hours until firm enough to scoop. Dust with cocoa powder and spoon into glass dishes. Decorate with chocolate curls, and serve.

2 Put the mascarpone into a bowl. Beat it with a spoon until it is soft, then stir in the fromage frais. Add the chilled sugar syrup, a little at a time, then stir in the vanilla essence.

3 By hand: Spoon the mixture into a plastic tub or similar freezerproof container and freeze for 4 hours, beating once with a fork, electric mixer or in a food processor to break up the ice crystals.

VARIATION
If you are using an ice cream maker: Churn the mascarpone mixture until it is thick but too soft to scoop.

Energy 323Kcal/1367kJ; Protein 11.8g; Carbohydrate 53.8g, of which sugars 49.6g; Fat 8.3g, of which saturates 4.7g; Cholesterol 74mg; Calcium 228mg; Fibre 0.2g; Sodium 97mg.

MARBLED CHOCOLATE CHEESECAKE

BAKED CHEESECAKE IS PLEASING TO PREPARE AND THIS CHOCOLATE-VANILLA COMBO IS SUPERLATIVE.

SERVES SIX

INGREDIENTS
  50g/2oz/½ cup cocoa powder
  75ml/5 tbsp hot water
  900g/2lb cream cheese, at room
    temperature
  200g/7oz/scant 1 cup caster
    (superfine) sugar
  4 eggs
  5ml/1 tsp vanilla essence (extract)
  75g/3oz digestive biscuits, crushed

1 Preheat the oven to 180°C/350°F/
Gas 4.

2 Line a 20 x 8 cm/8 x 3in cake tin
with baking paper. Grease the paper.

3 Sift the cocoa powder into a bowl.
Pour over the hot water and stir until
mixed and smooth.

4 Beat the cheese until smooth, then
beat in the sugar, followed by the eggs,
one at a time. Do not overmix.

5 Divide the mixture evenly between
two bowls. Stir the chocolate mixture
into one bowl, then add the vanilla
essence to the remaining mixture.

6 Pour a cup or ladleful of the plain
mixture into the centre of the tin; it will
spread out into an even layer. Slowly
pour over a cupful of chocolate mixture
in the centre. Continue to alternate the
cake mixtures in this way until both
are used up. Draw a thin metal
skewer through the cake mixture for a
marbled effect.

7 Set the tin in a roasting pan and pour
in hot water to come 4cm/1½in up the
sides of the cake tin.

8 Bake the cheesecake for about
1½ hours, until the top is golden. (The
cake will rise during baking and sink
later.) Cool in the tin on a wire rack.

9 Run a knife around the inside edge
of the cake. Invert a flat plate over the
tin and turn out the cake.

10 Sprinkle the crushed biscuits
evenly over the cheesecake. Gently
invert another plate on top, and turn
both cake and plates over again. Cover
and place in the fridge for at least 3
hours, preferably overnight.

Energy 933Kcal/3869kJ; Protein 12.2g; Carbohydrate 44.4g, of which sugars 36.5g; Fat 80g, of which saturates 48g; Cholesterol 300mg; Calcium 210mg; Fibre 1.3g; Sodium 662mg.

LEMON CHEESECAKE <u>WITH</u> FOREST FRUITS

THIS ZESTY CHEESECAKE HAS A LIGHT CORNFLAKE BASE AND A COLOURFUL TOPPING OF LUSCIOUS, FOREST FRUITS. IT IS THE PERFECT REVIVER – SLIGHTLY NAUGHTY BUT FULL OF GOOD INGREDIENTS.

SERVES EIGHT

INGREDIENTS

50g/2oz/¼ cup unsalted
  (sweet) butter
25g/1oz/2 tbsp soft light brown sugar
45ml/3 tbsp golden (light corn) syrup
115g/4oz/generous 1 cup cornflakes
11g/¼oz sachet powdered gelatine
225g/8oz/1 cup soft cheese
150g/5oz/generous ½ cup Greek (US
  strained plain) yogurt
150ml/¼ pint/⅔ cup single
  (light) cream
finely grated rind and juice of
  2 lemons
75g/3oz/6 tbsp caster
  (superfine) sugar
2 eggs, separated
225g/8oz/2 cups mixed, prepared
  fresh forest fruits, such as
  blackberries, raspberries and
  redcurrants, to decorate
icing (confectioners') sugar,
  for dusting

1 Place the butter, brown sugar and syrup in a pan and heat over a low heat, stirring, until the mixture has melted and is well blended. Remove from the heat and stir in the cornflakes.

2 Press the mixture over the base of a deep 20cm/8in loose-based round cake tin (pan). Chill for 30 minutes.

VARIATION
Use unsweetened puffed rice cereal or rice crispies in place of the cornflakes.

3 Sprinkle the gelatine over 45ml/ 3 tbsp water in a bowl and leave to soak for a few minutes. Place the bowl over a pan of simmering water and stir until the gelatine has dissolved. Place the cheese, yogurt, cream, lemon rind and juice, caster sugar and egg yolks in a large bowl and beat until smooth and thoroughly mixed.

4 Add the hot gelatine to the cheese and lemon mixture and beat well.

5 Whisk the egg whites until stiff, then fold into the cheese mixture.

6 Pour the cheese mixture over the cornflake base and level the surface. Chill for 4–5 hours, or until the filling has set.

7 Carefully remove the cheesecake from the tin and place on a serving plate. Decorate with the mixed fresh fruits, dust with icing sugar and serve.

Energy 340Kcal/1422kJ; Protein 7.7g; Carbohydrate 32.5g, of which sugars 20.8g; Fat 21.1g, of which saturates 12.5g; Cholesterol 106mg; Calcium 104mg; Fibre 1.1g; Sodium 331mg.

LEMON MERINGUE PIE

CRISP SHORTCRUST IS FILLED WITH A MOUTHWATERING LEMON CREAM FILLING AND HEAPED WITH SOFT GOLDEN-TOPPED MERINGUE. THIS CLASSIC DESSERT NEVER FAILS TO PLEASE.

SERVES SIX

INGREDIENTS
- 3 large (US extra large) eggs, separated
- 150g/5oz/⅔ cup caster (superfine) sugar
- grated rind and juice of 1 lemon
- 25g/1oz/½ cup fresh breadcrumbs
- 250ml/8fl oz/1 cup milk

For the pastry
- 115g/4oz/1 cup plain (all-purpose) flour
- pinch of salt
- 50g/2oz/¼ cup butter, diced
- 50g/2oz/¼ cup lard (shortening) or white vegetable fat, diced
- 15ml/1 tbsp caster (superfine) sugar
- 15ml/1 tbsp chilled water

1 To make the pastry, sift the flour and salt into a mixing bowl. Rub or cut in the fats until the mixture resembles fine breadcrumbs. Stir in the caster sugar and enough chilled water to make a soft dough. Roll it out on a lightly floured surface and use to line a 21cm/8½in pie plate. Chill until required.

2 Meanwhile, place the egg yolks and 30ml/2 tbsp of the caster sugar in a bowl. Add the lemon rind and juice, the breadcrumbs and milk, mix lightly and leave to soak for 1 hour.

3 Preheat the oven to 200°C/400°F/ Gas 6. Beat the filling until smooth and pour into the chilled pastry case. Bake for 20 minutes, or until the filling has just set. Remove the pie from the oven and cool on a wire rack for 30 minutes or until a slight skin has formed on the surface. Lower the oven temperature to 180°C/350°F/Gas 4.

4 Whisk the egg whites until stiff peaks form. Gradually whisk in the remaining caster sugar to form a glossy meringue. Spoon on top of the lemon filling and spread right to the edge of the pastry, using the back of a spoon. Swirl the meringue slightly.

5 Bake the pie for 20–25 minutes, or until the meringue is crisp and golden brown. Allow to cool on a wire rack for 10 minutes before serving.

Energy 378Kcal/1586kJ; Protein 7.6g; Carbohydrate 46.3g, of which sugars 28.5g; Fat 19.5g, of which saturates 9.1g; Cholesterol 142mg; Calcium 114mg; Fibre 0.7g; Sodium 144mg.

KEY LIME PIE

THIS SPLENDID TART WITH ITS RICH LIME FILLING IS ONE OF AMERICA'S FAVOURITES. AS THE NAME SUGGESTS, IT ORIGINATED IN THE FLORIDA KEYS. FORGET ABOUT BEING BLUE, THINK SUN AND ENJOY!

SERVES TEN

INGREDIENTS
 4 eggs, separated
 400g/14oz can condensed milk
 grated rind and juice of 3 limes
 a few drops of green food
   colouring (optional)
 30ml/2 tbsp caster (superfine) sugar
 thinly pared lime rind and fresh mint
   leaves, to decorate
For the pastry
 225g/8oz/2 cups plain
   (all-purpose) flour
 115g/4oz/½ cup chilled butter, diced
 30ml/2 tbsp caster (superfine) sugar
 2 egg yolks
 pinch of salt
 30ml/2 tbsp chilled water
For the topping
 300ml/½ pint/1¼ cups double
   (heavy) cream
 2–3 limes, thinly sliced

1 To make the pastry, sift the flour into a mixing bowl, add the butter and rub in with your fingertips until the mixture resembles fine breadcrumbs. Add the sugar, egg yolks, salt and water, then mix to a soft dough.

2 Roll out the pastry on a lightly floured surface and use to line a deep 21cm/8½in fluted flan tin (tart pan), allowing the excess pastry to hang over the edge. Prick the pastry base with a fork and chill for at least 30 minutes.

3 Preheat the oven to 200°C/400°F/Gas 6. Trim off the excess pastry from around the edge of the pastry case (pie shell) using a sharp knife. If using a metal flan tin, you can just roll over the rim with a rolling pin. Line the pastry case with baking parchment or foil and baking beans.

4 Bake the pastry case blind for about 10 minutes. Remove the parchment or foil and beans and return the pastry case to the oven for 10 minutes more, until just cooked but not browned.

5 Meanwhile, beat the egg yolks in a large bowl until light and creamy, then beat in the condensed milk, with the lime rind and juice, until thoroughly combined. Add the food colouring, if using, and continue to beat until the mixture is thick.

6 In a grease-free bowl, whisk the egg whites to stiff peaks. Whisk in the caster sugar until the meringue is stiff, then fold into the lime mixture.

7 Lower the oven temperature to 160°C/325°F/Gas 3. Pour the lime filling into the pastry case, smoothing the top. Bake for 20–25 minutes until it has set and is turning brown. Cool, then chill.

8 Whip the cream for the topping and spoon it around the edge of the pie. Cut each lime slice from the centre to the edge, then twist it and arrange between the spoonfuls of cream. Decorate with lime rind and mint leaves.

Energy 508Kcal/2121kJ; Protein 9.1g; Carbohydrate 47.8g, of which sugars 30.6g; Fat 32.6g, of which saturates 19.3g; Cholesterol 171g; Calcium 182mg; Fibre 0.7g; Sodium 167mg.

CHILLED CHOCOLATE MOUSSE

HEADY, AROMATIC ESPRESSO COFFEE ADDS A DISTINCTIVE FLAVOUR TO THIS SMOOTH, RICH MOUSSE.
SERVE IT IN STYLISH CHOCOLATE CUPS TO BRING A SENSE OF OCCASION TO THE DESSERT COURSE.

SERVES FOUR

INGREDIENTS
    225g/8oz plain (semisweet) chocolate
    45ml/3 tbsp brewed espresso
    25g/1oz/2 tbsp unsalted
      (sweet) butter
    4 eggs, separated
    mascarpone or clotted cream,
      to serve (optional)
    mint sprigs, to decorate (optional)
For the chocolate cups
    225g/8oz plain (semisweet) chocolate

1 For each chocolate cup, cut a double thickness 15cm/6in square of foil. Mould it around a small orange, leaving the edges and corners loose to make a cup shape. Remove the orange and press the base of the foil case (shell) gently on the work surface to make a flat base. Repeat to make four foil cups.

2 For the cups, break the chocolate into small pieces and place in a bowl set over very hot, but not boiling, water. Stir occasionally until the chocolate is smooth and has melted.

3 Spoon the chocolate into the foil cups, spreading it up the sides with the back of a spoon to give a ragged edge. Chill for 30 minutes or until set hard. Gently peel away the foil, starting at the top edge.

4 To make the chocolate mousse, put the plain chocolate and brewed espresso into a bowl set over a pan of hot water and melt as before. When smooth and liquid, add the unsalted butter, a little at a time. Remove the pan from the heat then stir in the egg yolks.

5 Whisk the egg whites in a bowl until stiff, but not dry, then fold into the chocolate mixture. Pour into a bowl and chill for at least 3 hours.

6 To serve, scoop the chilled mousse carefully into the chocolate cups. Add a scoop of mascarpone or clotted cream and decorate with a sprig of fresh mint, if using.

Energy 709Kcal/2963kJ; Protein 13.2g; Carbohydrate 71.5g, of which sugars 70.5g; Fat 43.3g, of which saturates 24g; Cholesterol 248mg; Calcium 73mg; Fibre 2.8g; Sodium 129mg.

RASPBERRY MOUSSE GÂTEAU

A LAVISH QUANTITY OF RASPBERRIES GIVES THIS GÂTEAU ITS VIBRANT COLOUR AND FULL FLAVOUR.
MAKE IT AT THE HEIGHT OF SUMMER, WHEN RASPBERRIES ARE PLENTIFUL.

SERVES EIGHT TO TEN

INGREDIENTS
  2 eggs
  50g/2oz/¼ cup caster (superfine)
  sugar
  50g/2oz/½ cup plain (all-purpose)
  flour
  30ml/2 tbsp cocoa powder
  600g/1lb 5oz/3½ cups raspberries
  115g/4oz/1 cup icing (confectioners')
  sugar
  60ml/4 tbsp whisky (optional)
  300ml/½ pint/1¼ cups
  whipping cream
  2 egg whites

1 Preheat the oven to 180°C/350°F/
Gas 4. Grease and line a 23cm/9in
springform cake tin. Whisk the eggs and
sugar in a heatproof bowl set over a pan
of gently simmering water until the
whisk leaves a trail when lifted. Remove
the bowl from the heat and continue to
whisk the mixture for 2 minutes.

2 Sift the flour and cocoa powder over
the mixture and fold it in with a large
metal spoon. Spoon the mixture into the
tin and spread it gently to the edges.
Bake for 12–15 minutes until just firm.

3 Leave to cool, then remove the cake
from the tin and place it on a wire rack.
Wash and dry the tin.

4 Line the sides of the clean tin with a
strip of greaseproof paper and carefully
lower the cake back into it. Freeze until
the raspberry filling is ready.

5 Set aside 200g/7oz/generous 1 cup
of the raspberries. Put the remainder in
a clean bowl, stir in the icing sugar,
process to a purée in a food processor
or blender. Sieve the purée into a bowl,
then stir in the whisky, if using.

6 Whip the cream to form soft peaks.
Whisk the egg whites until they are stiff.
Using a large metal spoon, fold the
cream, then the egg whites into the
raspberry purée.

7 Spread half the raspberry mixture
over the cake. Sprinkle with the
reserved raspberries. Spread the
remaining raspberry mixture on top and
level the surface. Cover and freeze the
gâteau overnight.

8 Transfer the gâteau to the fridge at
least 1 hour before serving. Remove it
from the tin, place on a serving plate
and serve in slices.

Energy 301Kcal/1260kJ; Protein 5.7g; Carbohydrate 31.4g, of which sugars 26g; Fat 17.9g, of which saturates 10.5g; Cholesterol 96mg; Calcium 67mg; Fibre 2.5g; Sodium 86mg.

BAKED CARAMEL CUSTARD

CUSTARDS ARE CLASSIC NURSERY PUDDINGS: THIS IS A MORE SOPHISTICATED TAKE ON THESE SIMPLE, NOURISHING DESSERTS. KNOWN AS CRÈME CARAMEL IN FRANCE AND FLAN IN SPAIN, THIS CHILLED CUSTARD HAS A RICH CARAMEL FLAVOUR WHICH IS WONDERFUL WITH CREAM AND STRAWBERRIES.

SERVES SIX TO EIGHT

INGREDIENTS
   250g/9oz/1¼ cups granulated sugar
   1 vanilla pod or 10ml/2 tsp
     vanilla essence (extract)
   425ml/15fl oz/1¾ cups double
     (heavy) cream
   5 large eggs, plus 2 extra yolks
   thick cream and fresh strawberries,
     to serve

1 Put 175g/6oz/generous ¾ cup of the sugar in a small heavy pan with just enough water to moisten the sugar. Bring to the boil over a high heat, swirling the pan until the sugar is dissolved completely. Boil for about 5 minutes, without stirring, until the syrup turns a dark caramel colour.

2 Working quickly, pour the caramel into a 1 litre/1¾ pint/4 cup soufflé dish. Holding the dish with oven gloves, carefully swirl the dish to coat the base and sides evenly with the hot caramel mixture. Work quickly as the caramel soon sets and becomes hard. Set the dish aside to cool.

3 Preheat the oven to 160°C/325°F/ Gas 3. With a small sharp knife, carefully split the vanilla pod lengthways and scrape the black seeds into a pan. Add the cream and bring just to the boil over a medium-high heat, stirring frequently. Remove the pan from the heat, cover and set aside for about 20 minutes to cool.

4 In a bowl, whisk the eggs and egg yolks with the remaining sugar for 2–3 minutes until smooth and creamy.

5 Whisk in the hot cream and carefully strain the mixture into the caramel-lined dish. Cover tightly with foil.

VARIATION
For a special occasion, make individual baked custards in ramekin dishes. Coat 6–8 ramekins with the caramel and divide the custard mixture among them. Bake, in a roasting tin of water, for 25–30 minutes or until set. Slice the strawberries and marinate them in a little sugar and a liqueur or dessert wine, such as Amaretto or Muscat wine.

6 Place the dish in a roasting tin and pour in just enough boiling water to come halfway up the side of the dish.

7 Bake the custard for 40–45 minutes until just set. To test whether the custard is set, insert a knife about 5cm/2in from the edge; if it comes out clean, the custard should be ready.

8 Remove the soufflé dish from the roasting tin and leave to cool for at least 30 minutes, then place in the fridge and chill overnight.

9 To turn out, carefully run a sharp knife around the edge of the dish to loosen the custard.

10 Cover the dish with a serving plate and, holding them together very tightly, invert the dish and plate, allowing the custard to drop down on to the plate.

11 Gently lift one edge of the dish, allowing the caramel to run down over the sides and on to the plate, then carefully lift off the dish. Serve with thick cream and fresh strawberries.

Energy 622Kcal/2587kJ; Protein 9.6g; Carbohydrate 44.8g, of which sugars 44.8g; Fat 46.4g, of which saturates 26g; Cholesterol 386mg; Calcium 98mg; Fibre 0g; Sodium 103mg.

SUMMER PUDDING

*THIS IS ONE OF THOSE GLORIOUS DESSERTS THAT WORKS WONDERS AND MAKES YOU FEEL A MILLION
DOLLARS. FIRST — AND FOREMOST WHEN LIFE IS A LITTLE GLUM — IT LOOKS AND TASTES IRRESISTIBLE.
SECOND, IT IS PACKED FULL OF FRUIT GOODNESS — VITAMINS GALORE TO PROTECT AND RESTORE.*

SERVES FOUR TO SIX

INGREDIENTS

8 x 1cm/½in thick slices of day-old
   white bread, crusts removed
800g/1¾lb/6–7 cups mixed berry
   fruit, such as strawberries,
   raspberries, blackcurrants,
   redcurrants and blueberries
50g/2oz/¼ cup golden caster
   (superfine) sugar
lightly whipped double (heavy) cream
   or crème fraîche, to serve

3 Fold over the excess bread, then
cover the fruit with the remaining bread
slices, trimming them to fit. Place a
small plate or saucer directly on top of
the pudding, fitting it inside the basin.
Weight it with a 900g/2lb weight if you
have one, or use a couple of full cans.

4 Leave the pudding in the fridge for
at least 8 hours or overnight. To serve,
run a knife between the pudding and
the basin and turn it out on to a plate.
Spoon any reserved juices over the top
and serve with whipped cream or
crème fraîche.

1 Trim a slice of bread to fit in the base
of a 1.2 litre/2 pint/5 cup pudding
basin, then trim another 5–6 slices to
line the sides of the basin.

2 Place all the fruit in a pan with the
sugar. Cook gently for 4–5 minutes until
the juices begin to run. Do not add any
water. Allow the mixture to cool slightly,
then spoon the berries and enough
of their juices to moisten into the bread-
lined pudding basin. Save any leftover
juice to serve with the pudding.

Energy 230Kcal/977kJ; Protein 6.2g; Carbohydrate 51.7g, of which sugars 26.5g; Fat 1.2g, of which saturates 0g; Cholesterol 0mg; Calcium 98mg; Fibre 3g; Sodium 294mg.

BRANDIED APPLE CHARLOTTE

LOOSELY BASED ON A TRADITIONAL APPLE CHARLOTTE, THIS ICED VERSION COMBINES BRANDY-STEEPED DRIED APPLE WITH A SPICY RICOTTA CREAM TO MAKE AN UNUSUAL AND INSPIRING DESSERT.

SERVES EIGHT TO TEN

INGREDIENTS
130g/4½oz/¾ cup dried apples
75ml/5 tbsp brandy
50g/2oz/¼ cup unsalted (sweet) butter
115g/4oz/½ cup light muscovado (brown) sugar
2.5ml/½ tsp mixed (apple-pie) spice
60ml/4 tbsp water
75g/3oz/½ cup sultanas (golden raisins)
300g/11oz Madeira cake, cut into 1cm/½in slices
250g/9oz/generous 1 cup ricotta cheese
30ml/2 tbsp lemon juice
150ml/¼ pint/⅔ cup double (heavy) or whipping cream
icing (confectioners') sugar and fresh mint sprigs, to decorate

1 Roughly chop the dried apples, then transfer them to a clean bowl. Pour over the brandy and set aside for about 1 hour or until most of the brandy has been absorbed.

2 Melt the butter in a frying pan. Add the sugar and stir over a low heat for 1 minute. Add the mixed spice, water and soaked apples, with any remaining brandy. Heat until just simmering, reduce the heat slightly, if necessary, and then cook gently for about 5 minutes or until the apples are tender. Stir in the sultanas and leave to cool completely.

3 Use the Madeira cake slices to line the sides of a 20cm/8in square or 20cm/8in round springform or loose-based cake tin (pan). Place in the freezer while you make the filling.

4 Beat the ricotta in a bowl until it has softened, then stir in the apple mixture and lemon juice. Whip the cream in a separate bowl and fold it in. Spoon the mixture into the lined tin and level the surface. Cover and freeze overnight.

5 Transfer the charlotte to the fridge 1 hour before serving. Invert it on to a serving plate, dust with sugar, and decorate with mint sprigs.

COOK'S TIP
Line the tin with clear film (plastic wrap) before placing the cake in it if you are concerned that the dessert will not turn out easily when it is frozen.

Energy 446Kcal/1869kJ; Protein 6g; Carbohydrate 54.4g, of which sugars 46.2g; Fat 21.9g, of which saturates 13.3g; Cholesterol 49mg; Calcium 119mg; Fibre 2.1g; Sodium 222mg.

MISSISSIPPI MUD PIE

THIS IS THE ULTIMATE IN CHOCOLATE DESSERTS — A DEEP PASTRY CASE, FILLED WITH CHOCOLATE
CUSTARD AND TOPPED WITH A FLUFFY RUM MOUSSE AND A SMOTHERING OF WHIPPED CREAM.

SERVES SIX TO EIGHT

INGREDIENTS
  3 eggs, separated
  20ml/4 tsp cornflour (cornstarch)
  75g/3oz/6 tbsp caster
    (superfine) sugar
  400ml/14fl oz/1⅔ cups milk
  150g/5oz plain (semisweet)
    chocolate, broken up
  5ml/1 tsp vanilla essence (extract)
  15ml/1 tbsp powdered gelatine
  45ml/3 tbsp water
  30ml/2 tbsp dark rum
  175g/6fl oz/¾ cup double (heavy)
    cream, whipped
  a few chocolate curls,
    to decorate
For the pastry
  250g/9oz/2¼ cups plain
    (all-purpose) flour
  150g/5oz/⅔ cup butter, diced
  2 egg yolks
  15–30ml/1–2 tbsp chilled water

1 To make the pastry, sift the flour into a bowl and rub or cut in the butter until the mixture resembles breadcrumbs. Stir in the egg yolks with just enough chilled water to make a soft dough.

2 Roll out on a lightly floured surface and use to line a deep 23cm/9in flan tin (quiche pan). Chill for 30 minutes. Preheat the oven to 190°C/375°F/Gas 5. Prick the pastry all over with a fork, line with foil and baking beans, then bake blind for 10 minutes.

3 Remove the foil and beans, return the pie to the oven and bake for about 10 minutes more until the pastry is crisp and golden. Cool in the tin.

4 To make the custard filling, mix the egg yolks, cornflour and 30ml/2 tbsp of the sugar in a bowl. Heat the milk in a pan until almost boiling, then beat into the egg mixture.

5 Return the custard mixture to the cleaned pan and stir over a low heat until the custard has thickened and is smooth. Pour half the custard into a bowl.

6 Melt the chocolate in a heatproof bowl set over a pan of hot water, then add to the custard in the bowl. Add the vanilla essence and mix well. Spread in the pastry case, cover closely with some baking parchment to prevent a skin from forming, cool, then chill until set.

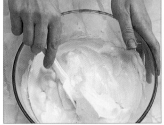

7 Sprinkle the gelatine over the water in a small bowl, leave until spongy, then place over a pan of simmering water until all the gelatine has dissolved. Stir into the remaining custard, along with the rum. Whisk the egg whites until stiff peaks form, whisk in the remaining sugar, then quickly fold into the custard before it sets.

8 Spoon the mixture over the chocolate custard to cover completely. Chill until set, then remove the pie from the tin to serve. Spread whipped cream over the top and decorate with chocolate curls.

Energy 827Kcal/3454kJ; Protein 13g; Carbohydrate 83.5g, of which sugars 33.1g; Fat 50.2g, of which saturates 29.2g; Cholesterol 280mg; Calcium 200mg; Fibre 1.9g; Sodium 246mg.

BOSTON BANOFFEE PIE

SIMPLY PRESS THIS WONDERFULLY BISCUITY PASTRY INTO THE TIN, RATHER THAN ROLLING IT OUT.
ADD THE FUDGE-TOFFEE FILLING AND SLICED BANANA TOPPING AND IT'LL PROVE IRRESISTIBLE.

SERVES SIX

INGREDIENTS
  115g/4oz/½ cup butter, diced
  200g/7oz can skimmed, sweetened
    condensed milk
  115g/4oz/½ cup soft brown sugar
  30ml/2 tbsp golden (light corn) syrup
  2 small bananas, sliced
  a little lemon juice
  whipped cream, to decorate
  5ml/1 tsp grated plain
    (semisweet) chocolate
For the pastry
  150g/5oz/1¼ cups plain
    (all-purpose) flour
  115g/4oz/½ cup butter, diced
  50g/2oz/¼ cup caster
    (superfine) sugar

1 Preheat the oven to 160°C/325°F/
Gas 3. In a food processor, process the
flour and diced butter until crumbed.
Stir in the caster sugar and mix to form
a soft, pliable dough.

2 Press into a 20cm/8in loose-based
flan tin (tart pan). Bake for 30 minutes.

3 To make the filling, place the butter
in a pan with the condensed milk,
brown sugar and syrup. Heat gently,
stirring, until the butter has melted and
the sugar has completely dissolved.

4 Bring to a gentle boil and cook for
7–10 minutes, stirring constantly, until
the mixture thickens and turns a light
caramel colour.

5 Pour the hot caramel filling into the
pastry case and leave until completely
cold. Sprinkle the banana slices with
lemon juice to prevent them from
discolouring and arrange them in
overlapping circles on top of the filling,
leaving a gap in the centre. Pipe a
generous swirl of whipped cream in the
centre and sprinkle with the grated
chocolate. Serve freshly decorated.

Energy 608Kcal/2547kJ; Protein 6.4g; Carbohydrate 78.5g, of which sugars 58.9g; Fat 32g, of which saturates 20.1g; Cholesterol 82mg; Calcium 169mg; Fibre 1.1g; Sodium 299mg.

HOT PUDDINGS, DESSERTS AND DRINKS

Look no further than here for classic comforters.
Here are the nursery puddings, the steaming
mugs of toddy or nectar and the bedtime drinks
that encouraged happy childhood dreams.

CRÊPES <u>WITH</u> ORANGE SAUCE

CRÊPE-MAKING CAN BE VERY RELAXING ONCE THE FIRST COUPLE OF REJECTS ARE OUT OF THE WAY
AND THE PAN TEMPERATURE IS JUST RIGHT. THIS IS ONE OF THE BEST WAYS TO ENJOY THIN CRÊPE.

SERVES SIX

INGREDIENTS
   115g/4oz/1 cup plain
   (all-purpose) flour
   1.5ml/¼ tsp salt
   25g/1oz/2 tbsp caster
   (superfine) sugar
   2 eggs, lightly beaten
   about 250ml/8fl oz/1 cup milk
   about 60ml/4 tbsp water
   30ml/2 tbsp orange flower water,
   Cointreau or other orange liqueur
   25g/1oz/2 tbsp unsalted (sweet)
   butter, melted, plus extra for frying
For the sauce
   75g/3oz/6 tbsp unsalted
   (sweet) butter
   50g/2oz/¼ cup caster
   (superfine) sugar
   grated rind and juice of
   1 large orange
   grated rind and juice of 1 lemon
   150ml/¼ pint/⅔ cup freshly
   squeezed orange juice
   60ml/4 tbsp Cointreau or other
   orange liqueur, plus more for
   flaming (optional)
   brandy, for flaming (optional)
   orange segments, to decorate

1 Sift the flour, salt and sugar into a large bowl. Make a well in the centre and pour in the eggs. Beat the eggs, gradually incorporating the flour.

2 Whisk in the milk, water and orange flower water or liqueur to make a very smooth batter. Strain into a jug (pitcher) and set aside for 20–30 minutes.

3 Heat an 18–20cm/7–8in crêpe pan (preferably non-stick) over a medium heat. If the crêpe batter has thickened, add a little more water or milk to thin it. Stir the melted butter into the batter.

4 Brush the hot pan with a little extra melted butter and pour in about 30ml/ 2 tbsp of batter. Quickly tilt and rotate the pan to cover the base evenly with a thin layer of batter. Cook for about 1 minute, or until the top is set and the base is golden. With a metal spatula, lift the edge to check the colour, then carefully turn over the crêpe and cook for 20–30 seconds, just to set. Tip out on to a plate.

5 Continue cooking the crêpes, stirring the batter occasionally and brushing the pan with a little more melted butter as and when necessary. Place a sheet of clear film (plastic wrap) or baking parchment between each crêpe as they are stacked to prevent them from sticking. (The crêpes can be prepared ahead to this point – put them in a plastic bag and chill until ready to use.)

6 To make the sauce, melt the butter in a large frying pan over a medium-low heat, then stir in the sugar, orange and lemon rind and juice, the additional orange juice and the orange liqueur.

7 Place a crêpe in the pan browned-side down, swirling gently to coat with the sauce. Fold it in half, then in half again to form a triangle, and push to the side of the pan. Continue heating and folding the crêpes until all are warm and covered with the sauce.

8 To flame the crêpes, heat 30–45ml/ 2–3 tbsp each of orange liqueur and brandy in a small pan over a medium heat. Remove the pan from the heat, carefully ignite the liquid with a match then pour evenly over the crêpes. Sprinkle over the orange segments and serve immediately.

COOK'S TIP
Cointreau is the world's leading brand of orange liqueur. It is colourless and flavoured with a mixture of bitter orange peel and sweet oranges.

Energy 303Kcal/1269kJ; Protein 5.9g; Carbohydrate 32.4g, of which sugars 17.8g; Fat 16.9g, of which saturates 9.8g; Cholesterol 114mg; Calcium 99mg; Fibre 0.6g; Sodium 248mg.

DEEP-DISH APPLE PIE

THIS IS PIE LIKE MOTHER USED TO MAKE, WITH MELT-IN-THE-MOUTH SHORTCRUST PASTRY. INSIDE,
SUGAR, SPICES AND FLOUR CREATE A DELICIOUSLY THICK AND SYRUPY SAUCE WITH THE APPLE JUICES.

4 Put a baking sheet in the oven and preheat to 200°C/400°F/Gas 6. Roll out just over half the pastry and use to line a 23cm/9in pie dish that is 4cm/1½in deep, allowing the pastry to overhang the edges slightly. Spoon in the filling, doming the apple slices in the centre.

5 Roll out the remaining pastry to form the lid. Lightly brush the edges of the pastry case with a little water, then place the lid over the apple filling.

6 Trim the pastry with a sharp knife. Gently press the edges together to seal, then knock up the edge. Re-roll the pastry trimmings and cut out apple and leaf shapes. Brush the top of the pie with egg white. Arrange the pastry apples and leaves on top.

7 Brush again with egg white, then sprinkle with golden granulated sugar. Make two small slits in the top of the pie to allow steam to escape.

8 Bake for 30 minutes, then lower the oven temperature to 180°C/350°F/Gas 4 and bake for a further 15 minutes until the pastry is golden and the apples are soft – check by inserting a small sharp knife or skewer through one of the slits in the top of the pie. Serve hot, with some whipped cream.

SERVES SIX

INGREDIENTS
115g/4oz/½ cup caster
  (superfine) sugar
45ml/3 tbsp plain (all-purpose) flour
2.5ml/½ tsp ground cinnamon
finely grated rind of 1 orange
900g/2lb tart cooking apples
1 egg white, lightly beaten
30ml/2 tbsp golden granulated sugar
whipped cream, to serve
For the pastry
350g/12oz/3 cups plain
  (all-purpose) flour
pinch of salt
175g/6oz/¾ cup butter, diced
about 75ml/5 tbsp chilled water

1 To make the pastry, sift the flour and salt into a mixing bowl and rub or cut in the butter until the mixture resembles fine breadcrumbs.

2 Sprinkle over the water and mix to a firm, soft dough. Knead lightly for a few seconds until smooth. Wrap in clear film (plastic wrap) and chill for 30 minutes.

3 Combine the caster sugar, flour, cinnamon and orange rind in a bowl. Peel, core and thinly slice the apples. Add to the sugar mixture in the bowl, then toss gently with your fingertips until they are all evenly coated.

Energy 600Kcal/2524kJ; Protein 7.7g; Carbohydrate 91.9g, of which sugars 39.8g; Fat 25g, of which saturates 15.3g; Cholesterol 62mg; Calcium 120mg; Fibre 4.5g; Sodium 193mg.

SPICED APPLE CRUMBLE

ANY FRUIT CAN BE USED IN THIS POPULAR PUD, BUT AUTUMNAL BLACKBERRY AND APPLE ARE A REASSURINGLY FAMILIAR DUO. HAZELNUT AND CARDAMOM BRING CRUNCH AND ZING TO THE TOPPING.

SERVES FOUR TO SIX

INGREDIENTS
  butter, for greasing
  450g/1lb cooking apples
  115g/4oz/1 cup blackberries
  grated rind and juice of 1 orange
  50g/2oz/⅓ cup light muscovado
    (brown) sugar
  custard, to serve
For the topping
  175g/6oz/1½ cups plain (all-purpose)
    flour
  75g/3oz/⅓ cup butter
  75g/3oz/⅓ cup caster sugar
  25g/1oz/¼ cup chopped hazelnuts
  2.5ml/½ tsp crushed cardamom
    seeds

1 Preheat the oven to 200°C/400°F/ Gas 6. Generously butter a 1.2 litre/ 2 pint/5 cup baking dish. Peel and core the apples, then slice them into the prepared baking dish. Level the surface, then scatter the blackberries over. Sprinkle the orange rind and light muscovado sugar evenly over the top, then pour over the orange juice. Set the fruit mixture aside while you make the crumble topping.

2 Make the topping. Sift the flour into a bowl and rub in the butter until the mixture resembles coarse breadcrumbs. Stir in the caster sugar, hazelnuts and cardamom seeds. Scatter the topping over the top of the fruit.

3 Press the topping around the edges of the dish to seal in the juices. Bake for 30–35 minutes or until the crumble is golden. Serve hot, with custard.

Energy 504Kcal/2120kJ; Protein 5.9g; Carbohydrate 79.7g, of which sugars 46.3g; Fat 20.1g, of which saturates 10.2g; Cholesterol 40g; Calcium 108mg; Fibre 4.5g; Sodium 121mg.

BLACKBERRY CHARLOTTE

THE PERFECT WARMER FOR COLD DAYS, SERVE THIS CHARLOTTE WITH WHIPPED CREAM OR HOME-MADE CUSTARD.

SERVES FOUR

INGREDIENTS
  65g/2½oz/5 tbsp unsalted (sweet)
    butter
  175g/6oz/3 cups fresh white
    breadcrumbs
  50g/2oz/4 tbsp soft brown sugar
  60ml/4 tbsp golden (light corn) syrup
  finely grated rind and juice of
    2 lemons
  50g/2oz walnut halves
  450g/1lb blackberries
  450g/1lb cooking apples, peeled,
    cored and finely sliced

1 Preheat the oven to 180°C/350°F/
Gas 4. Grease a 450ml/¾ pint/2 cup
dish with 15g/½oz/1 tbsp of the butter.
Melt the remaining butter and add the
breadcrumbs. Sauté them for 5–7
minutes, until the crumbs are a little
crisp and golden. Leave to cool slightly.

2 Place the sugar, syrup, lemon rind
and juice in a small pan and gently
warm them. Add the crumbs.

3 Process the walnuts until they are
finely ground.

4 Arrange a thin layer of blackberries
on the dish. Top with a thin layer
of crumbs.

5 Add a thin layer of apple, topping it
with another thin layer of crumbs.

6 Repeat the process with another
layer of blackberries, followed by a layer
of crumbs. Continue until you have
used up all the ingredients, finishing
with a layer of crumbs. The mixture
should be piled well above the top edge
of the dish, because it shrinks during
cooking. Bake for 30 minutes, until the
crumbs are golden and the fruit is soft.

Energy 546Kcal/2294kJ; Protein 8.5g; Carbohydrate 81g, of which sugars 48.2g; Fat 23.1g, of which saturates 9.2g; Cholesterol 35mg; Calcium 133mg; Fibre 6.7g; Sodium 498mg.

FRESH CURRANT BREAD AND BUTTER PUDDING

FRESH MIXED CURRANTS BRING A WIDE-AWAKE CHARACTER TO THIS SCRUMPTIOUS HOT PUDDING.

SERVES SIX

INGREDIENTS

8 medium-thick slices day-old bread,
crusts removed
50g/2oz/¼ cup butter, softened
115g/4oz/1 cup redcurrants
115g/4oz/1 cup blackcurrants
4 eggs, beaten
75g/3oz/6 tbsp caster (superfine)
sugar
475ml/16fl oz/2 cups creamy milk
5ml/1 tsp pure vanilla essence
(extract)
freshly grated nutmeg
30ml/2 tbsp demerara sugar
single (light) cream, to serve

1 Preheat the oven to 160°C/325°F/
Gas 3. Generously butter a 1.2 litre/
2 pint/5 cup oval baking dish.

2 Spread the slices of bread generously with the butter, then cut them in half diagonally. Layer the slices in the dish, buttered side up, scattering the currants between the layers.

3 Beat the eggs and caster sugar lightly together in a large mixing bowl, then gradually whisk in the milk, vanilla essence and a large pinch of freshly grated nutmeg.

4 Pour the milk mixture over the bread, pushing the slices down. Scatter the demerara sugar and a little nutmeg over the top. Place the dish in a baking tin and fill with hot water to come halfway up the sides of the dish. Bake for 40 minutes, then increase the oven temperature to 180°C/350°F/Gas 4 and bake for 20–25 minutes more or until the top is golden. Cool slightly, then serve with single cream.

Energy 335Kcal/1406kJ; Protein 11.2g; Carbohydrate 41.3g, of which sugars 24.5g; Fat 15.1g, of which saturates 7.6g; Cholesterol 181mg; Calcium 180mg; Fibre 1.9g; Sodium 330mg

CHOCOLATE PUDDING WITH RUM CUSTARD

WITH MELTING MOMENTS OF CHOCOLATE IN EVERY MOUTHFUL, THESE LITTLE PUDDINGS WON'T LAST LONG. THE RUM CUSTARD TURNS THEM INTO A MORE ADULT PUDDING; FOR A FAMILY DESSERT, FLAVOUR THE CUSTARD WITH VANILLA OR ORANGE RIND INSTEAD.

SERVES SIX

INGREDIENTS
    115g/4oz/½ cup butter, plus extra
      for greasing
    115g/4oz/½ cup soft light
      brown sugar
    2 eggs, beaten
    drops of vanilla essence (extract)
    45ml/3 tbsp cocoa powder, sifted
    115g/4oz/1 cup self-raising (self-
      rising) flour
    75g/3oz bitter (semisweet) chocolate,
      chopped
    a little milk, warmed
For the rum custard
    250ml/8fl oz/1 cup milk
    15ml/1 tbsp caster (superfine) sugar
    2 egg yolks
    10ml/2 tsp cornflour (cornstarch)
    30–45ml/2–3 tbsp rum

1 Lightly grease a 1.2 litre/2 pint/5 cup heatproof bowl or six individual dariole moulds. Cream the butter and sugar until pale and creamy. Gently blend in the eggs and the vanilla essence.

2 Sift together the cocoa and flour, and fold gently into the egg mixture with the chopped chocolate and sufficient milk to give a soft dropping consistency.

3 Spoon the mixture into the basin or moulds, cover with buttered greaseproof paper and tie down. Fill a pan with 2.5–5cm/1–2in water, place the puddings in the pan, cover with a lid and bring to the boil. Steam the large pudding for 1½–2 hours and the individual puddings for 45–50 minutes, topping up with water if necessary. When firm, turn out on to warm plates.

4 To make the rum custard, bring the milk and sugar to the boil. Whisk together the egg yolks and cornflour, then pour on the hot milk, whisking constantly. Return the mixture to the pan and stir continuously while it slowly comes back to the boil. Allow the sauce to simmer gently as it thickens, stirring all the time. Remove from the heat and stir in the rum.

COOK'S TIP
To microwave, spoon the mixture into a microwave-proof basin (at least 300ml/½ pint/1¼ cups larger than necessary). Cover loosely with clear film (plastic wrap) and microwave on full power for 5 minutes. Leave to stand for 5 minutes.

Energy 458Kcal/1915kJ; Protein 8.3g; Carbohydrate 49g, of which sugars 31.5g; Fat 25.6g, of which saturates 14.5g; Cholesterol 186mg; Calcium 145mg; Fibre 1.8g; Sodium 302mg.

STICKY COFFEE AND GINGER PUDDING

THIS COFFEE-CAPPED FEATHER-LIGHT SPONGE IS MADE WITH BREADCRUMBS AND GROUND ALMONDS.
SERVE WITH CREAMY CUSTARD OR SCOOPS OF VANILLA ICE CREAM FOR GROWN-UP NURSERY PUDDING.

SERVES FOUR

INGREDIENTS
30ml/2 tbsp soft light brown sugar
25g/1oz/2 tbsp preserved stem
  ginger, chopped, plus 75ml/5 tbsp
  ginger syrup
30ml/2 tbsp mild-flavoured
  ground coffee
115g/4oz/generous ½ cup caster
  (superfine) sugar
3 eggs, separated
25g/1oz/¼ cup plain (all-purpose)
  flour
5ml/1 tsp ground ginger
65g/2½oz/generous 1 cup fresh
  white breadcrumbs
25g/1oz/¼ cup ground almonds

1 Preheat the oven to 180°C/350°F/
Gas 4. Grease and line the base of a
750ml/1¼ pint/3 cup ovenproof bowl,
then sprinkle in the sugar and chopped
stem ginger.

2 Put the ground coffee in a small
bowl. Heat the ginger syrup until almost
boiling; pour into the coffee. Stir well
and leave for 4 minutes. Pour through
a fine sieve (strainer) into the
ovenproof bowl.

3 Beat half the sugar with the egg yolks
until light and fluffy. Sift the flour and
ground ginger together and fold into the
egg yolk mixture with the breadcrumbs
and ground almonds.

4 Whisk the egg whites until stiff, then
gradually whisk in the remaining caster
sugar. Fold into the mixture, in two
batches. Spoon into the pudding basin
and smooth the top.

5 Cover the basin with a piece of
pleated greased baking parchment and
secure with string. Bake for 40 minutes,
or until the sponge is firm to the touch.
Turn out and serve immediately.

COOK'S TIP
This pudding can also be baked in a
900ml/1½ pint/3¾ cup loaf tin (pan)
and served thickly sliced.

Energy 382Kcal/1617kJ; Protein 9.7g; Carbohydrate 70.6g, of which sugars 53.5g; Fat 8.9g, of which saturates 1.7g; Cholesterol 171mg; Calcium 93mg; Fibre 1g; Sodium 240mg.

STICKY TOFFEE PUDDING

FORGET THE MAIN COURSE BECAUSE THIS IS GOOEY AND GORGEOUS FOR A SWEET-COURSE-ONLY MEAL.

SERVES SIX

INGREDIENTS
115g/4oz/1 cup toasted walnuts,
   chopped
175g/6oz/¾ cup butter
175g/6oz/scant 1 cup soft brown
   sugar
60ml/4 tbsp double (heavy) cream
30ml/2 tbsp lemon juice
2 eggs, beaten
115g/4oz/1 cup self-raising (self-
   rising) flour

1 Grease a 900ml/1½ pint/¾ cup
heatproof bowl and add half the nuts.

2 Heat 50g/2oz/4 tbsp of the butter
with 50g/2oz/4 tbsp of the sugar, the
cream and 15ml/1 tbsp lemon juice in a
small pan, stirring until smooth. Pour
half into the heatproof bowl, then swirl
to coat it a little way up the sides.

3 Beat the remaining butter and sugar
until fluffy, then beat in the eggs. Fold
in the flour, remaining nuts and lemon
juice and spoon into the basin.

4 Cover the bowl with greaseproof
(waxed) paper with a pleat folded in the
centre, then tie securely with string.

5 Steam the pudding for about
1¼ hours, until set in the centre.

6 Just before serving, gently warm the
remaining sauce. Unmould the pudding
on to a warm plate and pour over the
warm sauce.

Energy 606Kcal/2523kJ; Protein 7.5g; Carbohydrate 46g, of which sugars 31.6g; Fat 44.9g, of which saturates 20.3g; Cholesterol 152mg; Calcium 122mg; Fibre 1.3g; Sodium 279mg.

CUSTARD

WHEN MAKING A CUSTARD, WHETHER YOU WANT A THIN POURING CUSTARD OR A THICK CUSTARD FOR A TRIFLE, ADDING A LITTLE CORNFLOUR WILL STABILIZE THE EGG AND HELP TO PREVENT CURDLING. THIS RECIPE USES A REASONABLE AMOUNT OF CORNFLOUR FOR SURE SUCCESS — SIMPLE TO MAKE AND SERIOUSLY COMFORTING TO EAT WITH ALL SORTS OF HEARTWARMING HOT PUDDINGS.

SERVES FOUR TO SIX

INGREDIENTS
   450ml/¾ pint/scant 2 cups milk
   few drops of vanilla essence (extract)
   2 eggs plus 1 egg yolk
   15–30ml/1–2 tbsp caster (superfine)
   sugar)
   15ml/1 tbsp cornflour (cornstarch)
   30ml/2 tbsp water

1 In a pan heat the milk with the vanilla essence and remove from the heat just as the milk comes to the boil.

2 Whisk the eggs and yolk in a bowl with the caster sugar until well combined but not frothy. In a separate bowl, blend together the cornflour with the water and mix into the eggs. Whisk in a little of the hot milk, then mix in all the remaining milk.

COOK'S TIP
If you are not serving the custard immediately, cover the surface of the sauce with clear film (plastic wrap) to prevent a skin from forming and keep warm in a heatproof bowl over a pan of hot water.

3 Strain the egg and milk mixture back into the pan and heat gently, stirring frequently. Take care not to overheat the mixture or it will curdle.

4 Continue stirring until the custard thickens sufficiently to coat the back of a wooden spoon. Do not allow to boil or it will curdle. Serve immediately.

Energy 156Kcal/656kJ; Protein 8g; Carbohydrate 17.9g, of which sugars 11g; Fat 6.5g, of which saturates 2.4g; Cholesterol 170mg; Calcium 147mg; Fibre 0g; Sodium 92mg.

TRADITIONAL ENGLISH RICE PUDDING

MEMORIES OF SCHOOL-DAYS RICE PUDDING ARE EITHER THE BEST OR WORST AND THIS IS THE RECIPE FOR DESSERTS THAT FEATURE IN DAYDREAMS. A PROPER RICE PUDDING IS SMOOTH AND CREAMY WITH JUST A HINT OF FRAGRANT SPICES. SERVE IT WITH A SPOONFUL OF THICK CHERRY JAM, IF YOU LIKE.

SERVES FOUR

INGREDIENTS
  600ml/1 pint/2½ cups creamy milk
  1 vanilla pod (bean)
  50g/2oz/generous ¼ cup short grain
    pudding rice
  45ml/3 tbsp caster (superfine) sugar
  25g/1oz/2 tbsp butter
  freshly grated nutmeg

1 Pour the milk into a pan and add the vanilla pod. Bring to simmering point, then remove from the heat, cover and leave to infuse for 1 hour. Preheat the oven to 150°C/300°F/Gas 2.

2 Put the rice and sugar in an oven-proof dish. Strain the milk over the rice, discarding the vanilla pod. Stir to mix, then dot the surface with the butter.

3 Bake, uncovered, for 2 hours. After about 40 minutes, stir the surface skin into the pudding, and repeat this after a further 40 minutes. At this point, sprinkle the surface of the pudding with grated nutmeg. Allow the pudding to finish cooking without stirring.

COOK'S TIP
If possible, always use a non-stick pan when heating milk, otherwise it is likely to stick to the bottom of the pan and burn.

Energy 233Kcal/972kJ; Protein 5.9g; Carbohydrate 28.2g, of which sugars 18.6g; Fat 11.1g, of which saturates 7g; Cholesterol 34mg; Calcium 187mg; Fibre 0g; Sodium 103mg.

BAKED BANANAS WITH ICE CREAM

BAKED BANANAS MAKE THE PERFECT PARTNERS FOR DELICIOUS VANILLA ICE CREAM TOPPED WITH A TOASTED HAZELNUT SAUCE. THIS IS QUICK AND EASY FOR TIMES WHEN ONLY SWEET TREATS WILL DO.

SERVES FOUR

INGREDIENTS
    4 large bananas
    15ml/1 tbsp lemon juice
    4 large scoops of vanilla ice cream
For the sauce
    25g/1oz/2 tbsp unsalted (sweet)
    butter
    50g/2oz/½ cup hazelnuts, toasted
    and roughly chopped
    45ml/3 tbsp golden (light corn) syrup
    30ml/2 tbsp lemon juice

1 Preheat the oven to 180°C/350°F/ Gas 4. Place the unpeeled bananas on a baking sheet and brush them with the lemon juice. Bake for about 20 minutes until the skins are turning black and the flesh gives a little when the bananas are gently squeezed.

2 Meanwhile, make the sauce. Melt the butter in a small pan. Add the hazelnuts and cook gently for 1 minute. Add the syrup and lemon juice and heat, stirring, for 1 minute more.

3 To serve, slit each banana open with a knife and open out the skins to reveal the tender flesh. Transfer to serving plates and serve with scoops of ice cream. Pour the sauce over.

Energy 382Kcal/1598kJ; Protein 5.4g; Carbohydrate 49.4g, of which sugars 45.7g; Fat 18.6g, of which saturates 7.6g; Cholesterol 28mg; Calcium 88mg; Fibre 2.1g; Sodium 106mg.

YORKSHIRE CURD TART

THE DISTINGUISHING FLAVOUR IN YORKSHIRE CURD TARTS IS ALLSPICE, OR "CLOVE PEPPER" AS IT WAS KNOWN LOCALLY. THIS TART IS SO GOOD THAT IT IS DIFFICULT TO RESIST SECOND HELPINGS.

2 Put the dough on a floured surface, knead lightly and briefly, then form into a ball. Roll out the pastry thinly and use to line a 20cm/8in fluted loose-based flan tin (tart pan). Cover with clear film (plastic wrap) and chill for about 15 minutes.

3 Preheat the oven to 190°C/375°F/ Gas 5. Mix the sugar with the ground allspice in a bowl, then stir in the eggs, lemon rind and juice, butter, curd cheese and raisins. Mix well.

4 Pour the filling into the pastry case, then bake for 40 minutes, or until the pastry is cooked and the filling is lightly set and golden brown. Cut the tart into wedges while it is still slightly warm, and serve with cream, if you like.

SERVES EIGHT

INGREDIENTS
90g/3½oz/scant ½ cup soft light
  brown sugar
large pinch of ground allspice
3 eggs, beaten
grated rind and juice of 1 lemon
40g/1½oz/3 tbsp butter, melted
450g/1lb/2 cups curd
  (farmer's) cheese
75g/3oz/scant ½ cup raisins
For the pastry
225g/8oz/2 cups plain
  (all-purpose) flour
115g/4oz/½ cup butter, diced
1 egg yolk
15–30ml/1–2 tbsp chilled water

1 To make the pastry, place the flour in a large mixing bowl and rub or cut in the butter until the mixture resembles fine breadcrumbs. Stir the egg yolk into the flour and add just enough of the water to bind the mixture together to form a dough.

COOK'S TIP
Although it is not traditional, mixed spice (apple pie spice) would make a good substitute for the ground allspice.

Energy 406Kcal/1700kJ; Protein 14g; Carbohydrate 41.4g, of which sugars 20g; Fat 21.7g, of which saturates 12.4g; Cholesterol 159mg; Calcium 110mg; Fibre 1.1g; Sodium 371mg.

TREACLE TART

TRADITIONAL SHORTCRUST PASTRY IS PERFECT FOR THIS OLD-FASHIONED FAVOURITE, WITH ITS STICKY LEMON AND GOLDEN SYRUP FILLING AND TWISTED LATTICE TOPPING.

SERVES FOUR TO SIX

INGREDIENTS
   260g/9½oz/generous ¾ cup golden
     (light corn) syrup
   75g/3oz/1½ cups fresh
     white breadcrumbs
   grated rind of 1 lemon
   30ml/2 tbsp lemon juice
For the pastry
   150g/5oz/1¼ cups plain
     (all-purpose) flour
   2.5ml/½ tsp salt
   130g/4½oz/9 tbsp chilled
     butter, diced
   45–60/3–4 tbsp chilled water

1 To make the pastry, combine the flour and salt in a bowl. Rub or cut in the butter until the mixture resembles coarse breadcrumbs.

2 With a fork, stir in just enough water to bind the dough. Gather into a smooth ball, knead lightly for a few seconds until smooth then wrap in clear film (plastic wrap) and chill for at least 20 minutes.

3 On a lightly floured surface, roll out the pastry to a thickness of 3mm/⅛in. Transfer to a 20cm/8in fluted flan tin (tart pan) and trim off the overhang. Chill the pastry case for 20 minutes. Reserve the pastry trimmings.

4 Put a baking sheet in the oven and preheat to 200°C/400°F/Gas 6. To make the filling, warm the syrup in a pan until it melts.

5 Remove the syrup from the heat and stir in the breadcrumbs and lemon rind. Leave to stand for 10 minutes, then add more breadcrumbs if the mixture is too thin and moist. Stir in the lemon juice, then spread the mixture evenly in the pastry case.

6 Roll out the pastry trimmings and cut into 10–12 thin strips.

7 Twist the strips into spirals, then lay half of them on the filling. Arrange the remaining strips at right angles to form a lattice. Press the ends on to the rim.

8 Place the tart on the hot baking sheet and bake for 10 minutes. Lower the oven temperature to 190°C/375°F/Gas 5. Bake for 15 minutes more, until golden. Serve warm with custard.

Energy 630Kcal/2646kJ; Protein 6.1g; Carbohydrate 95.2g, of which sugars 52.6g; Fat 27.6g, of which saturates 17g; Cholesterol 69mg; Calcium 93mg; Fibre 1.6g; Sodium 762mg.

BAKEWELL TART

ALTHOUGH THIS IS A TART, IN THE ENGLISH VILLAGE OF BAKEWELL IT ORIGINATED AS BAKEWELL PUDDING. THE NAME MAY VARY BUT THE RESULT IS ALWAYS UNDENIABLY GOOD.

SERVES FOUR

INGREDIENTS
225g/8oz puff pastry
30ml/2 tbsp raspberry or apricot jam
2 eggs, plus 2 egg yolks
115g/4oz/½ cup caster
   (superfine) sugar
115g/4oz/½ cup butter, melted
50g/2oz/⅔ cup ground almonds
a few drops of almond
   essence (extract)
icing (confectioners') sugar,
   for dusting

1 Preheat the oven to 200°C/400°F Gas 6. Roll out the pastry on a lightly floured surface and use to line an 18cm/7in pie plate. Trim the edge.

2 Re-roll the pastry trimmings and cut out wide strips of pastry. Use these to decorate the edge of the pastry case by gently twisting them around the rim, joining the strips together as necessary. Prick the pastry case all over, then spread the jam over the base.

3 Whisk the eggs, egg yolks and sugar together in a bowl until the mixture is thick and pale.

4 Gently stir the melted butter, ground almonds and almond essence into the whisked egg mixture.

5 Pour the mixture into the pastry case and bake for 30 minutes, or until the filling is just set and is lightly browned. Dust with icing sugar before serving hot, warm or cold.

COOK'S TIP
Since this pastry case is not baked blind before being filled, place a baking sheet in the oven while it preheats, then place the tart on the hot sheet. This will ensure that the base of the pastry case cooks right through.

Energy 417Kcal/1753kJ; Protein 8.6g; Carbohydrate 56.1g, of which sugars 36g; Fat 19.9g, of which saturates 1.7g; Cholesterol 215mg; Calcium 78mg; Fibre 0g; Sodium 226mg.

LEMON AND ALMOND TART

THIS REFRESHING, TANGY TART HAS A RICH, CREAMY LEMON FILLING SET OFF BY A CARAMELIZED
SUGAR TOP. SERVE WARM OR COLD WITH A DOLLOP OF CRÈME FRAÎCHE OR NATURAL YOGURT.

SERVES EIGHT TO TEN

INGREDIENTS

2 eggs
50g/2oz/¼ cup golden caster
  (superfine) sugar
finely grated rind and juice of
  4 unwaxed lemons
2.5ml/½ tsp vanilla essence (extract)
50g/2oz/½ cup ground almonds
120ml/4fl oz/½ cup single (light)
  cream

For the pastry

225g/8oz/2 cups plain (all-purpose)
  flour
75g/3oz/¾ cup icing (confectioners')
  sugar, plus extra for dusting
130g/4½oz/9 tbsp butter
1 egg, beaten
a pinch of salt

1 Preheat the oven to 180°C/350°F/
Gas 4. To make the pastry, sift together
the flour and sugar in a bowl. Rub in the
butter with your fingers until the mixture
resembles fine breadcrumbs. Add the egg
and salt, then mix to a smooth dough.

2 Knead the dough lightly on a floured
work surface and form into a smooth
flat round. Wrap the dough in clear film
(plastic wrap) and chill for 15 minutes.

3 Roll out the dough on a lightly
floured work surface and use to line a
23cm/9in loose-bottomed flan tin (tart
pan). Prick the pastry base and chill for
a further 15 minutes.

4 Line the pastry case with non-stick
baking paper. Tip in some baking beans
and bake blind for 10 minutes. Remove
the paper and beans and return the
pastry case to the oven for a further
10 minutes or until it is light golden.

5 Meanwhile, make the filling. Beat the
eggs with the sugar until the mixture
leaves a thin ribbon trail. Gently stir in
the lemon rind and juice, vanilla
essence, almonds and cream.

6 Pour the filling into the pastry case
and level the surface. Bake for about
25 minutes or until the filling is set.

7 Heat the grill (broiler) to high. Sift a
thick layer of icing sugar over the tart
and grill (broil) until it caramelizes.

8 Decorate the tart with a little extra
sifted icing sugar before serving it warm
or cold with generous dollops of crème
fraîche or natural (plain) yogurt.

Energy 379Kcal/1583kJ; Protein 7.4g; Carbohydrate 39.1g, of which sugars 17.4g; Fat 22.6g, of which saturates 11.3g; Cholesterol 129mg; Calcium 87mg; Fibre 1.3g; Sodium 138mg.

MINCE PIES WITH ORANGE WHISKY BUTTER

MINCEMEAT GETS THE LUXURY TREATMENT WITH THE ADDITION OF GLACÉ CITRUS PEEL, CHERRIES AND WHISKY TO MAKE A MARVELLOUS FILLING FOR TRADITIONAL FESTIVE PIES. WHEN SEASONAL ACTIVITIES ARE ALL A BIT MUCH, TAKE TIME OUT TO RELAX OVER A COUPLE OF THESE SPIRIT-LIFTING PIES.

MAKES TWELVE TO FIFTEEN

INGREDIENTS
225g/8oz/⅔ cup mincemeat
50g/2oz/¼ cup glacé (candied) citrus
  peel, chopped
50g/2oz/¼ cup glacé (candied)
  cherries, chopped
30ml/2 tbsp whisky
1 egg, beaten or a little milk
icing (confectioners') sugar,
  for dusting
For the pastry
1 egg yolk
5ml/1 tsp grated orange rind
15ml/1 tbsp caster (superfine) sugar
10ml/2 tsp chilled water
225g/8oz/2 cups plain
  (all-purpose) flour
150g/5oz/10 tbsp butter, diced
For the orange whisky butter
75g/3oz/6 tbsp butter, softened
175g/6oz/1½ cups icing
  (confectioners') sugar, sifted
30ml/2 tbsp whisky
5ml/1 tsp grated orange rind

1 To make the pastry, lightly beat the egg yolk in a bowl, then add the grated orange rind, caster sugar and water and mix together. Cover and set aside. Sift the flour into a separate mixing bowl.

VARIATIONS
• Use either puff or filo pastry instead of shortcrust for a change.
• Replace the whisky in both the filling and the flavoured butter with Cointreau or brandy, if you like.

2 Using your fingertips, rub the diced butter into the flour until the mixture resembles fine breadcrumbs. Stir in the egg mixture and mix to a dough. Wrap in clear film (plastic wrap) and chill for 30 minutes.

3 Mix together the mincemeat, glacé peel and cherries, then add the whisky.

4 Roll out three-quarters of the pastry. With a fluted pastry (cookie) cutter stamp out rounds and line 12–15 patty tins (muffin pans). Re-roll the trimmings thinly and stamp out star shapes.

5 Preheat the oven to 200°C/400°F/ Gas 6. Spoon a little filling into each pastry case (pie shell) and top with a star shape. Brush with a little beaten egg or milk and bake for 20–25 minutes, or until golden. Leave to cool.

6 Meanwhile, make the orange whisky butter. Place the softened butter, icing sugar, whisky and grated orange rind in a bowl and beat with a wooden spoon until light and fluffy.

7 To serve, lift off each pastry star, pipe a whirl of whisky butter on top of the filling, then replace the star. Lightly dust the mince pies with a little icing sugar.

COOK'S TIP
There is a wide range of small, shaped pastry cutters available from kitchenware stores and special seasonal packs with a festive theme also include stars and Christmas trees. While metal cutters are usually the wiser buy, as these will be used only annually, cheaper plastic cutters are fine.

Energy 356Kcal/1491kJ; Protein 2.9g; Carbohydrate 46.9g, of which sugars 32.4g; Fat 17.5g, of which saturates 10.1g; Cholesterol 77mg; Calcium 49mg; Fibre 1.1g; Sodium 140mg.

VANILLA CAFFÈ LATTE

THIS LUXURIOUS VANILLA AND CHOCOLATE VERSION OF THE CLASSIC COFFEE DRINK CAN BE SERVED AT ANY TIME OF THE DAY TOPPED WITH WHIPPED CREAM, WITH CINNAMON STICKS TO STIR AND FLAVOUR THE DRINK. CAFFÈ LATTE IS A POPULAR BREAKFAST DRINK IN ITALY AND FRANCE, AND IS NOW WIDELY AVAILABLE ELSEWHERE.

SERVES TWO

INGREDIENTS
    700ml/1¼ pints/scant 3 cups milk
    250ml/8fl oz/1 cup espresso or very
        strong coffee
    45ml/3 tbsp vanilla sugar, plus extra
        to taste
    115g/4oz dark (bittersweet)
        chocolate, grated

1 Pour the milk into a small pan and bring to the boil, then remove from the heat. Mix the espresso or very strong coffee with 500ml/16fl oz/2 cups of the boiled milk in a large heatproof jug (pitcher). Sweeten with vanilla sugar to taste.

2 Return the remaining boiled milk in the pan to the heat and add the 45ml/ 3 tbsp vanilla sugar. Stir constantly until dissolved. Bring to the boil, then reduce the heat. Add the dark chocolate and continue to heat, stirring constantly until all the chocolate has melted and the mixture is smooth and glossy.

3 Pour the chocolate milk into the jug of coffee and whisk thoroughly. Serve in tall mugs or glasses topped with whipped cream and with cinnamon sticks to stir.

Energy 543Kcal/2290kJ; Protein 14.9g; Carbohydrate 76.5g, of which sugars 76g; Fat 22.1g, of which saturates 13.4g; Cholesterol 24mg; Calcium 451mg; Fibre 1.5g; Sodium 156mg.

FROTHY HOT CHOCOLATE

REALLY GOOD HOT CHOCOLATE DOESN'T COME AS A POWDER IN A PACKET — IT IS MADE WITH THE BEST CHOCOLATE YOU CAN AFFORD, WHISKED IN HOT MILK UNTIL REALLY FROTHY. LARGE MUGS ARE ESSENTIAL FOR PLENTY OF ROOM TO ACCOMMODATE THE LIP-SMACKINGLY GOOD FROTH AS WELL AS THE DARK, RICH CHOCOLATE UNDERNEATH. THIS IS TRUE COMFORT IN A MUG.

SERVES FOUR

INGREDIENTS

1 litre/1¾ pints/4 cups milk
1 vanilla pod (bean)
50–115g/2–4oz dark (bittersweet)
  chocolate, grated

1 Pour the milk into a pan. Split the vanilla pod lengthways using a sharp knife to reveal the seeds, and add it to the milk; the vanilla seeds and the pod will flavour the milk.

2 Add the chocolate. The amount to use depends on personal taste – start with a smaller amount if you are unsure of the flavour and taste at the beginning of step 3, adding more if necessary.

3 Heat the chocolate milk gently, stirring until all the chocolate has melted and the mixture is smooth, then whisk with a wire whisk until the mixture boils. Remove the vanilla pod from the pan and divide the drink among four mugs or heatproof glasses. Serve the hot chocolate immediately.

Energy 179Kcal/755kJ; Protein 9.1g; Carbohydrate 19.7g, of which sugars 19.6g; Fat 7.8g, of which saturates 4.8g; Cholesterol 16mg; Calcium 304mg; Fibre 0.3g; Sodium 108mg.

HOT TODDY

HOT TODDIES ARE NORMALLY MADE WITH WHISKY BUT RUM WORKS REALLY WELL TOO AND PRODUCES A DELICIOUSLY WARMING DRINK THAT'S PERFECT FOR A COLD WINTER EVENING — OR EVEN A WINTER AFTERNOON AFTER A HEARTY WALK OUT IN THE FREEZING COLD COUNTRYSIDE. YOU CAN ALSO FLAVOUR THIS TODDY WITH DIFFERENT SPICES SUCH AS A VANILLA POD (BEAN) OR CINNAMON STICK.

SERVES FOUR

INGREDIENTS
   300ml/½ pint/1¼ cups dark rum
   45ml/3 tbsp caster
      (superfine) sugar
   1 star anise

1 Pour the rum into a heatproof jug (pitcher) and add the sugar and star anise. Pour in 450ml/¾ pint/scant 2 cups boiling water and stir thoroughly until the sugar has dissolved.

2 Carefully pour the hot toddy into heatproof glasses or mugs and serve immediately.

Energy 211Kcal/878kJ; Protein 0.1g; Carbohydrate 11.8g, of which sugars 11.8g; Fat 0g, of which saturates 0g; Cholesterol 0mg; Calcium 6mg; Fibre 0g; Sodium 1mg.

COFFEE EGG-NOG

CHILL OUT WHEN THE AFTERNOON HEAT TURNS TO STRESS AND SIP THIS RATHER SPECIAL GROWN-UP COFFEE DRINK, WHICH IS PARTICULARLY SUITABLE FOR DAYTIME SUMMER-HOLIDAY FESTIVITIES.

SERVES SIX TO EIGHT

INGREDIENTS
8 eggs, separated
225g/8oz sugar
250ml/8fl oz cold strong coffee
(espresso strength or filter/cafetière
(press pot) brewed at 75g/3oz
coffee per 1 litre/1¾ pints/4 cups
water)
220ml/7½fl oz Scotch or bourbon
220ml/7½fl oz double (heavy) cream
120ml/4fl oz whipped cream
ground nutmeg, to decorate

1 Thoroughly beat the egg yolks, then add the sugar mixing well.

2 Heat the egg mixture gently in a pan over a low heat, stirring with a wooden spoon. Allow to cool a few minutes, stir in the coffee and whisky, and then slowly add the cream, stirring well.

3 Beat the egg whites until stiff and stir into the egg-nog, mixing well. Pour into small round cups, top each with a small dollop of whipped cream and sprinkle nutmeg on top.

Energy 605Kcal/2519kJ; Protein 11.2g; Carbohydrate 40.4g, of which sugars 40.4g; Fat 36.6g, of which saturates 19.8g; Cholesterol 376mg; Calcium 95mg; Fibre 0g; Sodium 127mg.

IRISH CHOCOLATE VELVET

THIS IS A LUXURIOUS CREAMY HOT CHOCOLATE DRINK, WITH JUST A TOUCH OF ALCOHOL TO FORTIFY IT. IT WOULD BE THE PERFECT ANTIDOTE TO A BOUT OF FLAGGING WINTER SPIRITS.

SERVES FOUR

INGREDIENTS
250ml/8fl oz/1 cup double (heavy)
cream
400ml/14fl oz milk
115g/4oz milk chocolate, chopped
into small pieces
30ml/2 tbsp cocoa powder
60ml/4 tbsp Irish whiskey
whipped cream, for topping
chocolate curls, to decorate

1 Whip half the cream in a bowl until it is thick enough to hold its shape.

2 Place the milk and chocolate in a heavy based pan and heat gently, stirring all the time, until the chocolate has melted. Whisk in the cocoa, then bring to the boil.

3 Remove from the heat and stir in the remaining cream and the Irish whiskey. Pour into four warmed heatproof mugs or glasses and top each serving with a generous spoonful of the whipped cream, finishing with a garnish of milk chocolate curls.

Energy 559Kcal/2321kJ; Protein 7.2g; Carbohydrate 24.9g, of which sugars 23.8g; Fat 45g, of which saturates 27.7g; Cholesterol 93mg; Calcium 170mg; Fibre 1.6g; Sodium 130mg.

TEATIME TREATS, CAKES AND BREADS

*Baking is positive and wholesome. Wafts of
sweet aromas baking are uplifting and tease the
senses. From beating, mixing or kneading
through to enjoying the results, baking is a
brilliant way to feel good and creative.*

CHEWY FLAPJACK BARS

INSTEAD OF BUYING CEREAL BARS, THESE ARE EASY, FAR MORE TASTY AND MORE NUTRITIOUS THAN BOUGHT TYPES. GOOD FOR YOUR BODY AS WELL AS YOUR SPIRITS, THEY WILL KEEP IN AN AIRTIGHT CONTAINER FOR UP TO FOUR DAYS BUT ARE USUALLY EATEN FAR QUICKER THAN THAT.

MAKES TWELVE

INGREDIENTS
270g/10oz jar apple sauce
115g/4oz/½ cup ready-to-eat dried apricots, chopped
115g/4oz/¾ cup raisins
50g/2oz/¼ cup demerara (raw) sugar
50g/2oz/⅓ cup sunflower seeds
25g/1oz/2 tbsp sesame seeds
25g/1oz/¼ cup pumpkin seeds
75g/3oz/scant 1 cup rolled oats
75g/3oz/⅔ cup self-raising (self-rising) wholemeal (whole-wheat) flour
50g/2oz/⅔ cup desiccated (dry unsweetened shredded) coconut
2 eggs

1 Preheat the oven to 200°C/400°F/ Gas 6. Grease a 20cm/8in square shallow baking tin (pan) and line with baking parchment.

2 Put the apple sauce in a large bowl with the apricots, raisins, sugar and the sunflower, sesame and pumpkin seeds and stir together with a wooden spoon until thoroughly mixed.

3 Add the oats, flour, coconut and eggs to the fruit mixture and gently stir together until evenly combined.

4 Turn the mixture into the tin and spread to the edges in an even layer. Bake for about 25 minutes or until golden and just firm to the touch.

5 Leave to cool in the tin, then lift out on to a board and cut into bars.

COOK'S TIP
Allow the baking parchment to hang over the edges of the tin; this makes baked bars easier to remove.

Energy 194Kcal/816kJ; Protein 4.8g; Carbohydrate 28.9g, of which sugars 18.7g; Fat 7.4g, of which saturates 2.9g; Cholesterol 31mg; Calcium 52mg; Fibre 2.6g; Sodium 48mg.

PECAN TOFFEE SHORTBREAD

COFFEE SHORTBREAD TOPPED WITH PECAN-STUDDED TOFFEE IS JUST DIVINE ... AND NUTS ARE VERY GOOD FOR YOU. CORNFLOUR GIVES A LIGHT TEXTURE, BUT ALL PLAIN FLOUR CAN BE USED INSTEAD.

MAKES TWENTY

INGREDIENTS
    15ml/1 tbsp ground coffee
    15ml/1 tbsp nearly boiling water
    115g/4oz/8 tbsp butter, softened
    30ml/2 tbsp smooth peanut butter
    75g/3oz/scant ½ cup caster
        (superfine) sugar
    75g/3oz/⅔ cup cornflour (cornstarch)
    185g/6½oz/1⅔ cups plain (all-
        purpose) flour
For the topping
    175g/6oz/12 tbsp butter
    175g/6oz/¾ cup soft light
        brown sugar
    30ml/2 tbsp golden (light corn) syrup
    175g/6oz/1 cup shelled pecan nuts,
        roughly chopped

1 Preheat the oven to 180°C/350°F/Gas 4. Lightly grease and line the base of a 18 x 28cm/7 x 11in tin (pan) with baking parchment.

2 Put the coffee in a bowl and pour the hot water over. Leave to infuse for 4 minutes, then strain through a fine sieve (strainer).

3 Cream the butter, peanut butter, sugar and coffee together until light. Sift the cornflour and flour together and mix in to make a smooth dough.

4 Press into the base of the tin and prick all over with a fork. Bake for 20 minutes. To make the topping, put the butter, sugar and syrup in a pan and heat until melted. Bring to the boil.

5 Allow to simmer for 5 minutes, then stir in the chopped nuts. Spread the topping over the base. Leave in the tin until cold, then cut into fingers. Remove from the tin and serve.

Energy 278Kcal/1160kJ; Protein 2.3g; Carbohydrate 25.7g, of which sugars 15g; Fat 19.2g, of which saturates 8.3g; Cholesterol 31mg; Calcium 29mg; Fibre 0.8g; Sodium 102mg.

OATY CHOCOLATE-CHIP COOKIES

THESE CRUNCHY COOKIES ARE EASY ENOUGH FOR CHILDREN TO MAKE AND ARE SURE TO DISAPPEAR AS SOON AS THEY ARE BAKED. COOK WITH THE CHILDREN TO CREATE THEIR FUTURE COMFORT FOOD.

MAKES ABOUT TWENTY

INGREDIENTS
115g/4oz/½ cup butter, plus extra
for greasing
115g/4oz/½ cup soft
dark brown sugar
2 eggs, lightly beaten
45–60ml/3–4 tbsp milk
5ml/1 tsp vanilla essence (extract)
150g/5oz/1¼ cups plain (all-
purpose) flour
5ml/1 tsp baking powder
pinch of salt
115g/4oz/generous 1 cup
rolled oats
175g/6oz plain (semisweet) chocolate
chips
115g/4oz/1 cup pecan nuts, chopped

1 Cream the butter and sugar in a large bowl until pale and fluffy. Add the beaten eggs, milk and vanilla essence, and beat thoroughly.

2 Sift in the flour, baking powder and salt, and stir in until well mixed. Fold in the rolled oats, chocolate chips and chopped pecan nuts.

3 Chill the mixture for at least 1 hour. Preheat the oven to 180°C/350°F/Gas 4. Grease two large baking trays.

4 Using two teaspoons, place mounds well apart on the trays and flatten with a spoon or fork. Bake for 10–12 minutes until the edges are just colouring, then cool on wire racks.

Energy 208Kcal/871kJ; Protein 3.3g; Carbohydrate 22.1g, of which sugars 12g; Fat 12.5g, of which saturates 5g; Cholesterol 36mg; Calcium 30mg; Fibre 1.1g; Sodium 47mg.

GIANT TRIPLE CHOCOLATE COOKIES

HERE IS THE ULTIMATE COOKIE. PACKED WITH CHOCOLATE AND MACADAMIA NUTS, EACH COOKIE IS A SUPER-STRESS BUSTER. YOU WILL HAVE TO BE PATIENT WHEN THEY COME OUT OF THE OVEN, AS THEY ARE TOO SOFT TO MOVE UNTIL COMPLETELY COLD: THAT'S STRESS ENOUGH TO DESERVE AT LEAST TWO!

MAKES TWELVE LARGE COOKIES

INGREDIENTS

- 90g/3½oz milk chocolate
- 90g/3½oz white chocolate
- 300g/11oz dark (bittersweet) chocolate (minimum 70 per cent cocoa solids)
- 90g/3½oz/7 tbsp unsalted (sweet) butter, at room temperature, diced
- 5ml/1 tsp vanilla essence (extract)
- 150g/5oz/¾ cup light muscovado (brown) sugar
- 150g/5oz/1¼ cups self-raising (self-rising) flour
- 100g/3½oz/scant 1 cup macadamia nut halves

1 Preheat the oven to 180°C/350°F/Gas 4. Line two baking sheets with baking parchment. Coarsely chop the milk and white chocolate and put them in a bowl.

2 Chop 200g/7oz of the dark chocolate into very large chunks, at least 2cm/¾in in size. Set aside.

3 Break up the remaining dark chocolate and place in a heatproof bowl set over a pan of barely simmering water. Stir until melted and smooth. Remove from the heat and stir in the butter, then the vanilla essence and muscovado sugar.

4 Add the flour and mix gently. Add half the dark chocolate chunks, all the milk and white chocolate and the nuts and fold together.

5 Spoon 12 mounds on to the baking sheets. Press the remaining dark chocolate chunks into the top of each cookie. Bake for about 12 minutes until just beginning to colour. Cool on the baking sheets.

Energy 413Kcal/1727kJ; Protein 3.9g; Carbohydrate 48.4g, of which sugars 38.6g; Fat 24g, of which saturates 11.6g; Cholesterol 18mg; Calcium 69mg; Fibre 1.8g; Sodium 117mg.

CHOCOLATE POTATO CAKE

ANONYMOUS MASHED POTATO MAKES THIS RICH CAKE ESPECIALLY MOIST AND DELICIOUS. USE A GOOD-QUALITY DARK CHOCOLATE FOR BEST RESULTS AND SERVE WITH WHIPPED CREAM.

MAKES A 23CM/9IN CAKE

INGREDIENTS
oil, for greasing
200g/7oz/1 cup sugar
250g/9oz/1 cup and 2 tbsp butter
4 eggs, separated
275g/10oz dark (bittersweet) chocolate
75g/3oz/¾ cup ground almonds
165g/5½oz mashed potato
225g/8oz/2 cups self-raising (self-rising) flour
5ml/1 tsp cinnamon
45ml/3 tbsp milk
white and dark (bittersweet) chocolate shavings, to garnish
whipped cream, to serve

3 Finely chop or grate 175g/6oz of the chocolate and stir it into the creamed mixture with the ground almonds. Pass the mashed potato through a sieve or ricer and stir it into the creamed chocolate mixture.

5 Whisk the egg whites until they hold stiff but not dry peaks, and fold into the cake mixture.

6 Spoon into the prepared tin and smooth over the top, but make a slight hollow in the middle to help keep the surface of the cake level during cooking. Bake in the oven for 1¼ hours until a wooden toothpick inserted in the centre comes out clean. Allow the cake to cool slightly in the tin, then turn out and cool on a wire rack.

1 Preheat the oven to 180°C/350°F/ Gas 4. Grease and line a 23cm/9in round cake tin with baking parchment.

2 In a bowl, cream together the sugar and 225g/8oz/1 cup of the butter until light and fluffy. Then beat the egg yolks into the creamed mixture one at a time until it is smooth and creamy.

4 Sift together the flour and cinnamon and fold into the mixture with the milk.

COOK'S TIP
Chocolate can be melted very successfully in the microwave. Place the pieces of chocolate in a plastic measuring jug or bowl. The chocolate may scorch if placed in a glass bowl. Microwave on high for 1 minute, stir, and then heat again for up to 1 minute, checking halfway through to see if it is done.

7 Meanwhile break up the remaining chocolate into a heatproof bowl and stand it over a pan of hot water. Add the remaining butter in small pieces and stir well until the chocolate has melted and the mixture is smooth and glossy.

8 Peel off the lining paper and trim the top of the cake so that it is level. Smooth over the chocolate icing and allow to set. Decorate with white and dark chocolate shavings and serve with lashings of whipped cream.

Energy 5749Kcal/24034kJ; Protein 87.1g; Carbohydrate 590.9g, of which sugars 391.8g; Fat 354.8g, of which saturates 188.1g; Cholesterol 1465mg; Calcium 1408mg; Fibre 21.5g; Sodium 2731mg.

CHOCOLATE CHEESECAKE BROWNIES

A VERY DENSE CHOCOLATE BROWNIE MIXTURE IS SWIRLED WITH CREAMY CHEESECAKE MIXTURE TO GIVE A MARBLED EFFECT. CUT INTO TINY SQUARES FOR LITTLE MOUTHFULS OF ABSOLUTE HEAVEN.

MAKES SIXTEEN

INGREDIENTS

For the cheesecake mixture
1 egg
225g/8oz/1 cup full-fat
   cream cheese
50g/2oz/¼ cup caster
   (superfine) sugar
5ml/1 tsp vanilla essence (extract)

For the brownie mixture
115g/4oz dark (bittersweet)
   chocolate (minimum 70 per cent
   cocoa solids)
115g/4oz/½ cup unsalted
   (sweet) butter
150g/5oz/¾ cup light muscovado
   (brown) sugar
2 eggs, beaten
50g/2oz/½ cup plain (all-purpose)
   flour

1 Preheat the oven to 160°C/325°F/ Gas 3. Line the base and sides of a 20cm/8in cake tin (pan) with baking parchment.

2 To make the cheesecake mixture, beat the egg in a mixing bowl, then add the cream cheese, caster sugar and vanilla essence. Beat together until smooth and creamy.

3 To make the brownie mixture, melt the chocolate and butter together in the microwave or in a heatproof bowl set over a pan of gently simmering water. When the mixture is melted, remove from the heat, stir well, then add the sugar. Gradually pour in the beaten eggs, a little at a time, and beat well until thoroughly combined. Gently stir in the flour.

4 Spread two-thirds of the brownie mixture over the base of the tin. Spread the cheesecake mixture on top, then spoon on the remaining brownie mixture in heaps. Using a skewer, swirl the mixtures together.

5 Bake for 30–35 minutes, or until just set in the centre. Leave to cool in the tin, then cut into squares.

Energy 228Kcal/952kJ; Protein 2.6g; Carbohydrate 20.1g, of which sugars 17.7g; Fat 15.9g, of which saturates 9.5g; Cholesterol 72mg; Calcium 35mg; Fibre 0.3g; Sodium 103mg.

WHITE CHOCOLATE BROWNIES

THESE IRRESISTIBLE BROWNIES ARE PACKED FULL OF CREAMY WHITE CHOCOLATE AND JUICY DRIED FRUIT. THEY ARE BEST SERVED CUT INTO VERY SMALL PORTIONS AS THEY ARE INCREDIBLY RICH.

MAKES EIGHTEEN

INGREDIENTS
75g/3oz/6 tbsp unsalted (sweet)
  butter, diced
400g/14oz white chocolate, chopped
3 eggs
90g/3½oz/½ cup golden caster
  (superfine) sugar
10ml/2 tsp vanilla essence (extract)
90g/3½oz/¾ cup sultanas
  (golden raisins)
coarsely grated rind of 1 lemon, plus
  15ml/1 tbsp juice
200g/7oz/1¾ cups plain
  (all-purpose) flour

1 Preheat the oven to 190°C/375°F/
Gas 5. Grease and line a 28 x 20cm/
11 x 8in shallow baking tin (pan) with
baking parchment.

2 Put the butter and 300g/11oz of the
chocolate in a bowl and melt over a pan
of gently simmering water, stirring
frequently.

3 Remove from the heat and beat in
the eggs and sugar, then add the vanilla
essence, sultanas, lemon rind and juice,
flour and the remaining chocolate.

4 Tip the mixture into the tin and
spread into the corners. Bake for about
20 minutes until slightly risen and the
surface is only just turning golden. The
centre should still be slightly soft. Leave
to cool in the tin.

5 Cut the brownies into small squares
and remove from the tin.

Energy 235Kcal/984kJ; Protein 4.3g; Carbohydrate 30.3g, of which sugars 21.8g; Fat 11.6g, of which saturates 6.6g; Cholesterol 47mg; Calcium 88mg; Fibre 0.4g; Sodium 65mg.

CHOCOLATE ECLAIRS

MANY OF THE ÉCLAIRS SOLD IN FRENCH CAKE SHOPS ARE FILLED WITH CRÈME PÂTISSIÈRE. HERE, THE CRISP CHOUX PASTRY FINGERS ARE FILLED WITH FRESH CREAM, SLIGHTLY SWEETENED AND FLAVOURED WITH VANILLA, AND THE ÉCLAIRS ARE THICKLY COATED IN DARK CHOCOLATE.

MAKES TWELVE

INGREDIENTS
    300ml/½ pint/1¼ cups double
       (heavy) cream
    10ml/2 tsp icing (confectioners')
       sugar, sifted
    1.5ml/¼ tsp vanilla essence (extract)
    115g/4oz plain (semisweet)
       chocolate
    30ml/2 tbsp water
    25g/1oz/2 tbsp butter
For the pastry
    65g/2½oz/9 tbsp plain
       (all-purpose) flour
    pinch of salt
    50g/2oz/¼ cup butter, diced
    150ml/¼ pint/⅔ cup water
    2 eggs, lightly beaten

3 Return the pan to a low heat, then beat the mixture until it leaves the sides of the pan and forms a ball. Set the pan aside and allow to cool for 2–3 minutes.

4 Add the beaten eggs, a little at a time, beating well after each addition, until you have a smooth, shiny paste, which is thick enough to hold its shape.

5 Spoon the choux pastry into a piping (pastry) bag fitted with a 2.5cm/1in plain nozzle. Pipe 10cm/4in lengths on to the prepared baking sheet. Use a wet knife to cut off the pastry at the nozzle.

6 Bake for 25–30 minutes, or until the pastries are well risen and golden brown. Remove from the oven and make a neat slit along the side of each to release the steam. Lower the oven temperature to 180°C/350°F/Gas 4 and bake for a further 5 minutes. Cool on a wire rack.

7 To make the filling, whip the cream with the icing sugar and vanilla essence until it just holds its shape. Spoon into a piping bag fitted with a 1cm/½in plain nozzle and use to fill the éclairs.

8 Place the chocolate and water in a small bowl set over a pan of hot water. Melt, stirring until smooth. Remove from the heat and gradually stir in the butter.

9 Carefully dip the top of each éclair in the melted chocolate, then place on a wire rack. Leave in a cool place until the chocolate is set. The éclairs are best served within 2 hours of being made, but they can be stored in the refrigerator for up to 24 hours.

1 Preheat the oven to 200°C/400°F/Gas 6. Grease a large baking sheet and line with baking parchment. To make the pastry, sift the flour and salt on to a small sheet of baking parchment. Heat the butter and water in a pan very gently until the butter melts.

2 Increase the heat and bring to a rolling boil. Remove the pan from the heat and immediately tip in all the flour. Beat vigorously with a wooden spoon until the flour is mixed into the liquid.

COOK'S TIP
When melting the chocolate, ensure that the bowl does not touch the hot water and keep the heat low. If the chocolate gets too hot, it will become unworkable.

GREEK HONEY CRUNCH CREAMS

WITH ITS SCENT OF LIQUORICE AND ANISEED, GREEK HONEY LENDS A WONDERFUL FLAVOUR TO THESE COOKIES. IF YOU LIKE YOUR HONEY LESS STRONG, TRY USING ORANGE BLOSSOM OR LAVENDER INSTEAD.

MAKES TWENTY

INGREDIENTS
- 250g/9oz/2¼ cups self-raising (self-rising) flour
- 10ml/2 tsp bicarbonate of soda (baking soda)
- 50g/2oz/¼ cup caster (superfine) sugar
- 115g/4oz/½ cup unsalted (sweet) butter, diced
- finely grated rind of 1 large orange
- 115g/4oz/½ cup Greek honey
- 25g/1oz/¼ cup pine nuts or chopped walnuts

For the filling
- 50g/2oz/¼ cup unsalted (sweet) butter, at room temperature, diced
- 115g/4oz/1 cup icing (confectioners') sugar, sifted
- 15ml/1 tbsp Greek honey

1 Preheat the oven to 200°C/400°F/Gas 6. Line three or four baking sheets with baking parchment. Sift the flour, bicarbonate of soda and caster sugar into a bowl. Add the butter and rub in until the mixture resembles breadcrumbs. Stir in the orange rind.

2 Put the honey in a small pan and heat until just runny but not hot. Pour over the dry mixture and mix to a firm dough.

3 Divide the dough in half and shape one half into 20 small balls about the size of a hazelnut in its shell. Place the balls on the baking sheets, spaced well apart, and gently flatten. Bake for 6–8 minutes, until golden brown. Leave to cool and firm up on the baking sheets. Use a palette knife (metal spatula) to transfer the cookies to a wire rack to allow them to cool completely.

4 Shape the remaining dough into 20 balls and dip one side of each one into the pine nuts or walnuts. Place the cookies, nut sides up, on the baking sheets, gently flatten and bake for 6–8 minutes, until golden brown. Leave to cool and firm up slightly on the baking sheets before carefully transferring the cookies to a wire rack, still nut sides up, to cool completely.

5 To make the filling, put the butter, sugar and honey in a bowl and beat together until light and fluffy.

6 Use the honey and butter mixture to sandwich the cookies together in pairs. Spread a little filling on a plain cookie for the base and place a nut-coated one on top. Press the cookies together gently without squeezing out the filling.

Energy 164Kcal/688kJ; Protein 1.4g; Carbohydrate 23.5g, of which sugars 14.2g; Fat 7.8g, of which saturates 4.4g; Cholesterol 18mg; Calcium 47mg; Fibre 0.4g; Sodium 97mg.

LEMON TART

THIS CLASSIC FRENCH TART IS ONE OF THE MOST DELICIOUS DESSERTS. A RICH LEMON CURD IS ENCASED IN A CRISP PASTRY CASE. CRÈME FRAÎCHE IS AN OPTIONAL — BUT NICE — EXTRA.

SERVES SIX

INGREDIENTS
    6 eggs, beaten
    350g/12oz/1½ cups caster
      (superfine) sugar
    115g/4oz/½ cup butter
    grated rind and juice of 4 lemons
    icing (confectioners') sugar
      for dusting
For the pastry
    225g/8oz/2 cups plain
      (all-purpose) flour
    115g/4oz/½ cup butter, diced
    30ml/2 tbsp icing
      (confectioners') sugar
    1 egg
    5ml/1 tsp vanilla
      essence (extract)
    15ml/1 tbsp chilled water

1 Preheat the oven to 200°C/400°F/ Gas 6. To make the pastry, sift the flour into a mixing bowl and rub or cut in the butter until the mixture resembles fine breadcrumbs. Stir in the icing sugar.

2 Add the egg, vanilla and most of the chilled water, then work to a soft dough. Add a few more drops of water if needed. Knead quickly and lightly until smooth.

3 Roll out the pastry on a floured surface and use to line a 23cm/9in flan tin (tart pan). Prick the base all over with a fork. Line with baking parchment and fill with baking beans. Bake in the oven for 10 minutes. Remove the paper and beans and set the pastry case (pie shell) aside while you make the filling.

4 Put the eggs, sugar and butter into a pan, and stir over a low heat until all the sugar has dissolved. Add the lemon rind and juice, and continue cooking, stirring constantly, until the lemon curd has thickened slightly.

5 Pour the curd mixture into the pastry case. Bake for about 20 minutes, or until the lemon curd filling is just set. Transfer the tart to a wire rack to cool. Dust the surface of the tart generously with icing sugar just before serving.

Energy 623Kcal/2623kJ; Protein 12.7g; Carbohydrate 95.5g, of which sugars 66.8g; Fat 24g, of which saturates 12.2g; Cholesterol 307mg; Calcium 127mg; Fibre 1.2g; Sodium 219mg.

MADEIRA CAKE WITH LEMON SYRUP

THIS SUGAR-CRUSTED CAKE IS SOAKED IN LEMON SYRUP, SO IT STAYS MOIST AND IS INFUSED WITH TANGY CITRUS. SERVE IT SLICED WITH TEA FOR ONE OF THOSE "CARING AND SHARING" SESSIONS.

SERVES TEN

INGREDIENTS
   250g/9oz/1 cup plus 2 tbsp
   butter, softened
   225g/8oz/generous 1 cup
   caster (superfine) sugar
   5 eggs
   275g/10oz/2½ cups plain
   (all-purpose) flour, sifted
   10ml/2 tsp baking powder
   salt
For the sugar crust
   60ml/4 tbsp lemon juice
   15ml/1 tbsp golden (light corn) syrup
   30ml/2 tbsp granulated sugar

COOK'S TIP
Make double the quantity of cake. Omit the syrup from one and leave plain. Simply cool, wrap and freeze.

1 Preheat the oven to 180°C/350°F/ Gas 4. Grease a 1kg/2¼lb loaf tin. Beat the butter and sugar until light and creamy, then gradually beat in the eggs.

2 Mix the sifted flour, baking powder and salt, and fold in gently. Spoon into the prepared tin, level the top and bake for 1¼ hours, until a skewer pushed into the middle comes out clean.

3 Remove the cake from the oven and, while still warm and in the tin, use a skewer to pierce it several times right the way through. Warm together the lemon juice and syrup, add the sugar and immediately spoon over the cake, so the flavoured syrup soaks through but leaves some sugar crystals on the top. Chill the cake for several hours or overnight before serving.

Energy 429Kcal/1796kJ; Protein 6.6g; Carbohydrate 49.4g, of which sugars 28.5g; Fat 24.2g, of which saturates 14g; Cholesterol 167mg; Calcium 74mg; Fibre 0.9g; Sodium 202mg.

PECAN CAKE

THIS CAKE IS AN EXAMPLE OF THE FRENCH INFLUENCE ON MEXICAN COOKING. IT IS TRADITIONALLY SERVED WITH CAJETA — SWEETENED BOILED MILK — BUT WHIPPED CREAM OR CRÈME FRAÎCHE CAN BE USED INSTEAD. SERVE THE CAKE WITH A FEW REDCURRANTS FOR A SPLASH OF UPLIFTING COLOUR.

SERVES EIGHT TO TEN

INGREDIENTS
   115g/4oz/1 cup pecan nuts
   115g/4oz/½ cup butter, softened
   115g/4oz/½ cup soft light
   brown sugar
   5ml/1 tsp natural vanilla essence
   (extract)
   4 large eggs, separated
   75g/3oz/¾ cup plain (all-purpose)
   flour
   pinch of salt
   12 whole pecan nuts, to decorate
   whipped cream or crème fraîche
For drizzling
   50g/2oz/¼ cup butter
   120ml/4fl oz/scant ½ cup clear honey

1 Preheat the oven to 180°C/350°F/ Gas 4. Grease a 20cm/8in round cake tin. Toast the nuts in a dry frying pan for 5 minutes, shaking frequently. Grind finely and place in a bowl.

2 Cream the butter with the sugar in a mixing bowl, then beat in the vanilla essence and egg yolks.

3 Add the flour to the ground nuts and mix well. Whisk the egg whites with the salt in a grease-free bowl until soft peaks form. Fold the whites into the butter mixture, then gently fold in the flour and nut mixture. Spoon the mixture into the prepared cake tin and bake for 30 minutes or until a skewer inserted in the centre comes out clean.

4 Cool the cake in the tin for 5 minutes, then remove the sides of the tin. Stand the cake on a wire rack until cold.

5 Remove the cake from the base of the tin if necessary, then return it to the rack and arrange the pecans on top. Transfer to a plate. Melt the butter in a small pan, add the honey and bring to the boil, stirring. Lower the heat and simmer for 3 minutes. Pour over the cake. Serve with whipped cream or crème fraîche.

Energy 428Kcal/1785kJ; Protein 6.2g; Carbohydrate 34.7g, of which sugars 27.4g; Fat 30.5g, of which saturates 12.5g; Cholesterol 158mg; Calcium 51mg; Fibre 1g; Sodium 170mg.

VICTORIA SANDWICH CAKE

SERVE THIS RICHLY FLAVOURED SPONGE CAKE SANDWICHED TOGETHER WITH YOUR FAVOURITE JAM (JELLY) OR PRESERVE. FOR SPECIAL OCCASIONS, FILL THE CAKE WITH PREPARED FRESH FRUIT, SUCH AS RASPBERRIES OR SLICED PEACHES, AS WELL AS JAM AND WHIPPED DAIRY CREAM OR FROMAGE FRAIS.

MAKES ONE 18CM/7IN CAKE

INGREDIENTS
175g/6oz/¾ cup soft butter
175g/6oz/¾ cup caster (superfine) sugar
3 eggs beaten
175g/6oz/1½ cups self-raising (self-rising) flour, sifted
60ml/4 tbsp jam (jelly)
150ml/¼pt/⅔ cup whipped cream or fromage frais
15–30ml/1–2 tbsp icing (confectioners') sugar, for dusting

3 Add the eggs, a little at a time, beating well after each addition. Fold in half the flour, using a metal spoon, then fold in the rest.

6 When the cakes are cool, sandwich them with the jam and whipped cream or fromage frais. Dust the top of the cake with sifted icing sugar and serve cut into slices. Store the cake in the refrigerator in an airtight container or wrapped in foil.

1 Preheat the oven to 180°C/350°F/Gas 4. Lightly grease and line the bottom of two 18cm/7in sandwich tins.

4 Divide the mixture between the two sandwich tins and level the surfaces with the back of a spoon.

VARIATIONS
• Replace 30ml/2 tbsp of the flour with sifted cocoa powder. Sandwich the cakes with chocolate butter icing. For a darker richer chocolate cake, add 90ml/6 tbsp cocoa powder without reducing the quantity of flour.
• To make a moist coffee cake, dissolve 15ml/1 tbsp instant coffee in 30ml/2 tbsp boiling water and fold this in at the end, when the flour has been incorporated. Sandwich together with a coffee butter icing or with cream whipped with a little dissolved instant coffee and sweetened with icing sugar.

2 Place the butter and caster sugar in a bowl and cream together until pale and fluffy. This can be done by hand using a mixing spoon or with a hand-held electric mixer, which is far quicker and easier.

5 Bake for 25–30 minutes, until the cakes have risen, feel just firm to the touch and are golden brown. Turn out and cool on a wire rack.

COOK'S TIP
The butter and sugar mixture can be creamed in a food processor. Some processors have a plastic attachment designed for creaming but the cutting knife can be used. Whichever attachment is used, it is very easy to overmix the ingredients, making it too liquid. Pulse the power to avoid this.

Energy 3553Kcal/14845kJ; Protein 42.5g; Carbohydrate 362.6g, of which sugars 232.5g; Fat 225.3g, of which saturates 43.8g; Cholesterol 842mg; Calcium 908mg; Fibre 5.4g; Sodium 2358mg.

FROSTED CARROT AND PARSNIP CAKE

THE GRATED CARROTS AND PARSNIPS IN THIS DELICIOUSLY LIGHT AND CRUMBLY CAKE HELP TO KEEP IT MOIST AND ACCOUNT FOR ITS VERY GOOD KEEPING QUALITIES. THE CREAMY SWEETNESS OF THE COOKED MERINGUE TOPPING MAKES A WONDERFUL CONTRAST TO THE CAKE'S LIGHT CRUMB.

SERVES EIGHT TO TEN

INGREDIENTS
oil, for greasing
1 lemon
1 orange
15ml/1 tbsp caster (superfine) sugar
225g/8oz/1 cup butter
225g/8oz/1 cup soft light brown
   sugar
4 eggs
225g/8oz/1⅔ cups carrot and
   parsnip, grated
115g/4oz/1¼ cups sultanas (golden
   raisins)
225g/8oz/2 cups self-raising (self-
   rising) wholemeal (whole-wheat)
   flour
5ml/1 tsp baking powder
For the topping
50g/2oz/¼ cup caster (superfine)
   sugar
1 egg white

1 Preheat the oven to 180°C/350°F/
Gas 4. Lightly grease a 20cm/8in loose-
based cake tin and line the base with a
circle of greaseproof paper.

VARIATION
If you do not like parsnips, you can make
this cake with just carrots, or replace the
parsnips with the same weight of
shredded courgettes. Add a pinch of
cinnamon and nutmeg to the mixture to
give a little extra flavour.

2 Finely grate the lemon and orange.
Put about half of the rind, selecting the
longest shreds, in a bowl and mix with
the caster sugar. Arrange the sugar-
coated rind on a sheet of greaseproof
paper and leave in a warm place, to
dry thoroughly.

3 Cream the butter and sugar until pale
and fluffy. Add the eggs gradually, then
beat well. Stir in the unsugared rinds,
the grated carrots and parsnips, 30ml/
2 tbsp orange juice and the sultanas.

4 Gradually fold in the flour and baking
powder, and tip into the prepared tin.
Bake for 1½ hours until risen, golden
and just firm.

5 Leave the cake to cool slightly in the
tin, then turn out on to a serving plate.

6 To make the topping, place the
caster sugar in a bowl over boiling water
with 30ml/2 tbsp of the remaining
orange juice. Stir over the heat until the
sugar begins to dissolve. Remove from
the heat, add the egg white and salt,
and whisk for 1 minute with an electric
beater.

7 Return to the heat and whisk for about
6 minutes until the mixture becomes stiff
and glossy, holding a good shape. Allow
to cool slightly, whisking frequently.

8 Swirl the cooked meringue topping
over the cake and leave to firm up for
about 1 hour. To serve, sprinkle with the
sugared lemon and orange rind, which
should now be dry and crumbly.

COOK'S TIP
When this cooked meringue frosting
cools, it becomes slightly hard on the
outside. The cake will keep well for a few
days until the crust is cut into.

Energy 540Kcal/2265kJ; Protein 7.5g; Carbohydrate 71.5g, of which sugars 50.5g; Fat 26.9g, of which saturates 15.7g; Cholesterol 174mg; Calcium 156mg; Fibre 1.8g; Sodium 333mg.

ORANGE CHOCOLATE LOAF

DO NOT BE ALARMED AT THE AMOUNT OF CREAM IN THIS RECIPE – IT'S NAUGHTY BUT NECESSARY, AND REPLACES BUTTER TO MAKE A DELICIOUSLY MOUTHWATERING, MOIST AND DARK CHOCOLATE CAKE. A BITTERSWEET STICKY MARMALADE FILLING AND TOPPING IS THE PERFECT FINISH.

SERVES EIGHT

INGREDIENTS
  115g/4oz dark (bittersweet) chocolate
  3 eggs
  175g/6oz/scant 1 cup unrefined
  caster (superfine) sugar
  175ml/6fl oz/¾ cup sour cream
  200g/7oz/1¾ cups self-raising
  (self-rising) flour
For the filling and topping
  200g/7oz/⅔ cup bitter orange
  marmalade
  115g/4oz dark (bittersweet) chocolate
  60ml/4 tbsp sour cream
  shredded orange rind, to decorate

1 Preheat the oven to 190°C/375°F/ Gas 5. Grease a 900g/2lb loaf tin (pan) lightly, then line the base with a piece of baking parchment.

2 Break the chocolate into pieces and place them in a heatproof bowl. Stand this over a pan of hot, not boiling, water and stir until melted.

3 Combine the eggs and sugar in a separate bowl. Using a hand-held electric mixer, beat the mixture until it is thick and creamy, then stir in the sour cream and melted chocolate. Fold in the flour evenly using a metal spoon.

4 Pour the mixture into the prepared tin and bake for about 1 hour, or until well risen and firm to the touch. Cool for a few minutes in the tin, then turn out on to a wire rack and let the loaf cool completely.

5 Make the filling. Spoon two-thirds of the marmalade into a small pan and melt over a low heat. Break the chocolate into pieces. Melt the chocolate in a heatproof bowl placed over hot water. Stir the chocolate into the marmalade with the sour cream.

6 Slice the cake across into three layers and sandwich back together with about half the marmalade filling. Spread the rest over the top of the cake and leave to set. Spoon the remaining marmalade over the cake and scatter with shredded orange rind, to decorate.

COOK'S TIP
A fantastic variety of different types of organic marmalades is available, including farmhouse and hand-made regional varieties.

Energy 474Kcal/1998kJ; Protein 7.5g; Carbohydrate 78.5g, of which sugars 59.7g; Fat 16.7g, of which saturates 9.3g; Cholesterol 105mg; Calcium 155mg; Fibre 1.6g; Sodium 153mg.

FRUITLOAF

DRIED FRUIT AND FLAKED ALMONDS ARE DELICIOUS IN THIS ENERGY-GIVING SWEET BREAD. SERVE IT THICKLY SLICED AND SPREAD WITH GOOD BUTTER TO REPLENISH SPENT ENERGY. IT IS A GREAT LOAF FOR WEEKEND BREAKFASTS, ESPECIALLY AFTER A LATE NIGHT, AND A GOOD CHOICE FOR AFTERNOON TEA WHEN THE CHILDREN COME HOME WITH RAGING APPETITES.

SERVES EIGHT TO TEN

INGREDIENTS
sunflower oil, for greasing
7 egg whites
175g/6oz/scant 1 cup caster
  (superfine) sugar
115g/4oz/1 cup flaked (sliced)
  almonds, toasted
115g/4oz/¾ cup sultanas (golden
  raisins)
grated rind of 1 lemon
165g/5½oz/1⅓ cups plain
  (all-purpose) flour, sifted, plus extra
  for flouring
75g/3oz/6 tbsp butter, melted

1 Preheat the oven to 180°C/350°F/ Gas 4 and grease and flour a 1kg/2¼lb loaf tin (pan). Whisk the egg whites until they are very stiff, but not crumbly. Fold in the sugar gradually, then add the almonds, sultanas and lemon rind.

2 Fold the flour and butter into the mixture and tip it into the prepared tin. Bake for about 45 minutes until well risen and pale golden brown. Cool for a few minutes in the tin, then turn out and serve warm or cold, in slices.

Energy 364Kcal/1529kJ; Protein 8.1g; Carbohydrate 49.9g, of which sugars 33.8g; Fat 16.1g, of which saturates 5.6g; Cholesterol 20mg; Calcium 87mg; Fibre 2g; Sodium 117mg.

MALTED CURRANT BREAD

*THIS SPICED CURRANT BREAD MAKES A GOOD TEA OR BREAKFAST BREAD, SLICED AND SPREAD WITH A
GENEROUS AMOUNT OF BUTTER. IT ALSO MAKES SUPERB TOAST FOR A MIDNIGHT SNACK.*

MAKES TWO LOAVES

INGREDIENTS
  50g/2oz/3 tbsp malt extract
  30ml/2 tbsp golden (light corn) syrup
  50g/2oz/¼ cup butter
  450g/1lb/4 cups unbleached white
    bread flour
  5ml/1 tsp mixed (apple pie) spice
  20g/¾ oz fresh yeast
  175ml/6fl oz/¾ cup lukewarm milk
  175g/6oz/¾ cup currants,
    slightly warmed
For the glaze
  30ml/2 tbsp milk
  30ml/2 tbsp caster (superfine) sugar

1 Lightly grease two 450g/1lb loaf tins
(pans). Place the malt extract, golden
syrup and butter in a pan and heat
gently until the butter has melted. Set
aside to cool completely.

2 Sift the flour and mixed spice together
into a large bowl and make a well in the
centre. Cream the yeast with a little of
the milk, then blend in the remaining
milk. Add the yeast mixture and cooled
malt mixture to the centre of the flour
and blend together to form a dough.

3 Turn out the dough on to a lightly
floured surface and knead for about
10 minutes until smooth and elastic.
Place in a lightly oiled bowl, cover with
lightly oiled clear film (plastic wrap) and
leave to rise, in a warm place, for
1½–2 hours, or until doubled in bulk.

4 Turn the dough out on to a lightly
floured surface, knock back (punch
down), then knead in the currants. Divide
the dough in two and shape into two
loaves. Place in the prepared tins. Cover
with oiled clear film and leave to rise, in a
warm place, for 2–3 hours, or until the
dough reaches the top of the tins.

5 Meanwhile, preheat the oven to
200°C/400°F/Gas 6. Bake for 35–40
minutes or until golden. While the
loaves are baking heat the milk and
sugar for the glaze in a small pan. Turn
out the loaves on to a wire rack, then
invert them, so that they are the right
way up. Immediately brush the glaze
evenly over the loaves and leave to cool.

COOK'S TIP
When you are making more than one
loaf, the easiest way to prove (rise) them
is to place the tins in a lightly oiled large
plastic bag.

Energy 1336Kcal/5659kJ; Protein 26.7g; Carbohydrate 267.1g, of which sugars 95.5g; Fat 25.3g, of which saturates 14.4g; Cholesterol 58mg; Calcium 646mg; Fibre 8.7g; Sodium 294mg

LARDY CAKE

THIS SPECIAL RICH FRUIT BREAD WAS ORIGINALLY MADE THROUGHOUT MANY COUNTIES OF ENGLAND FOR CELEBRATING THE HARVEST. USING LARD RATHER THAN BUTTER OR MARGARINE MAKES AN AUTHENTIC LARDY CAKE. IT IS FLAKY, RICH AND JUST WHAT THE DOCTOR ORDERED FOR CHEERING UP.

MAKES ONE LARGE LOAF

INGREDIENTS
    450g/1lb/4 cups unbleached white
      bread flour
    5ml/1 tsp salt
    15g/½oz/1 tbsp lard (shortening)
    25g/1oz/2 tbsp caster (superfine)
      sugar
    20g/¾oz fresh yeast
    300ml/½ pint/1¼ cups lukewarm
      water
For the filling
    75g/3oz/6 tbsp lard (shortening)
    75g/3oz/6 tbsp soft light brown sugar
    115g/4oz/½ cup currants,
      slightly warmed
    75g/3oz/½ cup sultanas (golden
      raisins), slightly warmed
    25g/1oz/3 tbsp mixed chopped
      (candied) peel
    5ml/1 tsp mixed (apple pie) spice
For the glaze
    10ml/2 tsp sunflower oil
    15–30ml/1–2 tbsp caster (superfine)
      sugar

1 Grease a 25 x 20cm/10 x 8in shallow roasting pan. Sift the flour and salt into a large bowl and rub in the lard. Stir in the sugar and make a well in the centre.

2 In a bowl, cream the yeast with half of the water, then blend in the remainder. Add to the centre of the flour and mix to a smooth dough.

3 Turn out on to a lightly floured surface and knead for 10 minutes until smooth and elastic. Place in a lightly oiled bowl, cover with oiled clear film (plastic wrap) and leave in a warm place for 1 hour, or until doubled in bulk.

4 Turn the dough out on to a lightly floured surface and knock back (punch down) until collapsed. Knead for 2–3 minutes. Roll into a rectangle about 5mm/¼in thick.

5 Using half the lard for the filling, cover the top two-thirds of the dough with flakes of lard. Sprinkle over half the sugar, half the dried fruits and peel and half the mixed spice. Fold the bottom third up and the top third down, sealing the edges with the rolling pin.

6 Turn the dough by 90 degrees. Repeat the rolling and cover with the remaining lard, fruit and peel and mixed spice. Fold, seal and turn as before. Roll out the dough to fit the prepared pan. Cover with lightly oiled clear film and leave to rise, in a warm place, for 30–45 minutes, or until doubled in size.

7 Meanwhile, preheat the oven to 200°C/400°F/Gas 6. Brush the top of the lardy cake with sunflower oil and sprinkle with caster sugar.

8 Score a criss-cross pattern on top using a sharp knife, then bake for 30–40 minutes until golden. Turn out on to a wire rack to cool slightly. Serve warm, cut into slices or squares.

Energy 3474Kcal/14663kJ; Protein 47.7g; Carbohydrate 630.3g, of which sugars 287.4g; Fat 101.9g, of which saturates 37.9g; Cholesterol 84mg; Calcium 888mg; Fibre 18.8g; Sodium 2080mg.

PANETTONE

*THIS CLASSIC ITALIAN BREAD CAN BE FOUND THROUGHOUT ITALY AROUND CHRISTMAS. IT IS A
SURPRISINGLY LIGHT BREAD EVEN THOUGH IT IS RICH WITH BUTTER AND DRIED FRUIT.*

MAKES ONE LOAF

INGREDIENTS
    400g/14oz/3½ cups unbleached
      white bread flour
    2.5ml/½ tsp salt
    15g/½oz fresh yeast
    120ml/4fl oz/½ cup lukewarm milk
    2 eggs plus 2 egg yolks
    75g/3oz/6 tbsp caster (superfine)
      sugar
    150g/5oz/⅔ cup butter, softened
    115g/4oz/⅔ cup mixed chopped
      (candied) peel
    75g/3oz/½ cup raisins
    melted butter, for brushing

COOK'S TIP
Once the dough has been enriched with
butter, do not prove (rise) in too warm a
place or the loaf will become greasy.

1 Using a double layer of baking
parchment, line and butter a 15cm/6in
deep cake tin (pan) or soufflé dish.
Finish the paper 7.5cm/3in above the
top of the tin.

2 Sift the flour and salt together into a
large bowl. Make a well in the centre.
Cream the yeast with 60ml/4 tbsp of the
milk, then mix in the remainder.

3 Pour the yeast mixture into the
centre of the flour, add the whole eggs
and mix in sufficient flour to make a
thick batter. Sprinkle a little of the
remaining flour over the top and leave
to "sponge", in a warm place, for
30 minutes.

4 Add the egg yolks and sugar and mix
to a soft dough. Work in the softened
butter, then turn out on to a lightly
floured surface and knead for 5 minutes
until smooth and elastic. Place in a
lightly oiled bowl, cover with lightly oiled
clear film (plastic wrap) and leave to
rise, in a slightly warm place, for
1½–2 hours, or until doubled in bulk.

5 Knock back (punch down) the dough
and turn out on to a lightly floured
surface. Gently knead in the peel and
raisins. Shape into a ball and place
in the prepared tin. Cover with lightly
oiled clear film and leave to rise, in a
slightly warm place, for about 1 hour, or
until doubled.

6 Meanwhile, preheat the oven to
190°C/375°F/Gas 5. Brush the surface
with melted butter and cut a cross in
the top using a sharp knife. Bake for
20 minutes, then reduce the oven
temperature to 180°C/350°F/Gas 4.
Brush the top with butter again and
bake for a further 25–30 minutes, or
until golden. Cool in the tin for 5–10
minutes, then turn out on to a wire rack
to cool.

Energy 3599Kcal/15123kJ; Protein 65.7g; Carbohydrate 515.7g, of which sugars 210.9g; Fat 156.2g, of which saturates 87.1g; Cholesterol 1187mg; Calcium 1070mg; Fibre 19.4g; Sodium 1530mg.

GREEK OLIVE BREAD

THE FLAVOURS OF THE MEDITERRANEAN SIMPLY OOZE FROM THIS DECORATIVE BREAD, SPECKLED WITH OLIVES, RED ONIONS AND HERBS. WITH A BOTTLE OF RED WINE IT BRINGS SUNSHINE TO THE TABLE.

MAKES TWO LOAVES

INGREDIENTS
675g/1½ lb/6 cups unbleached white
   bread flour, plus extra
   for dusting
10ml/2 tsp salt
25g/1oz fresh yeast
350ml/12fl oz/1½ cups lukewarm
   water
75ml/5 tbsp olive oil
175g/6oz/1½ cups pitted black
   olives, roughly chopped
1 red onion, finely chopped
30ml/2 tbsp chopped fresh coriander
   (cilantro) or mint

VARIATION
Make one large loaf and increase the
baking time by about 15 minutes.

1 Lightly grease two baking sheets. Sift
the flour and salt together into a large
bowl and make a well in the centre.

2 In a jug (pitcher), blend the yeast
with half of the water. Add to the centre
of the flour with the remaining water
and the olive oil; mix to a soft dough.

3 Turn out the dough on to a lightly
floured surface and knead for
8–10 minutes until smooth. Place in a
lightly oiled bowl, cover with lightly oiled
clear film (plastic wrap) and leave to
rise, in a warm place, for 1 hour, or
until doubled in bulk.

4 Turn out on to a lightly floured
surface and knock back (punch down).
Cut off a quarter of the dough, cover
with lightly oiled clear film and set aside.

5 Roll out the remaining, large piece of
dough to a round. Sprinkle the olives,
onion and herbs evenly over the surface,
then bring up the sides of the circle and
gently knead together. Cut the dough in
half and shape each piece into a plump
oval loaf, about 20cm/8in long. Place on
the prepared baking sheets.

6 Divide the reserved dough into four
equal pieces and roll each to a long
strand 60cm/24in long. Twist together
and cut in half. Brush the centre of
each loaf with water and place two
pieces of twisted dough on top of each,
tucking the ends underneath the loaves.

7 Cover with lightly oiled clear film and
leave to rise, in a warm place, for about
45 minutes, until nearly doubled in size.

8 Meanwhile, preheat the oven to
220°C/425°F/Gas 7. Dust the loaves
lightly with flour and bake for
35–40 minutes, or until golden and
sounding hollow when tapped on the
base. Transfer to a wire rack to cool.

Energy 1515Kcal/6392kJ; Protein 33.4g; Carbohydrate 268.2g, of which sugars 9.3g; Fat 41.7g, of which saturates 6.1g; Cholesterol 0mg; Calcium 545mg; Fibre 14.1g; Sodium 3946mg.

FRENCH BAGUETTES

*BAGUETTES ARE DIFFICULT TO REPRODUCE AT HOME AS THEY REQUIRE A VERY HOT OVEN AND STEAM.
HOWEVER, BY USING LESS YEAST AND A TRIPLE FERMENTATION YOU CAN PRODUCE A BREAD WITH A
SUPERIOR TASTE AND FAR BETTER TEXTURE THAN MASS-PRODUCED BAGUETTES. THERE IS NOTHING
LIKE POUNDING DOUGH TO RELIEVE STRESS AND THESE ARE FABULOUS EATEN ON THE DAY OF BAKING.*

MAKES THREE LOAVES

INGREDIENTS
  500g/1¼ lb/5 cups unbleached white
    bread flour
  115g/4oz/1 cup fine French plain
    (all-purpose) flour
  10ml/2 tsp salt
  15g/½ oz fresh yeast
  525ml/18fl oz/2¼ cups lukewarm
    water

VARIATION
If you make baguettes regularly you may
want to purchase baguette frames to
hold and bake the breads in, or long
bannetons in which to prove (rise) this
wonderful bread.

1 Sift the flours and salt into a large
bowl. Add the yeast to the water in
another bowl and stir to dissolve.
Gradually beat in half the flour mixture
to form a batter. Cover with clear film
(plastic wrap) and leave at room
temperature for about 3 hours, or until
nearly trebled in size and starting
to collapse.

2 Add the remaining flour a little at a
time, beating with your hand. Turn out
on to a lightly floured surface and
knead for 8–10 minutes to form a moist
dough. Place in a lightly oiled bowl,
cover with lightly oiled clear film and
leave to rise, in a warm place, for about
1 hour.

3 When the dough has almost doubled
in bulk, knock it back (punch it down),
turn out on to a lightly floured surface
and divide into three equal pieces.
Shape each into a ball and then into a
rectangle measuring about 15 x 7.5cm/
6 x 3in.

4 Fold the bottom third up lengthways
and the top third down and press down
to make sure the pieces of dough are in
contact. Seal the edges. Repeat two or
three more times until each loaf is an
oblong. Leave to rest in between folding
for a few minutes, if necessary, to avoid
tearing the dough.

5 Gently stretch each piece of dough
lengthways into a 33–35cm/13–14in
long loaf. Pleat a floured dishtowel on a
baking sheet to make three moulds for
the loaves. Place the breads between
the pleats of the towel, to help hold
their shape while rising. Cover with
lightly oiled clear film and leave to rise,
in a warm place, for 45–60 minutes.

6 Meanwhile, preheat the oven to
maximum, at least 230°C/450°F/Gas 8.
Roll the loaves on to a baking sheet,
spaced well apart. Using a sharp knife,
slash the top of each loaf several times
with long diagonal slits. Place at the top
of the oven, spray the inside of the oven
with water and bake for 20–25 minutes,
or until golden. Spray the oven twice
more during the first 5 minutes of
baking. Transfer the cooked loaves to a
wire rack to cool.

Energy 699Kcal/2973kJ; Protein 19.3g; Carbohydrate 159.3g, of which sugars 3.1g; Fat 2.7g, of which saturates 0.4g; Cholesterol 0mg; Calcium 287mg; Fibre 6.4g; Sodium 1327mg.

CIABATTA

THIS IRREGULAR-SHAPED ITALIAN BREAD IS SO CALLED BECAUSE IT LOOKS LIKE AN OLD SHOE OR SLIPPER. IT IS MADE WITH A VERY WET DOUGH FLAVOURED WITH OLIVE OIL; COOKING PRODUCES A BREAD WITH HOLES AND A WONDERFULLY CHEWY CRUST. IT'S FUN TO MAKE AND FABULOUS TO EAT.

MAKES THREE LOAVES

INGREDIENTS
For the starter
    7g/¼ oz fresh yeast
    175–200ml/6–7fl oz/¾–scant 1 cup
    lukewarm water
    350g/12oz/3 cups unbleached plain
    (all-purpose) flour, plus extra for
    dusting
For the dough
    15g/½ oz fresh yeast
    400ml/14fl oz/1⅔ cups lukewarm
    water
    60ml/4 tbsp lukewarm milk
    500g/1¼ lb/5 cups unbleached white
    bread flour
    10ml/2 tsp salt
    45ml/3 tbsp extra virgin olive oil

VARIATION
To make tomato-flavoured ciabatta, add 115g/4oz/1 cup chopped, drained sun-dried tomatoes in olive oil. Add with the olive oil in step 5.

1 For the starter, cream the yeast with a little of the water. Sift the flour into a large bowl. Gradually mix in the yeast mixture and sufficient of the remaining water to form a firm dough.

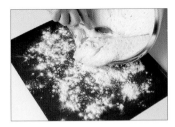

2 Turn out the biga starter dough on to a lightly floured surface and knead for about 5 minutes until smooth and elastic. Return the dough to the bowl, cover with lightly oiled clear film (plastic wrap) and leave in a warm place for 12–15 hours, or until the dough has risen and is starting to collapse.

3 Sprinkle three baking sheets with flour. Mix the yeast for the dough with a little of the water until creamy, then mix in the remainder. Add the yeast mixture to the biga and gradually mix in.

4 Mix in the milk, beating thoroughly with a wooden spoon. Using your hand, gradually beat in the flour, lifting the dough as you mix. Mixing the dough will take 15 minutes or more and form a very wet mix, impossible to knead on a work surface.

5 Beat in the salt and olive oil. Cover with lightly oiled clear film and leave to rise, in a warm place, for 1½–2 hours, or until doubled in bulk.

6 With a spoon, carefully tip one-third of the dough at a time on to the baking sheets without knocking back (punching down) the dough in the process.

7 Using floured hands, shape into rough oblong loaf shapes, about 2.5cm/1in thick. Flatten slightly with splayed fingers. Sprinkle with flour and leave to rise in a warm place for 30 minutes.

8 Meanwhile, preheat the oven to 220°C/425°F/Gas 7. Bake for 25–30 minutes, or until golden brown and sounding hollow when tapped on the base. Transfer to a wire rack to cool.

Energy 1084Kcal/4597kJ; Protein 27.6g; Carbohydrate 223.4g, of which sugars 5.2g; Fat 15.1g, of which saturates 2.4g; Cholesterol 1mg; Calcium 425mg; Fibre 8.9g; Sodium 1327mg

GARLIC AND HERB BREAD

THIS IRRESISTIBLE GARLIC BREAD INCLUDES PLENTY OF FRESH MIXED HERBS. YOU CAN VARY THE
OVERALL FLAVOUR ACCORDING TO THE COMBINATION OF HERBS YOU CHOOSE.

SERVES THREE TO FOUR

INGREDIENTS
  1 baguette or bloomer loaf
For the garlic and herb butter
  115g/4oz/½ cup unsalted (sweet)
    butter, softened
  5–6 large garlic cloves, finely
    chopped or crushed
  30–45ml/2–3 tbsp chopped fresh
    herbs (such as parsley, chervil and
    a little tarragon)
  15ml/1 tbsp chopped fresh chives
  coarse salt and ground black pepper

1 Preheat the oven to 200°C/400°F/
Gas 6. Make the garlic and herb butter
by beating the butter with the garlic,
herbs, chives and seasoning.

VARIATIONS
• Use 105ml/7 tbsp extra virgin olive oil
instead of the butter.
• Flavour the butter with garlic, a little
chopped fresh chilli, grated (shredded) lime
rind and chopped fresh coriander (cilantro).
• Add chopped, pitted black olives or
sun-dried tomatoes to the butter with a
little grated lemon rind.

2 Cut the bread into 1cm/½in thick
diagonal slices, but be sure to leave
them attached at the base so that the
loaf stays intact.

3 Spread the garlic and herb butter
between the slices evenly, being careful
not to detach them, and then spread
any remaining butter over the top of
the loaf.

4 Wrap the loaf in foil and bake in the
preheated oven for 20–25 minutes, until
the butter is melted and the crust is
golden and crisp. Cut the loaf into slices
to serve.

COOK'S TIP
This loaf makes an excellent addition to
a barbecue. If space permits, place the
foil-wrapped loaf on the top of the
barbecue and cook for about the same
length of time as for oven baking. Turn
the foil parcel over several times to
ensure it cooks evenly.

Energy 920Kcal/3877kJ; Protein 22.1g; Carbohydrate 135.1g, of which sugars 7.2g; Fat 36.2g, of which saturates 20.8g; Cholesterol 82mg; Calcium 317mg; Fibre 6.3g; Sodium 1714mg.

RED ONION WITH ROSEMARY FOCACCIA

THIS BREAD IS RICH IN OLIVE OIL AND IT HAS AN AROMATIC TOPPING OF RED ONION, FRESH ROSEMARY AND COARSE SALT. SERVE IT WITH A TOMATO AND BASIL SALAD FOR FLAVOUR THERAPY.

2 Set the yeast aside in a warm, but not hot, place for 10 minutes, until it has turned frothy.

3 Add the yeast, the remaining water, 15ml/1 tbsp of the oil and the chopped rosemary to the flour. Mix all the ingredients together to form a dough, then gather the dough into a ball and knead on a floured work surface for about 5 minutes, until smooth and elastic. You may need to add a little extra flour if the dough is very sticky.

4 Place the dough in a lightly oiled bowl and slip it into a polythene bag or cover with oiled clear film (plastic wrap) and leave to rise. The length of time you leave it for depends on the temperature: leave it all day in a cool place, overnight in the refrigerator, or for 1–2 hours in a warm, but not hot, place.

5 Lightly oil a baking sheet. Knead the dough to form a flat loaf that is about 30cm/12in round or square. Place on the baking sheet, cover with oiled polythene or clear film and leave to rise again in a warm place for a further 40–60 minutes.

6 Preheat the oven to 220°C/425°F/Gas 7. Toss the onion in 15ml/1 tbsp of the oil and scatter over the loaf with the rosemary sprigs and a scattering of coarse salt. Bake for 15–20 minutes until golden brown.

7 Serve the bread freshly baked or leave to cool on the baking sheet and serve warm.

SERVES FOUR TO FIVE

INGREDIENTS
- 450g/1lb/4 cups strong white bread flour, plus extra for dusting
- 5ml/1 tsp salt
- 7g/¼oz fresh yeast or generous 5ml/1 tsp dried yeast
- 2.5ml/½ tsp light muscovado (molasses) sugar
- 250ml/8fl oz/1 cup lukewarm water
- 60ml/4 tbsp extra virgin olive oil, plus extra for greasing
- 5ml/1 tsp very finely chopped fresh rosemary, plus 6–8 small sprigs
- 1 red onion, thinly sliced
- coarse salt

1 Sift the flour and salt into a bowl. Set aside. Cream the fresh yeast with the sugar, and gradually stir in half the water. If using dried yeast, stir the sugar into the water and sprinkle the dried yeast over.

Energy 496Kcal/2094kJ; Protein 11g; Carbohydrate 90.4g, of which sugars 3.8g; Fat 12.5g, of which saturates 1.8g; Cholesterol 0mg; Calcium 167mg; Fibre 4g; Sodium 496mg.

BAGELS

THESE RING-SHAPED ROLLS ARE ONE OF THE EASTERN EUROPEAN JEWS' BEST CONTRIBUTIONS TO THE GASTRONOMY. THE DOUGH IS FIRST BOILED TO GIVE IT A CHEWY TEXTURE AND THEN BAKED. THE BAGELS CAN BE TOPPED WITH ALMOST ANYTHING: CREAM CHEESE, SMOKED SALMON OR FRESH, CHOPPED VEGETABLES ARE JUST A FEW EXAMPLES.

MAKES TEN TO TWELVE

INGREDIENTS
7g packet easy-blend (rapid-rise)
 dried yeast
25ml/1½ tbsp salt
500g/1¼lb/4½ cups strong white
 bread flour
250ml/8fl oz/1 cup lukewarm water
oil for greasing
30ml/2 tbsp sugar
corn meal for sprinkling
1 egg yolk

1 In a bowl, combine the yeast, salt and flour. Pour the lukewarm water into a separate large bowl.

2 Gradually add half the flour to the lukewarm water, beating until it forms a smooth, soft batter.

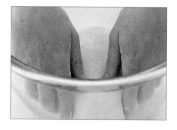

3 Knead the remaining flour into the batter until the mixture forms a fairly firm, smooth dough that is easy to handle without being too sticky.

4 On a lightly floured surface knead the dough by hand for 10–20 minutes or, if using a bread machine, 5–8 minutes, until shiny and smooth. If the dough is sticky, add a little more flour. (The dough should be much firmer than ordinary bread dough.)

5 Lightly oil a bowl. Place the dough in it and turn to coat it completely in oil. Cover with a clean dishtowel and leave in a warm place for about 40 minutes, or until doubled in size.

6 Turn the dough on to a lightly floured surface and punch down (knock back) with your fists. Knead for 3–4 minutes, or until smooth and elastic.

7 Divide the dough into 10–12 balls. Poke your thumb through each one then, working with your fingers, open the hole to form a bagel measuring 6–7.5cm/2½–3in diameter. Place on a floured board and leave to rise for 20 minutes, or until doubled in size.

8 Preheat the oven to 200°C/400°F/ Gas 6. Bring 3–4 litres/5–7 pints/ 2½–3½ quarts water to the boil in a large pan and add the sugar. Lower the heat to a gentle boil. Lightly oil a baking sheet and sprinkle with corn meal. Beat the egg yolk with 15ml/1 tbsp water.

9 Add the bagels, one at a time, to the boiling water, until you have a single layer of bagels, and cook for 8 minutes turning occasionally so that they cook evenly. Remove from the pan with a slotted spoon, drain and place on the prepared baking sheet.

10 Brush each bagel with the egg mixture. Bake for 25–30 minutes until well browned. Cool on a wire rack.

VARIATIONS
Add dried onions, garlic granules or poppy seeds to the bagel dough or top the bagels with poppy seeds, sesame seeds, caraway seeds, dried onion or garlic granules before baking.

Nutritional information per portion: Energy 188Kcal/801kJ; Protein 5g; Carbohydrate 42g, of which sugars 3.9g; Fat 1.2g, of which saturates 0.3g; Cholesterol 20mg; Calcium 74mg; Fibre 1.6g; Sodium 985mg.

SAN FRANCISCO-STYLE SOURDOUGH

HOME-BAKED BREAD IS ONE OF THE MOST DELICIOUS TREATS OF ALL TIME, ESPECIALLY WHEN IT'S STILL WARM AND FRESH FROM THE OVEN. BAKING A LOAF IS A PLEASANT WEEKEND TASK: THE REPETITIVE KNEADING ACTION IS BOTH THERAPEUTIC AND COMFORTING.

MAKES ONE LOAF

INGREDIENTS
For the starter
  25g/1oz/¼ cup organic plain (all-
    purpose) flour
  15–30ml/1–2 tbsp warm water
1st refreshment for the starter
  30ml/2 tbsp water
  15ml/1 tbsp milk
  50g/2oz/½ cup organic plain flour
2nd refreshment for the starter
  90ml/6 tbsp water
  15–30ml/1–2 tbsp milk
  175g/6oz/1½ cups organic white
    bread flour
For the dough
  100ml/3½fl oz/7 tbsp water
  175g/6oz/1½ cups organic white
    bread flour
1st refreshment for the dough
  100ml/3½fl oz/7 tbsp water
  175g/6oz/1½ cups organic white
    bread flour
  50g/2oz/½ cup organic wholemeal
    (whole-wheat) bread flour
  7.5ml/1½ tsp salt
  5ml/1 tsp granulated sugar
  unbleached white bread flour, for
    dusting

1 Place the flour in a bowl and stir in enough water for the starter to make a firm, moist dough. Knead for 5 minutes. Cover with a damp cloth. Leave for 2–3 days until a crust forms and the dough inflates with tiny bubbles. Remove the hardened crust and place the moist centre in a clean bowl. Add the water and milk for the 1st refreshment.

2 Gradually add the flour and mix to a firm but moist dough. Cover and leave for 1–2 days as before. Then repeat as for 1st refreshment using the ingredients for the 2nd refreshment. Leave for 8–12 hours in a warm place until well risen.

3 Pour the water for the dough into the pan. Add 200g/7oz/scant 1 cup of starter. If necessary for your machine, add the dry ingredients first. Sprinkle over the flour, covering the water. Set the machine to the dough setting; use basic dough setting (if available). Press Start.

4 Mix for 10 minutes then turn off the machine. Leave the dough in the machine for 8 hours. Add the water for the 1st dough refreshment to the pan, then sprinkle over the flours.

5 Add the salt and sugar in separate corners. Set the machine as before. Press Start. Lightly flour a baking sheet.

6 When the dough cycle ends put the dough on a floured surface. Knock it back (punch it down) gently; shape into a plump ball. Place on the baking sheet; cover with oiled clear film (plastic wrap). Leave for 2 hours, or until almost doubled in bulk.

7 Meanwhile, preheat the oven to 230°C/450°F/Gas 8. Dust the loaf with flour and slash the top in a star shape. Bake for 25 minutes, spraying the oven with water three times in the first 5 minutes. Reduce the oven temperature to 200°C/400°F/Gas 6. Bake the loaf for 10 minutes more or until golden and hollow-sounding. Allow the bread to cool on a wire rack.

Energy 2145Kcal/9121kJ; Protein 59.8g; Carbohydrate 487g, of which sugars 10.8g; Fat 8.6g, of which saturates 1.6g; Cholesterol 2mg; Calcium 912mg; Fibre 19.4g; Sodium 1997mg.

PITTA BREAD

Throughout the Mediterranean, pitta is the most common bread. There are many different types, from very flat examples, to those with distinct pockets and thicker cushions. The best pitta bread is always soft, tender and moist. Good to make and shape; and to eat.

MAKES TWELVE

INGREDIENTS

500g/1¼lb/4½ cups strong white
    bread flour, or half white and half
    wholemeal (whole-wheat)
7g packet easy-blend (rapid-rise)
    dried yeast
15ml/1 tbsp salt
15ml/1 tbsp olive oil
250ml/8fl oz/1 cup water

1 Combine the flour, yeast and salt. In a large bowl, mix together the oil and water, then stir in half of the flour mixture, stirring in the same direction, until the dough is stiff. Knead in the remaining flour.

2 Place the dough in a clean bowl, cover with a clean dishtowel and leave in a warm place for at least 30 minutes and up to 2 hours.

3 Knead the dough for 10 minutes, or until smooth. Lightly oil the bowl, place the dough in it, cover again and leave to rise in a warm place for about 1 hour, or until doubled in size.

4 Divide the dough into 12 equal-size pieces. With lightly floured hands, flatten each piece, then roll out into a round measuring about 20cm/8in and about 5mm–1cm/¼–½in thick. Keep the rolled breads covered with a clean dishtowel while you make the remaining pittas so that they do not begin to dry out on the surface.

5 Heat a large, heavy frying pan over a medium-high heat. When smoking hot, gently lay one piece of flattened dough in the pan and cook for 15–20 seconds. Carefully turn it over and cook the second side for about 1 minute.

6 When large bubbles start to form on the bread, turn it over again. It should puff up. Using a clean dishtowel, gently press on the bread where the bubbles have formed. Cook for 3 minutes, then remove the pitta from the pan. Repeat with the remaining dough until all the pittas have been cooked.

7 Wrap the pitta breads in a clean dishtowel, stacking them as each one is cooked. Serve the pittas hot while they are soft and moist.

VARIATION

To cook the breads in the oven, preheat the oven to 220°C/425°F/Gas 7. Fill an unglazed or partially glazed dish with hot water and place in the bottom of the oven. Alternatively, arrange a handful of unglazed tiles in the bottom of the oven. Use either a non-stick baking sheet or a lightly oiled ordinary baking sheet and heat in the oven for a few minutes. Place two or three pieces of flattened dough on to the baking sheet and place in the hottest part of the oven. Bake for 2–3 minutes. They should puff up. Repeat with the remaining dough until all the pittas have been cooked.

Energy 150Kcal/638kJ; Protein 3.9g; Carbohydrate 32.4g, of which sugars 0.6g; Fat 1.5g, of which saturates 0.2g; Cholesterol 0mg; Calcium 59mg; Fibre 1.3g; Sodium 493mg.

GARLIC AND CORIANDER NAAN

THIS VERSION OF THE POPULAR INDIAN FLAT BREAD IS PARTICULARLY TASTY AND WILL BECOME A GREAT FAVOURITE. THE BREAD IS TRADITIONALLY MADE IN A TANDOORI OVEN, BUT THIS METHOD HAS BEEN DEVELOPED TO GIVE ALMOST IDENTICAL RESULTS. BREAD MAKING IS VERY SOOTHING, AND THE ADVANTAGE OF NAAN IS THAT AFTER THE PREPARATION, IT COOKS QUICKLY AND IS AT ITS BEST FRESH.

MAKES THREE

INGREDIENTS
280g/10oz/2½ cups unbleached
  white bread flour
5ml/1 tsp easy-blend (rapid-rise)
  dried yeast
1 garlic clove, finely chopped
5ml/1 tsp black onion seeds
5ml/1 tsp ground coriander
5ml/1 tsp salt
100ml/3½fl oz/7 tbsp water
60ml/4 tbsp natural (plain) yogurt
10ml/2 tsp clear honey
15ml/1 tbsp melted ghee or butter,
  plus 30–45ml/2–3 tbsp
15ml/1 tbsp chopped fresh
  coriander (cilantro)

1 Place the flour in a bowl and mix in the easy-blend dried yeast. Add the garlic, black onion seeds, ground coriander and salt. Mix thoroughly.

2 Pour the water and natural yogurt into a jug (pitcher) and mix well. Add the honey and the 15ml/1 tbsp melted ghee or butter.

3 Pour the yogurt mixture into the dry ingredients and mix to a firm dough. Turn the dough out on to a lightly floured surface and knead for about 10 minutes, until smooth and elastic. Place in an oiled bowl, cover with oil clear film (plastic wrap) and leave to rise in a warm place until doubled in size.

4 Knock the naan dough back (punch it down) gently and leave it to rise for a second time as before.

5 Meanwhile, preheat the oven to 220°C/425°F/Gas 7. Place three baking sheets in the oven to heat. Knock back (punch down) the dough and then knead in the chopped fresh coriander.

6 Divide the dough into three equal pieces. Shape each piece into a ball and cover two of the pieces with oiled clear film (plastic wrap). Roll out the remaining piece of dough into a large teardrop shape, making it about 5–8mm/¼–⅜in thick. Cover with oiled clear film while you roll out the remaining two pieces of dough to make two more naan.

7 Preheat the grill (broiler) to its highest setting. Place the naan on the preheated baking sheets and then bake them for 4–5 minutes, until puffed up. Remove the baking sheets from the oven and place them under the hot grill for a few seconds, until the naan start to brown and blister. Brush the naan with melted ghee or butter and serve warm.

VARIATION
For a basic naan omit the coriander, garlic and black onion seeds. Include a little ground black pepper or chilli powder for a slightly piquant note. Add cumin seeds instead of onion seeds for a warm, spicy seasoning.

Energy 380Kcal/1611kJ; Protein 9.7g; Carbohydrate 77.9g, of which sugars 6.8g; Fat 5.5g, of which saturates 2.9g; Cholesterol 11mg; Calcium 164mg; Fibre 2.9g; Sodium 703mg.

CHAPATIS

These chewy, unleavened breads are eaten throughout Northern India. Try slapping the dough from one hand to the other instead of pressing it out — it's a great stress buster!

MAKES SIX CHAPATIS

INGREDIENTS

175g/6oz/1½ cups atta or wholemeal
  (whole-wheat) flour
2.5ml/½ tsp salt
100–120ml/scant 4fl oz/
  scant ½ cup water
5ml/1 tsp vegetable oil
melted ghee or butter, for brushing
  (optional)

1 Sift the flour and salt into a bowl. Add the water and mix to a soft dough. Knead in the oil, then turn out on to a lightly floured surface.

2 Knead for 5–6 minutes until smooth. Place in a lightly oiled bowl, cover with a damp dishtowel and leave to rest for 30 minutes. Turn out on to a floured surface. Divide the dough into six equal pieces. Shape each piece into a ball.

3 Press the dough into a larger round with your palm, or slap it from hand to hand to spread it out into a round. Then roll into a 13cm/5in round. Stack, layered between clear film (plastic wrap), to keep moist.

4 Heat a griddle or heavy frying pan over a medium heat for a few minutes until hot. Take one chapati, brush off any excess flour, and place on the griddle. Cook for 30–60 seconds, or until the top begins to bubble and white specks appear on the underside. If necessary, adjust the heat under the griddle fairly often at first, until it reaches a steady, medium temperature.

5 Turn the chapati over using a metal spatula and cook for a further 30 seconds. Remove from the pan and keep warm, layered between a folded dishtowel, while cooking the remaining chapatis. If you like, the chapatis can be brushed lightly with melted ghee or butter immediately after cooking. Serve warm.

COOK'S TIP
Atta or ata is a very fine wholemeal (whole-wheat) flour, which is found in Indian stores and supermarkets. It is sometimes simply labelled chapati flour. Atta can also be used for making rotis and other Indian flatbreads.

Energy 95Kcal/403kJ; Protein 3.7g; Carbohydrate 18.6g, of which sugars 0.6g; Fat 1.1g, of which saturates 0.2g; Cholesterol 0mg; Calcium 11mg; Fibre 2.6g; Sodium 165mg.

INDEX

ACKNOWLEDGEMENTS

Recipes: Catherine Atkinson, Mary Banks,
Alex Barker, Judy Bastyra, Angela
Boggiano, Maxine Clark, Roz Denny,
Joanna Farrow, Jennie Fleetwood, Brian
Glover, Nicola Graimes, Deh-ta Hsuing,
Christine Ingram, Becky Johnson, Lucy
Knox, Sally Mansfield, Christine McFadden,
Jane Milton, Sallie Morris, Keith Richmond,
Jenni Shapter, Marlena Spieler, Liz Trigg,
Jenny White, Kate Whiteman, Lucy
Whiteman, Jeni Wright.

Home economists: Eliza Baird, Alex Barker,
Caroline Barty, Joanna Farrow, Annabel
Ford, Christine France, Carole Handslip,
Kate Jay, Becky Johnson, Jill Jones, Bridget
Sargeson, Jennie Shapter, Carol Tennant,
Sunil Vijayakar, Jenny White.

Stylists: Nicki Dowey, Penny Markham,
Lucy McKelvie, Marion Price, Helen Trent,
Linda Tubby.

Photographers: Frank Adam, Tim Auty,
Martin Brigdale, Louisa Dare, Nicki Dowey,
Gus Filgate, John Heseltine, Amanda
Heywood, Janine Hosegood, Dave King,
William Lingwood, Thomas Odulate, Craig
Roberson, Simon Smith, Sam Stowell.

NOTES

NOTES

NOTES

NOTES

NOTES

NOTES

NOTES

Notes